Retrieving Charisms
for the Twenty-First Century

Retrieving Charisms
for the Twenty-First Century

Doris Donnelly
Editor

A Liturgical Press Book

THE LITURGICAL PRESS
Collegeville, Minnesota

343

Cover design by Greg Becker.

1	2	3	4	5	6	7	8	9

Library of Congress Cataloging-in-Publication Data

Retrieving charisms for the twenty-first century / Doris Donnelly,
    editor.
        p.   cm.
    Includes bibliographical references.
    ISBN 0-8146-2540-1 (alk. paper)
    1. Gifts, Spiritual—Congresses.   2. Catholic Church—Doctrines-
-Congresses.   I. Donnelly, Doris.
BT767.3.R48   1999
234'.13—dc21
                                                                99-18655
                                                                    CIP

Contents

Acknowledgments

Being in debt has never been so pleasant—or as overwhelming.

Our first and most obvious debt is to Cardinal Suenens. He is the continual source of insight, wisdom, and courage, always transparent to the Gospel of Jesus Christ, in the work we do at the center which bears his name.

We are also enormously indebted to Margie Grace whose friendship with the cardinal and whose understanding of his person and mission enable us to carry forth the cardinal's vision of faithful service to the Church.

In 1996, John Carroll University honored Leon-Joseph Cardinal Suenens at a symposium titled "Retrieving Charisms for the Twenty-First Century." The contributions to this volume were addresses at that event. The local committee which assisted in so many ways at the symposium deserves very special mention: Ann Coakley Anderson, Bobbie Bokman, Mary Bookman, Rev. Donald B. Cozzens, Marilyn Cunin, Marsha Daley, Kathy DiFranco, Gorman Duffett, Mary Ann Flannery, V.S.C.; Christine Gibbons, Mary Kay Kantz, Mary Michael, Mary Kay Oosdyke, O.P.; Louise Prochaska, S.N.D.; Klaus Romer, Madeline Shemo, H.M.; Rev. Thomas Schubeck, S.J.; Barbara Schubert, and Rev. Donald Snyder. In addition, deep gratitude is extended to John Shea, S.J.; Fred Travis, Paul Kantz, Carol and Bill Manning; Ann and Vincent Marotta; Gerry Coakley, Jean Keller, Diane Ferguson, Rev. Robert Marrone, Rev. John V. White, S.J.; William P. Gibbons, Sally Griswold, Jerry Sheehan, Alan Stephenson, Mary Beadle, and Liz Sander.

For the production of this book, help was provided by Joe Chernowski, Rosie Hudak, Eric Schild, Jessica Tummino, and Beth Yanko, student assistants in our office, and Mary Beth Brooks, secretary to the program. A most sincere thank you to each is in order.

Much has happened since the 1996 symposium. The Cardinal Suenens Program in Theology and Church Life has taken up residence at John

Carroll University where our president, Father Edward Glynn, S.J., provides us with leadership in the spirit of Vatican II. In addition, an international advisory committee provides creative counsel, and a local committee generously gives both time and energy to our programs. It is in this supportive setting that the work of the program continues.

Doris Donnelly
July 31, 1999
Feast of St. Ignatius

The Cardinal Suenens Program in Theology & Church Life
International Advisory Committee

Professor Giuseppe Alberigo
Istituto per le Scienze Religiose
Bologna, Italy

Reverend Joseph Famerée
Universitaire de Louvain-la-Neuve
Belgium

Reverend Gustavo Gutiérrez
Lima, Peru

Reverend John C. Haughey, S.J.
Loyola University of Chicago

Reverend J. Bryan Hehir
The Divinity School, Harvard University
Cambridge, Massachusetts

Dr. Monika Hellwig
Association of Catholic Colleges
    and Universities
Washington, D.C.

Reverend Joseph A. Komonchak
The Catholic University of America
Washington, D.C.

Professor Mathieu Lamberigts
Katholieke Universiteit Leuven
Belgium

Reverend John P. Meier
University of Notre Dame
South Bend, Indiana

Reverend Stanislaus Obirek, S.J.
Director, Center for Culture & Dialogue
Cracow, Poland

Reverend John W. O'Malley, S.J.
Weston Jesuit School of Theology
Cambridge, Massachusetts

Mrs. Margaret O'Brien Steinfels
Editor, *Commonweal*
New York, New York

Professor Geoffrey Wainwright
Duke University
Durham, North Carolina

Local Advisory Committee
Mary E. Beadle (JCU); Mary Bookman (Hunting Valley, Ohio); Lauren Bowen (JCU); Dee Christie (Ursuline College); Marilyn Cunin (Cleveland Heights, Ohio); Carol Edkins (Shaker Heights, Ohio); Mary Ann Flannery, V.S.C. (JCU); Christine Gibbons (JCU); William P. Gibbons (Cleveland, Ohio); Rev. Gregory N.P. Konz, S.J. (JCU); Rev. Stephen T. Krupa, S.J. (JCU); Rev. Mark A. Latcovich (Saint Mary's Seminary); Mary C. Michael (Pepper Pike, Ohio); Mary Kay Oosdyke, O.P. (Cleveland, Ohio); Patrick H. Rombalski (JCU); Frank Scardiglia (Shaker Heights, Ohio); Barbara Schubert (Cleveland Heights, Ohio); Priscilla M. Shields (Cleveland, Ohio); Brenda Wirkus (JCU)

Executive Committee
His Eminence Godfried Cardinal Danneels, Archdiocese of Mechelen-Brussels
Rev Edward Glynn, S.J., President, John Carroll University
Mrs. Margaret F. Grace, Manhasset, New York
Mr. Patrick P. Grace, New York, New York
Prof. Doris Donnelly, Director, The Cardinal Suenens Program, *ex officio*

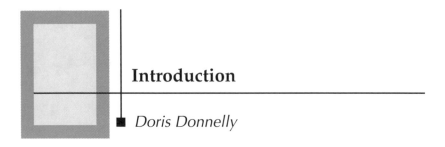

Introduction

Doris Donnelly

This is a book about a promise and the surprises that follow from it.

The promise belongs to Jesus who assured us that he would be with us always.

The surprises have to do with how he would continue that presence.

The clue to the "how" lies with *charisms*, an uncommon word which we might be tempted to equate with *gift* or *grace*, and even though it is these things, it is something different, too. At the risk of oversimplifying, *charisms* are a special variety of gifts dispensed through the Holy Spirit in Church and world, as needed, for the common good.

Therein lie at least three of the surprises about *charisms*, and a word about each seems in order.

The first surprise is that *charisms* emerge among people not only in the Church but also *in the world*. The gifts of the Spirit, apparently, are not confined exclusively to ecclesial institutions or to ecclesially affiliated persons, but may be unearthed in other settings, for example, among people who raise families, establish banking policies, organize unions, settle strikes, teach the inexperienced, promote the dignity of the disenfranchised, or care for the wounded—young or old.

The second surprise is that *charisms* may be found wherever there are human needs. If it does not seem so, if in fact it seems that human needs are unattended and that forces of evil and destruction are winning the day, we are invited, with renewed confidence in that promise of Jesus to be with us, to look harder and to be willing to find *charisms* often enough in the least likely places and among the least likely carriers. A special bonus is ours if we are able to take delight in how the Spirit maneuvers and does the arranging of these special gifts, for the

Spirit's activity in this regard is anything but predictable. More than one person in this volume will point out that the Holy Spirit is an unruly house guest, upsetting preconceived notions of how and where the Spirit should act.

A third surprise is that *charisms* are unique gifts given for the common good. Unlike graces dispensed for the good of the individual—and these certainly are many—*charisms* are never private possessions. Their *raison d'etre* is the upbuilding of others. Expect to find them where an instinct towards civility prevails, even if fragily, in conflict situations. Expect them where the mood is reconciling in the middle of discord and struggle. Expect to see them where some person is willing to sacrifice a personal agenda for the sake of the bigger picture. Expect them where someone surrenders plenty so that all may have some.

One of the persons who helped uncover these special gifts of God's spirit which we call *charisms* was Leon-Joseph Cardinal Suenens, archbishop of Malines-Brussels from 1961–1979. His life spanned nearly a century [1904–1996], and his leadership at the Vatican Council made him a major architect of twentieth-century Roman Catholicism. Certain that *charisms* lay undetected, unrecognized, and often devalued, the cardinal sought to retrieve them and re-establish them in the mainstream of Christian life. A highly respected Church leader with ample *charisms* of his own, the cardinal was able to discern them in others, and he spent a fair amount of his time doing just that: respecting and rejoicing in the placement of sparks from the Spirit of God.

Cardinal Suenens was aware that a mutual interdependence of charisms among the people of God of whatever rank or station was essential if the Holy Spirit were to renew the face of the earth. His vision prompted this collection of essays, originally given as addresses at an international symposium held at John Carroll University in 1996 and entitled *Retrieving Charisms for the Twenty-First Century.*

With the new millennium here, the task before us is precisely the retrieval of *charisms* which are needed for us all not merely to survive but to survive with courage and imagination. The contributors to this volume are well aware of the urgency of our survival as well as its style. In the spirit of Cardinal Suenens, their approaches are refreshing, balanced, nuanced, open to new possibilities and faithful to the Spirit who has surprises in store for those of us willing to be swept away by gusts of gracious wind.

1

Charisms:
An Ecclesiological Exploration

■ *John C. Haughey, S.J.*

Gathered in the upper room the 120 heard a mighty, rushing wind that filled the whole house and then saw tongues of fire divide and come to rest on each of them. "All were filled with the Holy Spirit. They began to express themselves in foreign tongues and make bold proclamation as the Spirit prompted them" (Acts 2:4). Years later Paul the apostle attested to the fact that "each [member of the Christian community here] has a charism, one this, another that" (1 Cor 7:7). The observation was made in the course of his advising the Christian Corinthians about their choice of marriage or celibacy.

Even in these two first references we can see that charisms are notoriously elusive. Trying to define them is like trying to bottle wind or package fire, since they take as many forms as there are individuals receiving them. In the first and last sections of this article I will attempt to locate and isolate their unique character. The middle sections will deal with their ecclesiological and societal implications, beginning with Vatican II and ending with some of the more helpful theological voices on the subject.

The *charismata*, it seems, are a species of which the *(charis)* grace or favor of God is the genus. One conclusion I have reached after studying much about the subject is that charisms enable many people to do ordinary things extraordinarily well. Occasionally, charisms enable a few people to do extraordinary things. If we think of them only in this latter sense, i.e., something out of the ordinary, we easily miss their presence among us and in us.

1

One of the distinctive traits of charisms is that they are given by the Holy Spirit to some for the sake of others.[1] Most of God's graces are given for the sake of those receiving them. But charisms are different insofar as they are God's way of building up families, communities, parishes, the Church, but also businesses, neighborhoods, cities. As Paul puts it, they are given not for the individual's good but for "the common good" (1 Cor 12:7). It does not appear that Paul had in mind the public as such when he wrote of the ecclesial arena of the charisms' exercise. The scope of the exercise of most charisms was (and is) more immediate, like families, even relationships. If we do not see that we will miss their frequency.

Devising a list of the *charismata* would be exhausting and probably wrongheaded since "each member has a charism." Maybe a matrix of charisms would be more accurate, since they seem individuated without being individualistic. It would be more instructive, it seems, to look at them as functioning where there are human needs. Since charisms meet needs, they are God's way of ministering to people. Charisms are conferred on those through whom God would minister. The importance of charisms should be linked to human needs which are universal and overwhelming. Peter's speech at Pentecost recalled Joel's prophecy that God would pour out "a portion of the Spirit on *all* humanity" in the form of many gifts (Acts 2:17). Where needs are, there the charisms should be, ministering to them.

The relationship of the charisms to natural talents or learned skills or inherited abilities is a difficult question. The old adage of grace building on nature might be a helpful starting point for understanding the relationship. A charism is often a power God's Spirit imbues human beings with that enables them to do better what nature or training or praxis has first equipped them to do, thus enhancing what is already there. You might say there is a *super additum*, something that cannot be humanly accounted for, where a charism is operating. It would be dualistic to say that "where nature ends charism begins," since this might show our ignorance of how graced nature is or how latent its obediential potency for charism. If we do not see how coincident charisms are with nature or the compenetration of one by the other, charisms will always reek of oddity.

Some, most charisms in fact, are role-enhancing, it seems. Others sear into the deepest marrow of a person and become life-consuming. The

---

[1] A medieval distinction was made between *gratia gratis data*, graces that were for others, and *gratia gratum faciens*, the grace that made the recipient pleasing to God. Cf. Karl Rahner, *The Dynamic Element in the Church*, chapter 2 "On the Charismatic Element in the Church" (New York: Herder & Herder, 1964) 55.

charisms of prophecy of the Old Testament prophets, for example, were life-consuming. I wonder too, in this connection, about Simon Peter and the charism of his office. "When you were young you went where you would. But when you are old another (the Spirit) will tie you fast and carry you off against your will" (John 21:18). What Jesus said indicated the sort of death by which Peter was to glorify God. All charisms are a person's way of glorifying God but, it seems, some are so all consuming that one can die acting on the energies it takes to exercise them.

A final introductory note: charisms, though from above, as our spatial imagery likes to put it, ordinarily follow human growth patterns. They take time, in other words, and attention and cultivation and desire and encouragement and perseverance and exercise to amount to something "the birds of the air" can find strength in. All this having been said, if this desire to cultivate them "for others" is lacking, it is hard to see how they would ever grow into effectiveness.

Vatican II on Charisms

Any orientation to charisms should begin with Vatican II's sporadic and brief attention to them. The term appears fourteen different times in the documents but in no consistent way. *Lumen gentium*'s §4 contended that "[the Spirit] furnishes and directs [the Church] with various gifts both hierarchical and charismatic. . . ." This is potentially a very significant statement, but since it is not spelled out, the ecclesiological implications of it are not immediately obvious.

In §12 of the same document it becomes even more obvious that there is considerable uncertainty about exactly where these charisms fit ecclesially. "[The Spirit] distributes special graces among the faithful of every rank. By these gifts He makes them fit and ready to undertake the various tasks or offices advantageous for the renewal and upbuilding of the Church. . . . These charismatic gifts, whether they be the most outstanding or the more simple and widely diffused, are to be received with thanksgiving and consolation for they are exceedingly suitable and useful for the needs of the Church." This passage isn't at all clear about the relationship between graces, gifts, offices and charisms; they are all smudged together. What, for example, does it mean in practice for "the faithful of every rank" to be receiving gifts to "undertake the various tasks and offices for the upbuilding of the Church"? Again, the ecclesiological implications are not pursued.

The Decree on the Apostolate of the Laity §3 again addresses the subject of the charisms but now broadens them to see them and their exercise for both Church and world. "From the reception of these charisms or gifts, there arise for each believer the right and duty to use them in

the Church and in the world for the good of mankind and the upbuilding of the Church." How has the "right" to use these charisms in the
Church been made operational?

Two other uses of the term "charisms" in the documents of Vatican II
are of great significance but again are not pursued. The charism of infallibility is said to be something the whole Church has received, but
the context of the assertion is related only to the pope. It is "individually
present" in him when he is expounding on or defending a doctrine of
the Catholic faith. *Lumen gentium,* §25. It would seem to be of enormous
importance for the members of the Church to know how they participate or share in this charism of infallibility if for no other reason than
they could then know how the pope's "infallibility" relates to them.

No less tantalizing is *Presbyterorum ordinis* §9, wherein priests are
exhorted to discover "with the instinct of faith, acknowledge with joy
and foster with diligence the various humble and exalted charisms of
the laity." How this exhortation has been heeded in our parishes since
Vatican II is an empirical question that is not likely to result in many af-
firmative answers.

The fact is the Council was quite unprepared to deal with the subject
of the charisms. They entered in by the back door, so to speak, and received no adequate treatment in the Council documents. Even more
broadly, they have had a very unsatisfactory treatment in the whole
history of theology. There were those in the Council, e.g., Cardinal
Ernesto Ruffini, who protested even the use of the term "charism,"
foreseeing disorder by reintroducing them. He explained to the assembled Council Fathers that charisms had ceased after the first years of
the Church. Betraying a deep clericalism with which the Fathers did
not concur, Ruffini observed: "We cannot stably and firmly rely on
charismatic lay persons for the advancement of the Church and the
apostolate, for charisms—contrary to the opinion of many separated
brethren who freely speak of the ministry of charismatics in the
Church—are today very rare and entirely singular."[2]

In a speech given several days later, Leon-Joseph Cardinal Suenens
objected to this position by insisting that "one should not think that the
gifts of the Spirit consist exclusively of extraordinary and astonishing
phenomena. . . . Do not all of us know, each in his own diocese, lay
people, men and women, who are truly called by God . . . and given
special gifts? . . ."[3] "Each and every Christian, whether lettered or un-

---

[2] *Acta Synodalia Concilii Vaticani II,* v. 10, pars 2 (Vatican City, 1972) 629–30.

[3] Leon-Joseph Cardinal Suenens, "The Charismatic Dimension of the Church," in
H. Kung *et alia* (eds.) *Council Speeches of Vatican II* (Glen Rock, N.J.: Paulist Press,
1964) 29–30.

lettered, has his charism in daily life."[4] The questions of how frequent or infrequent, extraordinary or ordinary, the charisms are remains with us to this day.

Perhaps the most important thing the Council did was to reiterate the still unexamined expression from Pius XII's *Mystici Corporis*, from 1943, that the living organism that is the Church is directed by two kinds of gifts, hierarchical and charismatic. Like Pius XII, the Council had a sense that hierarchical gifts keep the organism organic, while charismatic gifts keep it vital. The Dominican theologian Christian Duquoc puts the matter crisply: "The charisms bear witness at the core of the institution to the fact that it is necessary for its very survival not to lock itself up in a legal order or a rationally planned institution. The charism constitutes a bridge between the Church as event and the Church as institution, or the gratuitous and the legal, or the unpredictable and what is planned, or the Spirit and the structure."[5]

The Ecclesiology of Charisms

All of the above makes it obvious that charisms are not peripheral to the life of the Church but more like the yeast that makes the Church a Church. Still there is something deliciously unpredictable about the Spirit, while there is something predictably institutional about the Church within which the Spirit works through the charisms of its members. The charisms functioning independently of the structures of the institution would be chaos, while the institution without the charisms would be monotonous, uniform, lifeless. So each needs the other.

At their most enlightened the Church's priests and bishops know they must evoke the charisms of the people, since even its best programs and training don't automatically produce them. Furthermore, they must not be confined in their exercise to the inner life of the Church, since they are given by the Spirit to upbuild and enrich the institution, making it a more vital community. An institution which neither expects nor makes room for their exercise will inevitably make its own structure and order dominate the Spirit and its gifts. Charism reminds the Church what kind of an institution it is, how dependent it is on the unpredictable wind of the Spirit to blow where it would, when it would and whether it would. The Church's laws must be careful to create the conditions of possibility for the Spirit to function as It would. "Where the Spirit of the Lord is, there is freedom" (2 Cor 3:17).

[4] *Ibid.*

[5] Christian Duquoc, O.P., "Charism as the Social Expression of the Unpredictable Nature of Grace," in *Charisms in the Church,* Duquoc and Floristan (eds.), (New York: The Seabury Press, 1978) 93.

How could the Church make a law that would exclude *a priori* the freedom of the Spirit to seize some portion of the community to minister to the upbuilding of the rest of the community? One of the more troubling questions facing Catholic Christianity is whether the gratuitous and unpredictable character of charisms given by a very free Spirit should be inhibited by an *a priori* based on gender. And even more generally, we must inquire whether the serious dearth of vocations is due to laws written for previous generations rather than to an absence of such calls today or to an unwillingness of the called to follow them?

Obviously, every charism is a call. What if the call is being issued and the possibility of responding to it is being thwarted because of a law? The whole Church with its charism of infallibility needs to look at its *a priori* to see if it is guilty of trying to domesticate the Spirit, confining it to a house too small for It to operate in freely.

Getting this Pauline doctrine of the charisms right is a very tricky business. It is also a dangerous business. Charisms can be powerful if they are given a chance to be exercised. This power can be renewing or strong enough to destroy a community's order, as the early Church came to understand both in the Pauline communities and in the Montanist era a couple centuries later. To those who might think this issue of the charisms is being overdone, it should be instructive to see the phenomenal growth of the Churches that have the charisms as a constitutive part of their structures. The Pentecostal Churches, for example, which took their start in the twentieth century, already claim in excess of 470 million adherents, with far too many of them former Catholics.[6] These Churches have developed a very charismatic ecclesiology, meaning they fully expect and train their members personally to discover and exercise the charisms of the Spirit.[7]

What kind of community does Roman Catholicism experience? What kind of community does it expect in this matter of the powers of its members? There is either too little expectation or too much conflict about these and the present structures within which they operate or would operate. Discerning what powers are of the Spirit and what are not is essential to a healthy ecclesiology. The character of the powers in conflict are of two kinds, with two very different spirits motivating them. One is the spirit of power as the world knows it, which seeks to control, or to have its own way. The other is the spirit of power as the

---

[6] David B. Barrett, "Annual Statistical Table on Global Mission: 1995," *International Bulletin on Missionary Research* 19:1 (January 1955) 25.

[7] Guy Duffield and N. VanCleave, *Foundations of Pentecostal Theology* (Los Angeles: Life Bible College, 1983) chapter 6.

Gospels explain it, which is willing to be poured out like a libation for the many. Jesus is the embodiment of this second kind of power, which is the power of a servant. The powers of the charisms the Spirit of Christ confers, given their source, will be congenial and in continuity with Jesus' understanding and exercise of power. Those possessing them will not seek to "lord it over others" (Matt 20:25).

Catholic Christianity has always agreed that the one most responsible for keeping the powers in order is the bishop. And those responsible for receiving the powers are the rest of the members, who owe it to the bishops to hand them something increasingly powerful that they have to keep in order. The members do not owe the hierarchy acquiescence in an order that is merely juridical.

Historically, when there has been power without order there has been turmoil, division, chaos. And when there has been order without power there has been indifference, conformism, lifelessness. And there still are. It is estimated there are 20,800 separate Christian denominations.[8] How many of these came into being because of a failure to keep this dialectic between order and power in balance, would be instructive to know. Power can overwhelm order. And order can suffocate power. Balance in this dialectic is the only way to have a healthy ecclesial community.

It is far too simple to think one can deal with this dialectic by playing off church office against charism, as many have in the past. One of the reasons it isn't that simple is that so many office holders are not without notable charisms, and many of these are obviously in office because of their charisms. But by the same token there would appear to be office holders without any real charisms if we use the growth and up-building of the Church as any criterion of their presence.

I am not going to handle the liberal Protestant authors from the early part of this century on the relationship between office and charism. I have in mind such figures as R. Sohm, Adolph Von Harnack, Gotthold Hasenhuttl, Emil Brunner, and Auguste Sabatier who, generally speaking, pneumaticize their ecclesiologies while denigrating office as a human construct. Granted, a complete study of the matter of the dialectic operating here would have to take pneumatology into account. To be even more thorough, one would have to examine the sociological analyses of how charism functions within and over against institutions.

In a very Catholic appreciation of the issue, Hans Urs von Balthasar would stymie those who are all too ready to see office in the Church in

---

[8] David Barrett (ed.), *World Christian Encyclopedia* (New York: Oxford University Press, 1982) preface.

a negative light, since he finds these offices as already begun with the calling and training of the twelve by Christ. Office in the Church is "crystallized love" for him; it must take its cue in its exercise from this font and source.[9] Although he doesn't employ it, his contention might be reinforced if one recalls the unforgettable scene at the end of John's Gospel where Simon Peter is quizzed three times: "Do you love me?"— and with each affirmation is given the office: "Feed my sheep" (John 21:15-17). However, office as crystalized love might not hold up under historical scrutiny as well as it does scripturally. Von Balthasar also has as a major function of the charism of office the coordination and integration of the charisms into the unity of the Church.[10]

Most charisms are not interactive with church office and are not meant to be. They are given by God to be exercised in and for the world, and their scope is either the more immediate terrain of family, or the networks of relationship in neighborhood or job, with some extending to the larger, more complex terrain of the public, with its professions, civic structures, political institutions, etc. The Son was sent into the world not to condemn it but to minister to it, and he does this, it would appear, largely through these ministerial charismatic gifts.

Although much about them remains a mystery to us, we can always regain our footing by returning again to their purpose: the common good. We know that this is God's will and purpose in distributing them. The common good also happens to be what every community that would be more of a community strives for. If these assertions are true, we should expect that effective change will come about in communities where the change agents are acting from the particular charisms God gives them for their community's upbuilding, even if they haven't the slightest awareness that this is the source of their efficacy. In this connection one would have to be Rip Van Winkle to miss how often in the last couple of decades leadership has been the subject of conferences, books, seminars, studies in professional, business and political circles. The subject has become urgent because leadership is seen to be so scarce. Students of the subject might find much fruit in examining the untapped resources of the charisms without which our professions, cities and country find themselves seriously leaderless.

It should be said and said with emphasis that most charisms enrich circles that are not ecclesial. Most charisms are evoked by the encouragement of nurturers who seldom see themselves functioning religiously. Their essential role in upbuilding of individuals one by one,

---

[9] Von Balthasar, "Charis and Charism" *Explorations in Theology* vol. II (San Francisco: Ignatius Press, 1991) 313.

[10] *Loc. cit.*, 330.

and in small circles and large, goes largely unrecorded. Yet everyone exists in and functions from interlocking interdependencies. It is the varying degrees of indifference to one another in these interdependencies that keeps many charisms latent or undiscovered or underdeveloped. Conversely, the nurturing skills that "bring people out" go a long way in bringing charisms to bear on Church and society. Educators and therapists, parents and friends, are the people who spring to mind as the ones most likely to effect this calling forth. Important as these individuals are, it is in communities that charisms are recognized and strengthened.

A wider-than-church lens should be used for discerning the Spirit's distribution of the charisms. Some theologians would trace those charisms to the power of the Spirit in the energies of those who serve the common good. Through these energies, people are trying to build just structures, toppling unjust ones and winning agreements of reconciliation and peace between hostile factions, even between nations.[11]

History and the Charisms

We began this study by focusing mostly on charisms in the Church, not to become narrowly ecclesio-centric in how we view them but, better to understand them theologically. We will now return to this narrower focus because, again, if we can understand them better in the Church we will see how they can function more effectively in the world and for the sake of the world.

There is the unfortunately widespread thesis we have already heard that the *charismata* came about at a very early moment in the primitive Church and that that moment was superseded by the Church order we have now. So, from immature to mature! Certainly, the Churches that Paul oversaw did not have an ordained priesthood, and his understanding of ministry as charism-centered came from that very early moment. So it might be more accurate to ascribe immaturity to the present Churches that do not hold charism and order in tension very well.

The Lutheran exegete Ernst Käsemann wrote a hugely influential essay on charism some years ago (1949) that is still provocative.[12] He sees charism as something that goes with the territory of being a Christian so that you don't have some special Christians who are charismatic and then the rest of us, since the Spirit individuates and concretizes the grace each Christian receives in becoming a member of the body of

---

[11] E.g. Walter Hollenweger, "Creator Spiritus," *Theology,* January 1978, 38ff.

[12] Ernst Kasemann, "Ministry and Community in the New Testament," *Essays on New Testament Themes* (London: SCM Press, 1964) 63ff.

Christ by the distinct charism with which each is endowed. The distinctiveness of each one's charism creates a call to live and serve in a distinctive way within the community or society. "The general rule is each one should lead the life the Lord has assigned him or her" (1 Cor 7:17).

But before long this very egalitarian way of seeing and doing ministry seems to have been bypassed, and a more structured understanding of ministry followed in which it seems only some had a charism. 1 and 2 Timothy signal the change. Presbyters, a group unheard of in the beginning years, laid their hands on a new presbyter, Timothy, and he was exhorted to recall and "not neglect the gift [charism]" he received at that time (1 Tim 4:14). He was later exhorted to "stir into flame the gift [charism] of God bestowed when my hands were laid on you" (2 Tim 1:6). When we presumed these Pastoral Epistles were authored by Paul, this huge change in the meaning of charisms was not comprehended. But now the Corinthians' ministry of charisms seems to have been superseded by one exercised largely by the presbyters and bishops. And the legitimacy of their ministry is not due to their charisms but to their being in a continuum with the apostles. The real bearers of the Spirit to the Churches are now the officeholders.

There's a complex history behind these forty years of church experience between the Corinthian letters in the 50s and the Timothy's in the 90s, and it is only partly known. Without spelling out even the little we do know of what happened, the change raises the question of how many are seen to have charisms in this later moment of ministry.

It would obviously be totalitarian to have a Church in which the only legitimate initiatives and impulses given room to operate are those which come from the church's office holders, since the texts clearly indicate that it is the Spirit who directs the Church through *charismata* that are not linked to office or to office holders. To think or act otherwise is certain to stifle, quench, or extinguish the Spirit.

What happened to the charisms since Paul's enthusiastic Corinthian discourse about them is that they were absorbed only in part into the pastoral offices of the bishop and the presbyterate. More accurately, an episcopal overseer role as the coordinator of the charisms was inevitable lest they disappear, dissipate, or divide the congregations. Even staying just with Paul's experience we see how he became pragmatic about the various charisms. For example, he contrasts two charisms—speaking in tongues and prophecy—and assigns so much more value to the latter because it upbuilds, encourages and consoles hearers (1 Cor 14). Furthermore, once the office of bishop was in place, he was obviously responsible for discerning which prophets were false prophets and which true, which prophecies of true prophets were authentic and which off the wall. He would have to be seen as having the necessary insight into the Gospels and the faith that in itself was a form of prophecy. But endowed with that kind of insight, from the charism of discernment, it is easy to see how the charism of prophecy might come to be less important, and to some extent, leave prophets somewhat superfluous with sound doctrine prevenient.

The question that is always posed of Catholic ecclesiology by members of other Christian Churches is whether it was necessary to elevate the stature and job description of the overseers, the *episkopoi*, the bishops, to being in a continuum with the apostles, as the early Church eventually did. Certainly a continuity was of enormous importance, but the other side of this is that the simple faithful did not enjoy that kind of legitimacy. The bishops seem to have trumped them, in many ways.

As overseers, the *episkopoi* held offices so that the bearers of charisms could function through the structures the office holders oversaw. Catholic ecclesiology would not play off these two sources of authority against one another. It would see them both coming from the same Spirit. Furthermore, the office holders were themselves not bereft of charisms. Nonetheless, some conflict will inevitably happen between these two forms of the Spirit's actions, since one is moving toward unifying and consolidating, and the other toward upbuilding and enriching.

God's unities are always coming into being, it seems, rather than already constituted. Charisms certainly play into these ever-being-made unities. The incursion of a special charism into the Church or a community can be easily misjudged, especially by those whose function is a unitary one since it usually adds to the complexity of their unitary task. By the same token those with purported charisms can too easily dismiss the importance of unifiers, those with the complex task of unity.

Keeping these two actions of the Spirit, hierarchical and charismatic, in a fruitful tension is primarily but not exclusively the responsibility of the bishop. Tension, of course, does not have to mean conflict. It should be enriching. Assuming the episcopal order is no less of the Spirit than charisms, a belief that is foundational to a Catholic understanding of the faith, it appears that at present order and unity are in the ascendancy. A charism is a power, a ministerial empowerment. Is the ministry of the Church sufficiently charismatic, is it open to and resplendent with the manifold gifts of the Spirit? If it is not, why not? To what extent have the presbyterate, the episcopate and the papacy been either too dominant—or at least been perceived to be so? Either way, the result is that charismatic ministries are insufficiently forthcoming. A listless congregation, a passivity in liturgy, and an indifference about the service of others are all symptomatic of a tension relaxed in favor of order.

There is even better evidence of a failure in keeping the necessary tension between office and charism, namely when ministry does not have its center in the congregation but rather in office—presbyterial, episcopal, and papal. Good ecclesiology has the whole believing community participating in the ministry and mission of Christ through the exercise of the charisms. If the wind is not able to blow where it will (John 3:8), there will be a stillness and an un-freedom. Confining ministry to office ties charisms to office holders and the Spirit is left unfree.

What I am contending is that charism is both a call and an empowerment to do ministry in and beyond the Church. It would be too facile an explanation to blame clericalism for a felt absence here. Clericalism is much less the problem than ignorance, doctrinal ignorance. But even more than this, the dearth seems traceable to the willingness of far too many in the Church whose attitude has become, Let the clergy do it. The only antidote to all of these shortcomings is a radical change in expectation on the part of office holders and members alike about the frequency and power of charisms.

Three Theological Excursions

(A) Fr. Richard Dillon, an exegete from Fordham University, has developed an insight into charism that relieves us of the need to use the paradigm used in this article which holds charism and office in tension. He sees Jesus, who taught with authority, unlike the scribes and pharisees, as acting from a charismatic authority, from the prophetic charism of *exousia*. Jesus teaches and acts free of "an institutionalized orthodoxy which gives some people their exclusive claim to God's favor"; he is free of the need to impose "that most cherished and fortified of all boundaries . . . which distinguishes between good people and bad."[13] His authority, his *exousia*, derives from "the immediacy of the gift imparted with God's Spirit."[14]

According to Paul, this same charism of *exousia* was passed on to the followers of Jesus, who were redeemed, apart from the Law, through their faith in the Crucified (1 Cor 8:9; Rom 3:21-26; Phil. 3:4-11). Their freedom did not give Jesus' followers freedom to do as they chose. They

---

[13] Richard J. Dillon, "Speaking of Authority and Charism From the New Testament," from *Raising the Torch of Good News*, Bernard Prusak (ed.) *The Annual Publication of the College Theology Society,* 1986 (Lanham: University Press of America) 6–7.

[14] *Loc. cit.,* 5.

had to live under and according to the reign of God's own righteous-ness, a righteousness which had God already reigning in their hearts and in the communities that proclaimed Jesus "Lord." This new au-thority that Christians received "instilled an unconditional obligation rooted in an unconditional gift; it was a summons to full moral in-tegrity and authenticity."[15] It is from this vision of a new kind of and new source for authority that office and charism can be seen in a wholly different light. This gift of *exousia* never becomes the possession of those receiving it. Hence, authority "can never be severed from the lib-erating gift that has been received in Christ."[16] The Catholic temptation, therefore, to "apotheosize the Church and speak of her as a quasi-independent, self-contained teaching authority" is drastically dimin-ished.[17] Vatican II reminds us that "the teaching office is not above the word of God but serves it, teaching only what has been handed on . . ." (*Dei Verbum* §10).

(B) Karl Rahner's treatment of the subject of charisms is, as usual, trenchant. He saw the Church as the on-going concretization in history of the *charismata* whose author is the Spirit of Christ. And he saw "the institutional element in the Church simply as one of the regulating fac-tors (albeit a necessary one) for this charismatic element."[18] He con-trasts open to closed systems and sees the Church as having to be an open system, meaning one "that the definitive condition in which it ac-tually stands neither can nor should be defined in any adequate sense in terms of any one point immanent within the system itself."[19] An open system is defined by a point outside of itself. The point outside the system which defines the Church is "the dominion of God." It is also, to be sure, from outside the system that charisms come to it. "We use the term charismatic," Rahner suggests, "to stand for that ultimate incalculability which belongs to all the other elements in the Church in their mutual interplay. . . . the charismatic is transcendental in charac-ter, not one element in the system of the Church but a special character-istic of the system as a whole."[20] Rahner saw charisms as the point at which the lordship of Christ is most clearly exercised.

---

[15] *Ibid.*

[16] *Loc. cit.,* 8.

[17] *Loc. cit.,* 8.

[18] Karl Rahner, "Observations on the Factor of the Charismatic in the Church," *Theological Investigations,* vol. XII (New York: The Seabury Press, 1974) 86. This 1969 theologizing on charism is much more progressive than his 1957 article on the same subject noted in endnote #1.

[19] *Loc. cit.,* 89.

[20] *Ibid.*

In a sweeping ecclesiological assertion, he claims that "the institutional factor in the Church . . . remains encompassed by the charismatic movement of the Spirit in the Church, the Spirit who again and again ushers the Church as an open system into a future which God alone, and no one else has arranged."[21] Finally, Rahner contends that the charismatic element in the Church simply isn't on the same plane as the institutional but "is the first and the most ultimate among the formal characteristics inherent in the very nature of the Church as such."[22] He laments that Vatican II's *Lumen gentium* did not take the position that charisms belong to the constitution of the Church, but only that "they are exceedingly suitable and useful for the needs of the Church." He notes with regret that in Vatican II "the Church of officialdom still continues constantly to occupy the center of the ecclesiological stage" even after the Council itself had promisingly placed the People of God chapter ahead of the one concerned with "the Church's official functionaries."[23]

The eschatology of the charisms is a theme not as well attended to by theologians as by Paul, who saw the charisms, e.g., prophecy, tongues, ceasing (1 Cor 13:8). Could he have meant "ceasing" not in the eschaton but having accomplished what their exercise was meant to upbuild? Could it be that a charism is fire stolen from heaven that posits some thing of the reign of God in time? Jurgen Moltmann might be implying as much when he comments that the charisms are "designations of what is, not of what ought to be."[24] Like all of God's inbreaking actions in history they are sent in light of the definitive, future kingdom of God.

Meanwhile, if we see the charisms as making possible now whatever of the reign of God can exist in time while also being augurs of the final eschatological union God will have with "all flesh," then the importance we attach to them would escalate exponentially. "As the power of resurrection, the Spirit is the reviving presence of the future of eternal life in the midst of the history of death; or the presence of the future of the new creation in the midst of the dying life of this world and its evil state. Through the Spirit's powers the eschatological new thing—behold I make all things new—becomes the new thing in history."[25] This is a reminder that each charism bearer takes his or her place in an edifice of spirit like living stones that are being built into a chosen race, a royal priesthood, a holy nation, a people set apart.

[21] *Loc. cit.*, 94.

[22] *Loc. cit.*, 97.

[23] *Loc. cit.*, 98.

[24] Jurgen Moltmann, *The Church in the Power of the Spirit* (San Francisco: Harper & Row, 1977) 293.

[25] *Loc. cit.*, 294.

Isolating their Difference

I have left this part till the end because it is a complex matter. What are the "near misses" to charisms, i.e., akin to but not exactly charisms? We have already seen that they are unique gifts that people receive from God for the sake of others. How are the powers of faith, hope, and love—the supernatural virtues, as tradition calls them, *charismata*, as Paul calls them—different from charisms as understood in this paper? They would fail on the note of distinctiveness, since presumably all the faithful have received these powers at baptism and continue to be imbued with them. However, they could hardly fail totally on the note of being for others since the powers of faith, hope, and love not only perfect the one receiving them, but in the exercise of those powers others are obviously benefitted. So, this distinction about what benefits others *(gratia gratis data)* and what has the individual grow in grace *(gratia gratum faciens)* is helpful only up to a point in isolating charisms, since it would be hard to see how the benefitting of others would also not redound to one's growth in grace. Charisms and graces meld one into the other.

How do the charisms differ from the different dispositions of character or strengths of soul of a person that are usually called virtues? Since both are relied upon for developing strong bonds with others, they are similar. And since they are developed through praxis and give evidence of the assistance of God, they are similar. Scripture hints at their difference when it sees faith in two different ways, first as something all believers are presumed to have, but also it sees faith as something few have but on which many can rely. In this second sense, the charism would be faith to an extraordinary degree, like the faith to move mountains (1 Cor 13:2). "Through the Spirit one receives faith . . . another the gift of healing" (1 Cor 12:9).

Can the time-worn categories of "the grace of a calling" or "the grace of office" be seen as conferring charisms? This is even more difficult to answer yes or no to, since it brings up the question of the relationship between charisms and roles. We all have roles to play, and we can be sure God will not be stingy in supplying us with the graces we need to perform those roles for the sake of others. Are such role-related graces to be counted charisms? Possibly we could see them that way, but it might be better to see charisms relating to roles if the performance of the role is notably suffused with an energy that cannot be humanly accounted for.

When the roles we play come from states of life like spouse or parent or doctor or lawyer, etc., the same question resurfaces. Again, can we not piously presume that, since each of these is intrinsically other-directed and other-regarding, God would not be stingy in according the graces necessary for executing the duties of these states of life? We in fact do presume this, but would these graces be called charisms? Avery Dulles' terse comment on this is apposite: "Charisms can be seen as spiritual gifts proportioned to a person's office, state of life, and social responsibilities. It is characteristic of the Holy Spirit to be a source of creativity, energy, enthusiasm and freedom."[26]

In brief, there was much hope after Vatican II that the charisms would become a much greater source of ministerial power in the Church and in society. This seems not to have happened. One reason for this is the indefiniteness of the theology of the charisms we were left with before and after the Council. This article is an attempt to generate a new theological interest in them.

---

[26] Avery Dulles, "Institution and Charism in the Church," *A Church to Believe In* (New York: Crossroad Publishing Co., 1985) 30.

"'Be Zealous for the Greater *Charismata*': Pauline Advice for the Church of the Twenty-First Century"

■ *Margaret M. Mitchell*

Introduction

Like most Americans of my generation I have tended to think of my life as being constituted fundamentally by choices I have made for my family life, my education, and my professional vocation. In deeper moments of prayer I have more humbly and rightly acknowledged the power of divine guidance through those choices, and through the people who have generously populated my life. But in reflecting these past months in preparation for this conference, and reading about the life and ministry of Leon-Joseph Cardinal Suenens, I have been confronted with yet another astonishing way of making sense of my own life: for, were it not for the leadership and boldness of this cardinal from Belgium, whom I never dreamed of meeting, nor imagined that his life intersected with mine, I would not be who or what I am today.

Just a generation ago my vocation in the Church would have been unthinkable: a Roman Catholic laywoman with a doctorate in biblical studies from the University of Chicago Divinity School (to which Cardinal Suenens paid a ground-breaking ecumenical visit in May of 1964),[1] who teaches New Testament (specializing in Paul, of all things) at McCormick Theological Seminary, a seminary of the Presbyterian Church (U.S.A.) which prepares women and men from a range of Protestant denominations for a variety of ministries in the Church of Jesus Christ. The work of Cardinal Suenens, at Vatican II and in countless other

---

[1] For a full record of Cardinal Suenens' visit to the University of Chicago Divinity School on May 4–5, 1964, see *Criterion* 3 (Spring 1964). I have also received a privileged window into that remarkable event from conversations with Jerald C. Brauer and Martin E. Marty.

initiatives for ecumenism and empowering the laity, has profoundly paved the way for my vocation in the Church (and I am sure for many of those here present). May I echo to you and to him the words of the apostle Paul: "Thanks be to God for his indescribable gift!" (2 Cor 9:15).

1 Corinthians 12–14 on Charismata in the Church

My task is to assist in opening up Scripture to inform us about the nature of charisms for the twenty-first century. The text I have chosen for our study, 1 Corinthians 12-14, is the most sustained treatment of the subject of spiritual gifts, *charismata*, in the Bible. This passage not coincidentally surfaces two of the fundamental values which were at the heart of Cardinal Suenens' vision: co-responsibility and respect for the particular spiritual gifts of each member of the Church.

Our purpose is to examine what Paul says about *charismata* in these famous chapters, and ask what his advice to the Corinthians can teach us about *charismata* for the twenty-first century. We shall see that from very early on in the Church diverse *charismata* were a source of both life and strife. My procedure here will be to offer an exegetical reading of 1 Corinthians 12–14, inviting you to engage the passage yourself in the NRSV translation. From my exegetical analysis of the text I shall make a preliminary assessment of the positive contributions Paul makes to contemporary dialogue over these issues, and further give an honest eye to the limitations or potentially negative consequences for the Church of the next century of Paul's advice to the Corinthian church in the first century. It is my view that 1 Corinthians, which is the apostle's fervent attempt to reunite a church torn apart by factions, presents us with a dual legacy. On the one hand in this letter Paul paints what is perhaps the most eloquent call for ecclesial unity in the New Testament. On the other hand, the apostle's unifying strategy raises significant questions for contemporary churches about the nature of compromise in the pursuit of concord, the extent of conformity required for unity, and the social and power dynamics involved in such negotiations.

Text in Context

First we need to reacquaint ourselves with our conversation partner this afternoon, the text. 1 Corinthians 12–14 is a long section of Paul's First Letter to the Corinthians. This section is itself a literary unit which begins with the heading, "concerning spiritual gifts," in 12:1, and concludes in 14:40, "Let everything be done decently and in order." All three chapters deal with divisions caused in the church at Corinth by competing *charismata*. Chapter 12 begins with Paul's insistence that the

Spirit is what enables the confession of faith "Jesus is Lord." He then follows up in verses 4–11 with his exposition of the divine apportionment of gifts among the members of the ecclesia. In verses 12–27 Paul expounds on the famous Body of Christ imagery for the church, which appears first here in his writings (see also Rom 12). Chapter 12 ends with a pecking order of church offices and *charismata* (v. 28ff). Chapter 14 is a detailed discussion of liturgical spiritual gifts and their impact on the whole community. Paul wishes the Corinthians to recognize that while speaking in tongues is a *charisma*, it is also a potentially divisive *charisma* which must be tempered by the greater gift of prophecy, which builds up *the Church* instead of the individual believer.

These two chapters, 12 and 14, frame what is perhaps the most famous chapter of 1 Corinthians, the so-called hymn to love in chapter 13. It is a common practice for Paul to use such a sandwiching technique as this—that is, to put in the middle of his detailed treatment of a specific topic a more general exemplification of a higher principle which the situation calls forth, in this case, love[2] In arranging his argument in this way, Paul throws love into relief, and accents its key role for the Church.

Our focal chapters 12–14 cannot be understood correctly apart from the whole letter in which they are situated. One of the advances of Pauline scholarship of the last twenty-five years or so has been the emphasis on Paul's letters as genuine letters, as actual pieces of correspondence written in the heat of the joys and struggles of pastoral ministry. Thus Paul's letters should not be understood as time capsules of eternal, uncontextualized instructions, but rather as the apostle's considered theological and practical response to real issues in the life of actual churches. Today we would call Paul a "practical theologian," but he hasn't changed so much as we, perhaps, have finally caught up with him. 1 Corinthians in particular is what I would call a fundamental work of "practical ecclesiology," because Paul was forced, when faced with a Church he regarded as on the verge of destruction, to reflect upon the meaning of and fundamental values for the Church.

Why did Paul write 1 Corinthians?[3] In 1:11 Paul says he has heard from Chloe's people that there are "contentions" among the Corinthians. These contentions, among other things, seem to be rooted in allegiances to the different missionaries—Paul, Apollos, and Cephas (Peter).

---

[2] See also chapter 9 on freedom, in the midst of chapters 8 and 10, and, within chapter 7, the section 7:17-24 on "calling."

[3] The exegetical and historical reading here presented is based upon the research which is presented in my book, *Paul and the Rhetoric of Reconciliation* (Tübingen: J.C.B. Mohr [Paul Siebeck] 1991; Louisville, Ky.: Westminster/John Knox, 1993).

Recent research has also detected in the letter evidence of socio-economic dimensions of these conflicts (rich against poor, slave against free, Jewish-Christian against Gentile-Christian, male against female), and some geographical basis for conflict between local house-churches in the same city.

At the time he wrote this letter, Paul was in Ephesus in Asia Minor. Chloe's people have journeyed from Corinth to see him, as has another delegation of prominent Corinthians (16:17). Further, some of the Corinthians have written Paul a letter (7:1). Paul has also received oral reports or heard rumors concerning a case of sexual immorality, and divisions at the Lord's Supper (5:1; 11:19). Now, how are we to account for these numerous contacts between Paul and the Church at Corinth? Why did so many people make the roughly 175-mile sea voyage or take the months-long land route via Macedonia to reach Paul at Ephesus? The reason Paul has had so many contacts from the Corinthians, the reason that his in-box is full, so to speak, is because he is dealing with a divided church. People were not knocking down Paul's door in Ephesus merely to tell him that their church is divided, either. No, they were traveling and writing to Paul to enlist his support for their point of view. "Paul, tell them we're right, that they shouldn't speak in tongues during worship because we don't understand what they are saying . . . Paul, tell them that we're right, for after all, you spoke in tongues while you were here?" (cf. 14:18). So what was Paul to do?

Well, Paul first had to make a long-distance pastoral diagnosis. He decided that none of the disputes (which deal with matters ranging from liturgical behavior to marital mores to eating habits to hairstyles, to beliefs about the resurrection) is as important as what these disputes have caused: division and disunity in the Church. So, he wrote a letter in which he did not initially delve into and adjudicate the different issues, for he recognized that to do so would be both risky and futile. Instead, he wrote a letter which throughout urged the Corinthians toward unity, and sought compromise wherever possible on the subjects which divided the church members. Paul centered his appeal in the thematic sentence of 1:10: "I urge you, brothers and sisters, through the name of our Lord Jesus Christ, all to say the same thing, and let there not be factions (*schismata*) among you, but be reconciled in the same mind and in the same opinion" (my translation).

Exegesis and Appropriation

My procedure will be to study our passage in three large blocks, pausing after each brief set of exegetical comments to ask the significance of Paul's argument for the Church of the twenty-first century.

1 Corinthians 12—The Body of Christ. With the historical background we just rehearsed in mind it becomes immediately clear that we should not read chapters 12–14 as an abstract discussion of church order, but rather as a central part of Paul's unifying strategy for this divided Church. We can see from the text that the Corinthian Christians have become divided by their different spiritual gifts: some feel and act superior in their attainment of *charismata* while others feel and act inferior by comparison. The expression of superiority is stated twice in 12:21: "I have no need of you," and that of inferiority is repeated twice in verses 15 and 16: "because I am not a hand, I do not belong to the body." Paul considers both of these sentiments to be antithetical to his overarching view of the Church.

This formulation by Paul is his adaption of a Greco-Roman political commonplace for unity which goes back as far as the fifth century B.C.E. There is a famous fable of a Roman statesman Menenius Agrippa, who persuaded the plebs at Rome to end their factionalism and be reconciled with the patricians by telling them a parable about what happened to a body when the hands and feet went on strike and refused to feed the belly: the body died and they with it. As the story goes, the plebs immediately recognized the wisdom in this—that by cutting off the patricians (the belly) by their strike, they would kill themselves—and returned to work. What the body metaphor stresses is unity in diversity through mutual interdependence. Each member is necessary for the health of the body; each member plays its appropriate role, upon which all others depend.

You can see that this is precisely what Paul is doing in 12:12 and the following verses. All members depend on one another. Paul's christianizing of this Greco-Roman political concept of the society as a body can be seen in 12:13: one becomes a member of this body not by birth or by purchasing citizenship, but by baptism into one Spirit. The new social-theological entity, the very body of Christ, is to be characterized by its unity. For Paul unity in the body of Christ is rooted in its divine apportionment, as he says in 12:24-25: "But *God* has so arranged the body, giving the greater honor to the inferior member, that there may be no dissension *(schisma)* within the body, but the members may have the same care for one another." This unity is not a mere wish or fringe benefit, either; for Paul it is an organic, physical reality rooted in the very identity of the members of the body, as he says in 12:26: "If one member suffers, all suffer together with it; if one member is honored, all rejoice together with it." The members of the body of Christ are enlivened and united by the same spirit of baptism, that same Spirit which apportions *charismata* (as he said in 12:7) "for the common good."

Body Building for the Twenty-First Century

How interesting it is that this ecclesiological self-understanding, summarized in the body of Christ imagery, was honed by the apostle Paul, not from observing that harmony in action, but rather in seeking to foster unity when what he saw was contention. In reflecting on this, I would like to raise eight fundamental issues which emerge in Paul's argument in 1 Cor 12 which are of particular relevance for the topic of this conference:

How Common is the Common Good? According to Paul, *charismata,* spiritual gifts from God, are given to individuals (v. 11), but they are given *for the common good* (v. 7). This is a needed reminder that *charismata* are not private possessions. However, the pastoral question this raises is a fundamentally political one: who discerns or determines what is the common good? What happens to those who have this decided for them? How are alternative visions of the common good weighed and judged?

Which Gifts? There are different *charismata* in members of the Church. Paul names some representative gifts in 12:8-10, a rather unusual, and surely not complete, list: utterance of wisdom, utterance of knowledge, faith, gifts of healing, working of miracles, prophecy, discernment of spirits, tongues, interpreting tongues. This catalogue of gifts, with its emphasis on vocal expression, shows quite clearly that Paul's argument here is composed with the specific Corinthian situation in mind, where liturgical speech acts were a major cause of dissension. We might ask, what we would put on our list of essential and yet controversial *charismata* for the Church in our times?

Who Gets What Gift? Paul's exposition of the disposition of *charismata* by the Spirit in 12:8-10 does not presume to answer why the Spirit chooses to give one gift "to one" and another gift "to another." He does not clue us in to the Spirit's hiring practices, nor does he limit the gifts to any single category of person.

Diversity not Uniformity. The spirit who gives *diverse* gifts is the same Spirit who *unifies* the body. But the body of Christ itself is not monoform; it is made up of distinct and different members (as Paul writes in 12:19-20: "If all were a single member, where would the body be? As it is, there are many members, yet one body"). Therefore, unity in the Church through uniformity or simple lockstep conformity is ruled out from the start.

Hierarchy Upheld and Challenged. Within this diversity, though Paul urges that all members depend upon all the others, he does not deny that some members appear to have higher status than others. Indeed, the very choice of the body metaphor on his part involves an acceptance of some form of status distinctions (wouldn't it be better to be a hand than an ingrown toenail?). Paul deals with the inherent hierarchy of the members of the body in two paradoxical ways. First, twice Paul asserts that God has placed the members of the body as God wishes (see vv. 18 and 24; cf. 11). This would seem to indicate divine legitimation for ecclesial hierarchy, for the pecking order of body parts. But Paul at the same time announces that God has relativized the very status designations upon which a pecking order is based: "God has so arranged the body, giving the greater honor to the inferior member" (v. 24). The question we want to ask, of course, is how and when does God effect this revolution? And what does this have to do with the hierarchical order of church offices which Paul presents next in verses 28 and following ("first apostles, second prophets, third teachers . . .")? Does Paul ever resolve this paradox of a hierarchical body, which is understood in upside-down valuation? Have we?

Both Inferiority and Superiority Threaten the Church. Diversity of *charismata* caused contention in the church at Corinth because some thought their gift better than those possessed by others; the others in turn devalued their own gifts. Therefore, for Paul the unity of the Church in proper exercise of spiritual gifts is threatened, not just by the superiority of those who say (or think) "I have no need of you" but equally as much by those who accept for themselves an inferred position of inferiority, saying (or thinking), "I do not belong to the body." Unity in the Church depends upon a conversion of thinking *of both groups* to a unified vision of honor and suffering shared in common by the members of the body.

As Simple as the Trinity. Paul explores the unity in diversity of Christian spiritual gifts in verses 4–6 by reference to the triune divine (the same Spirit, the same Lord, the same God). In so doing Paul has defined one mystery with reference to another. But perhaps this gives us also a needed reminder that in asking about spiritual gifts in the lives of persons in the Church, and how best to cultivate them, that we are participating in a mysterious divine drama. Just as we Christians strangely believe that three persons make one God, so also it is perhaps only in God's peculiar logic (and arithmetic!) that diverse and sometimes competing gifts in varied individuals make a single united body of Christ.

Bodily Health. For Paul the body was a good metaphor for the Church because it insists that there is a common good—a common health—to the body which depends upon the cooperation and robustness of each constituent member. It may be fruitful for us to reflect not just upon the health of the body of Christ, but also its opposite: the ways in which the body may become ill. Medical anthropologists speak of two different types of "disease etiologies," or ways in which different cultures think about the body's vulnerability to disease: either from an invasion into the body of external agents which can bring sickness or disease ("germs"), or from an internal imbalance of the fluids, humors and temperatures of which the body is constituted.[4] We who worry about the health of the Church might ponder further how our theologies and our pastoral decisions appear to be governed by an implied choice about from what source the Church's health is most threatened—from without or from within. Unless we think carefully about this, preventive health care is impossible, and we may simply be rendered incapacitated by overwrought ecclesial hypochondria. In short, do we think and act as though the Church of the twenty-first century more needs a battery of flu shots, or a low-fat diet?

1 Corinthians 13—Love as the Greatest Charisma. Having just seen the precarious tension in chapter 12 between a hierarchical and a revolutionary view of God's governance of spiritual gifts in the Church, we turn to the famous chapter on love. That "chapter" actually begins in 12:31: "But strive for the *greater* gifts. And I will show you a still more excellent way." So, perhaps all gifts in the end are not equal, in Paul's view. In the discussion of love which follows, Paul presents love as the quintessential *charisma*, the highest spiritual gift. Love is contrasted in 13:1-2 with speaking in tongues and prophecy, the two most disputed liturgical gifts in this Corinthian church. Love is higher than those two *charismata* for two reasons. First, love unifies rather than divides. You can see this clearly in the familiar verses 4-8 ("love is patient, love is kind . . ."), which define love as the very opposite of contentiousness. Second, love remains (vv. 8, 13). The love which Paul urges the contentious Corinthians to pursue above all else is a dynamic force for unity.

The active power of love, for Paul, is the antidote to factionalism in the Church. Though chapter 12 stressed the diversity of *charismata* in the Church, chapter 13 emphasizes the single *charisma* that all Christians can share equally: the power of love. That is why Paul can say, "be zealous for the greater *charismata* in 12:31, even though in chapter 12 the various gifts were said to have been apportioned by the Spirit, and thus seem to be beyond individual practiced attainment. If you wish to

---

[4] See Dale B. Martin, *The Corinthian Body* (New Haven: Yale University Press, 1995) 139–62.

compete with one another, Paul says, you can compete in loving the most.

Love for the Twenty-First Century

For the Church of the twenty-first century, Paul's teaching has several implications, of which I shall name only three.

Saving Love. We need to rescue the word and concept of love from common cultural uses which have trivialized and depoliticized love. Love, for Paul, is profoundly social and profusely active. It bears little resemblance to the rapidly beating heart of Hallmark greeting cards, or the privatized sentimentalism of much popular cinema.

Love Whom? The love about which Paul was writing here was not directly love of spouse or child or even God (the uses to which we understandably like to put this passage), but rather the love for the other Christian with whom we are contending and bitterly disagreeing. It is love for the one in the Church who says, "I have no need of you" as equally for the one who says "I do not belong to the body." Love in the context of Paul's First Letter to the Corinthians, remember, is the antidote to factionalism in the Church; it is the sinews that bind together the kinetic members of the body.

Lasting Love. Love, for Paul, is genuine and lasting because it is tempered with humility. Look at the section in 13:8-12. Most human *charismata*—even the impressive divinely inspired gifts of tongues and prophecy—will pass away. Our present vision is only partial, and it is certainly temporary. "For now we see in a mirror, dimly, but then we will see face to face" (13:12). In verse 13 Paul says that only three things known to finite humanity are permanent: faith, hope and love. From wider reading in Paul's letters we know how he thinks of these three as rooted in time: faith is centered in a confession of what God has done in the past in the death and resurrection of Christ; hope is centered in the future in what God will do in the second coming of Christ; love is centered in the present in what God is now doing through the Spirit in the life of the Church. Love is the greatest of these. It is to be lived and, according to 14:1, pursued or "chased down."[5]

1 Corinthians 14—Seek the Upbuilding of the Church. After the "love intermezzo" Paul resumes the theme of competing spiritual gifts. From

---

[5] The Greek verb *diōkein* means both of these things. See W. Bauer, *et al., A Greek-English Lexicon of the New Testament and Other Early Christian Literature* (Chicago: University of Chicago Press, 1979) 202.

14:26 we get some picture of what Paul has heard was going on in Corinthian worship: "When you come together, each one has a hymn, a lesson, a revelation, a tongue, or an interpretation." There are so many wonderful gifts, so many lively signs of the spirit in this church, but Paul worries that the result is a cacophony, a riot of liturgical excesses which, though they may empower the individuals in their sense of giftedness, do not unify the Church. Paul zeroes in on this problem in 14:2-4 where he draws a contrast between speaking in tongues and prophesying: "For those who speak in a tongue do not speak to other people but to God; for nobody understands them, since they are speaking mysteries in the Spirit. On the other hand, those who prophesy speak to other people for their *upbuilding* and encouragement and consolation. Those who speak in a tongue *build up* themselves, but those who prophesy *build up* the Church." The leitmotif of this chapter, and indeed of all of 1 Corinthians, is the building up of the Church. We see this theme also in verse 5, at the end, "so that the Church may be built up"; in verse 12, "since you are eager for spiritual gifts, strive to excel in them for the building up of the Church"; and again in the formulation of the general rule in verse 26, "Let all things be done for building up."

Here we see Paul's second favorite image for the Church, which he had introduced in chapter 3 of this letter: "You are God's building" (3:10). Then he described himself as the master builder who had laid the singular foundation, Jesus Christ, and mentioned that others have built and will continue to build upon that foundation. In that context Paul catalogued the variety of building materials which may be used to construct the Church: gold, silver, precious stones, wood, grass, straw. And, further, Paul warned that each person's work would have to survive the test of time and of apocalyptic trials: "If what has been built on the foundation survives, the builder will receive a reward. If the work is burned up, the builder will suffer loss; the builder will be saved, but only as through fire" (3:14-15).

In order to recognize fully the power of Paul's image of the Church as God's building, we must remember that at this time there were no church buildings, no edifices set apart for Christian worship. The word we translate as "church," *ekklesia*, means "assembly," and refers to a collection of people. These *ekklesiai*, "churches," met in private homes. Paul calls this group of people metaphorically a "building." Since, for Paul, the Church is this (spiritualized) building, Christian decision-making should always be made with reference to a single priority: what will build up the Church.

In 1 Cor 14, what will build up the Church is exercise of one's *charismata* which first takes into account the full experience of the other members of the assembly with whom one is worshiping. Improper use of *charismata* creates divisions among people; in the words of verse 11, it makes "foreigners" (the Greek word is *barbaroi*, literally, "barbarians") of those who should be brothers and sisters. But the proper use of *charismata* builds up the Church. The rest of the chapter spells out in concrete ways what Paul thinks this should entail for the Corinthians. Prophecy is to be preferred to speaking in tongues because it can be understood. Interpretation of spirit-filled speech should always be a priority. Prophets and others who are filled with God's spirit should take turns and not monopolize the air-time. Women should be silent. "All things should be done decently and in order" (14:40). After all, "God is not of disorder [*akatastasia*, "instability"], but of peace" (14:33).

Architecture for the Twenty-First Century

Paul's advice to the Corinthians gives us much to think about as we contemplate the ways in which wise master builders might guide the construction, the "building up," of the Church from the *charismata* with which the members are gifted. I shall focus on five implications of Paul's arguments.

Building Materials. In the language of 3:12, the members of the Church bring different materials, different *charismata*, to the common exercise of building the Church: from gold and silver to wood, grass and hay. While all are useful, indeed all are necessary for building the Church, wise general contractors are required to work these diverse materials into a church building which is harmonious, habitable, and beautiful. Each material must be fitted into the total picture according to its unique attributes. Gold, for instance, would be disastrous in the foundation, while wooden two-by-fours would make poor window panes.

Adaptation to the Environment. One thing every architect knows is that no single plan fits each building. In designing a building (or a church) an architect (or pastoral leader) must know what features are most essential for *this building*. There is no universal blueprint, for there are many variables on each construction site: features of the natural terrain upon which the building is to be situated, the availability of natural resources, the deployment of special local materials and human power, existing structures in the neighborhood. The same is true of the *charismata* of individual Christians.

Functionality. Different buildings have different needs depending upon their uses, also. Skyscrapers overlooking Lake Erie can be tall and thin, but airplane hangers must be low and wide. No building is all things to all people (though in most of our parishes we do regard the church gym that way!). Cathedrals are built to be airy and magnificently open, but as a consequence are not particularly warm. Igloos are toasty warm, but small, dark and (I imagine) smoky. Construction engineers, working with their clients, must make choices which correspond to the activities which will take place in the edifice being designed.

Stability. In his First Letter to the Corinthians, Paul was concerned with one key value for the building of the church for which he had laid the foundation: stability. That is why for Paul unity in the Corinthian church was the most important consideration, for without it, he feared, the whole building would collapse. The saying of Jesus in Mark 3:25 echoed well-known ancient wisdom: "a house divided against itself cannot stand." With that wisdom in mind, Paul counseled the Corinthians to "build up" their church cautiously, and carefully, with an eye always to its solid unity, as he summarizes in 15:58: "Therefore, my beloved sisters and brothers, be firm, immovable, abounding in the (construction) work of the Lord always" (my translation).

Now, in our society, the most firm, immovable, and stable buildings are bomb shelters. After them, in short order, come prisons, hospitals, and public schools. These are buildings which are meant to stay up, no matter what happens. They are defensively poised, braced against disaster. Such buildings are made of concrete and have minimal windows with protective wire embedded in the glass. They are indeed firm and immovable, but they are also non-descript and prefabricated (that is why in many cities public schools are known simply by number). In a word, these oh-so-stable buildings, made of heavy and lasting concrete, are usually ugly, and unsurprisingly are *not* places where people dwell permanently. They are hardly expressive of the living human (let alone divine) spirit!

So, the question for the Church of the twenty-first century is what kind of architecture it will promote (and remember, we are speaking metaphorically here, as Paul was): churches which are firm and secure but not very beautiful or comfortable? Churches like McDonald's restaurants, which are uniform the world over, but poorly situated on their local sites? Churches which are made of one material, to the exclusion of other available resources? Churches which are suitable only for short-term and painful appointments, such as dentist offices or motor vehicle departments, or those which are meant for the leisurely dwelling of the spirit and spirit-filled people?

Competing Design Priorities. Paul's Letter to the Corinthians awakens us to the reality of this choice, and to the reality of his choice. Every building cannot have all the attributes. If we opt for lots of windows, we lose some privacy; if we select the ocean view, we must accept the risk of flooding. At Corinth, Paul opted for stability, for unity. In so doing, he tried to constrain and govern what essentially cannot be constrained—the power of the spirit—for, he feared, unbridled spirit-expression would divide and thus destroy the church. "Let everything be done decently and in order" makes great sense for the dentist and the motor vehicle department; also for the public grade school, and, above all, for the hospital. But the Church, as Paul himself taught, is the temple of the Holy Spirit (3:17), an unruly permanent house guest who may not keep to the house rules! Surely Paul himself knew that decency and order could not be the only design priorities, especially for a community of the spirit.

In the end, it comes down to deciding what "builds up" the Church. This requires looking back at the original blueprints and making the necessary adjustments for the new day. On this Paul is especially helpful as an architectural guide, for he states as an unequivocal requirement for a church edifice that its foundation be Jesus Christ (3:11). Further, his advice that decision-making must be based upon the criterion of *common edification* rather than that of the individual is welcome and fresh advice in a modern scene which consistently prizes the individual over the group. We need to work together, instead of trying to niche out our private condo in the suburbs of the church. Further, we must consult the structural blueprint in our quest to see what will build up the church for the twenty-first century, for it contains the necessary information about the history of this edifice. One needs to know where the electrical and sewer lines are hidden, where the beams are, to see what remodeling is possible, and how.

Most importantly, what builds up the Church for the twenty-first century must be decided on the basis of what is considered "the common good" of the whole, not just the special interests of the few. We noted previously that in 12:7 Paul said the manifestation of the spirit is given to each for the common good. Earlier in the letter, at 10:33, Paul had offered himself as an example of one who "seeks not his own advantage, but that of the many." But who defines the common good? The notorious passage in 14:33-36, in which Paul, in contradiction to what he wrote in chapter 11 of this same letter, tells women they must remain silent in the assembly, is an example of where some members of the Church have "the common good" defined for (or, rather, against) them.

Paul in this instance decided that the unity of the Corinthian church was *the* single index of the common good; he was willing to silence the women in the assembly in order to try to attain that common good. In the Corinthian church in the early 50s, Paul made a choice for unity, bought by compromise, a compromise which was not to be equally shared among members of the Church. That fateful choice should not be the Church's only choice, to be repeated perpetually. In fact, we can learn from 2 Corinthians that Paul's appeal for unity at such a cost in this letter, 1 Corinthians, was not successful.

Aren't there times when no compromise can be made, no matter how precious and necessary church unity is? For this we turn to the example of none other than Paul himself, who, when faced with what he considered defamation of the truth of the gospel at Galatia, did not offer compromise with his opponents, but stood his ground for the truth. When must justice, for one thing, take precedence over unity, as, for example, in churches in the American South in the 60s, where courageous pastors took stands against racial injustice, knowing that their churches would be (and they were) destroyed by division? Stability should be a design priority for the church, but it cannot be the only consideration, for *fidelity* to the right foundation is the essential rule of building up for Paul. A unity built on a foundation of false security in defiance of the gospel and its call for justice is only a movie-set facade. Such a building, in the words of Matthew, is set on sand, not concrete (Matt 7:26). But neither should the Church have feet of clay. Perhaps what is needed for the Church of the twenty-first century is some new type of architectural design which incorporates both the values of stability and adaptability, something like those skyscrapers in San Francisco which, I am told, are built on roller skates. They are firm but moveable—able to respond effectively to the vicissitudes of the seismic scene and thus to survive through change, not inertia.

Conclusion: Not Just a House, But a Home

Paul's 1 Corinthians is an essential text for our topic of *charismata* for the Church of the twenty-first century. His brilliant images of the Church as body and building fuel our burning urge for the unification we fervently desire (and we know is devastatingly lacking) in the Church, and they prod us forward in our thinking about how that vision should and should not be realized. Paul's call for love as the superior gift stimulates us all, encourages us all, and humbles us all. The Church of the twenty-first century will require that love to guide it in body building and in innovative architecture. We who are the Church need faithfully to cultivate *charismata* in such a way that we sensitively balance the dual realities of life and strife. But this focus on the Church as a building or a body can lead to a narrow ecclesiastical self-centeredness. I would like to close with a quotation from Cardinal Suenens, who reminds us of *why* the health of the Church is important.

In an interview in 1969, the cardinal, in expert Pauline fashion, talked about the church as a building—specifically, a home. The cardinal envisioned the Church as a home—not a refuge or retreat from the world, but a "home school" preparing persons for their rightful mission to all of God's creation:

> "Home," said Eliot, "is where one starts
> from" . . . To make our home [read: our church]
> most spacious, more airy, more habitable does
> not mean just putting in such amenities as
> central heating, but providing a family
> security which enables us to start out with
> the rest of [hu]mankind along the great highways
> of the world.[6]

In Cardinal Suenens' spirit, may we, by cultivating *charismata* wisely, build the Church of the twenty-first century to be not just a shelter in a sea of storms, but a home for us and for the spirit, from which we can embark for faithful service to the world.

---

[6] José de Broucker, *The Suenens Dossier* (Dublin: Gill & Macmillan, 1970) 45.

3

The Charism of the New Evangelizer

■ *Avery Dulles, S.J.*

What is a charism? What is the new evangelization? And how are the two related? Questions such as these, which must occupy our attention this morning, are suitably proposed in a symposium dedicated to the late Cardinal Léon Joseph Suenens. In his writings before Vatican II he dealt at some length with the urgency of evangelization, as may be seen from his book *The Gospel to Every Creature*, published in English in 1956 with a preface by Cardinal John Baptist Montini. In endorsing Cardinal Suenens' book the future Paul VI declared: "With clear vision and vigorous style, the writer marshals all his arguments to one conclusion, namely, the necessity, the possibility of that energy which, springing from above, can alone bring forth within the Church a new spirit of a missionary apostolate and thus save the world."[1]

At Vatican II Cardinal Suenens played a crucial part in obtaining due recognition for the charismatic gifts in the Dogmatic Constitution on the Church *(Lumen gentium)*. After the Council he became closely identified with the charismatic renewal, which he regarded as a partial fulfillment of the prayer of Pope John XXIII for a new Pentecost.[2] For this reason we may turn to Cardinal Suenens as a patron and a guide in the tasks assigned at this symposium. May he intercede for all of us that we may obtain an abundance of light regarding this theme!

---

[1] John Baptist Montini, Preface to Léon Joseph Suenens, *The Gospel to Every Creature* (Westminster, Md.: The Newman Press, 1963) viii.

[2] See L. J. Suenens, Foreword to Francis A. Sullivan, *Charisms and Charismatic Renewal* (Ann Arbor, Mich.: Servant Books, 1982) 7; cf. Idem, *A New Pentecost?* (New York: Seabury/Crossroad, 1974) passim.

What, then, is a charism? Father Haughey has already explained the essentials, but it may be helpful for me to review them in my own style.

The Greek term *charisma* means a freely bestowed gift. The term appears seventeen times in the New Testament, and all but one of these occurrences are in the Pauline corpus. The exception is 1 Pet 4:10. In a number of the Pauline passages the Greek term cannot be translated by the English word "charism" (e.g., Rom 1:11; 5:15; 6:23; 2 Cor 1:11), but there are several important passages in which Paul is speaking of what we today mean by "charism." This is notably the case in 1 Cor 7:7; 1 Cor 12:4-11; and Rom 12:3-8. In several other texts Paul is clearly speaking of charisms without actually using that word (e.g., Eph 4:11).

The contemporary Catholic concept of charism is authoritatively set forth in the Dogmatic Constitution on the Church, which speaks of "special graces by which God renders [the faithful] able and willing to undertake the various tasks and offices that help the renewal and up-building of the Church" (§12).

To clarify the concept of charism the following ten comments may be helpful.

(1) It has become customary to distinguish between *graces*, whether actual or sanctifying, which are intended to render their recipient pleasing in the sight of God, and *charisms*, which are conferred to equip a person to render some service. St. Thomas Aquinas used the terms *gratia gratum faciens* for what we call sanctifying grace, and *gratia gratis data* ("freely bestowed grace") for what we call a charism.

(2) Charisms are attributed to the Holy Spirit. In 1 Cor 12:4-6 Paul identifies the *charisms*, as coming from the Holy Spirit, on the one hand with activities or *operations*, which come from God the Father, and on the other hand with *services*, which come from Christ the Lord. The same gift, it would seem, can be under different aspects a charism, an operation, and a service. It comes under different aspects from the Holy Spirit, the Father, and the Son.

(3) The bestowal of charisms depends on God's good pleasure, not upon any law or ordinance. Paul in 1 Cor 12:11 says that the Spirit apportions the gifts to each one individually as he wills—a passage quoted by *Lumen gentium*. Charisms are often bestowed without any institutional office, as is clear from the statement of Vatican II that they are given to "the faithful of every rank" (*LG* §12). Neither Scripture nor Catholic tradition speaks of charisms given prior to baptism, but something analogous to charisms could be operative, I suspect, even among non-Christians.

(4) There is no opposition between charism and office. It would be a mistake to imagine that charisms are always given in an uncovenanted and unpredictable way, without regard for a person's status and official

responsibilities.[3] Paul himself in 1 Cor 12:28 mentions the charisms of apostle, prophet, and teacher, which appear to be identified with institutional offices. The vocation to office itself involves a charism.

In the Pastoral Letters a further shift toward the institutionalization of charism may be detected. Timothy is described as having received a charism of ministry through the laying on of hands, together with utterances of prophecy (1 Tim 4:14; cf. 2 Tim 1:6). In this case the institutional office lies at the basis of the charismatic gift, though the two do not fully coincide. Because the charism may be neglected even while the appointment remains, Timothy is exhorted to fan into flame the charism that he received at the moment of his "ordination."

The concept of a "charism of office" has been traditional in the Church since the days of Irenaeus of Lyons, who spoke of the "sure charism of truth" *(charisma veritatis certum)* bestowed on presbyter/bishops ordained in the apostolic Churches.[4] Vatican II, picking up this term, declares that all bishops "have received through episcopal succession the sure charism of truth" *(Dei Verbum* §8). Vatican I had already taught that Peter and his successors possess the charism of unfailing truth and faith *(veritatis et fidei numquam deficientis charisma)*."[5] In its Constitution on the Church, Vatican II asserted rather surprisingly that infallibility is a charism of the whole Church, individually present in the pope when he defines doctrine. The concept of a charism given to the whole Church seems to stand in tension with the generally accepted description of charism, as we shall presently see.

(5) Paul in 1 Cor 12 and elsewhere makes the point that although the Spirit is one, the charisms are diverse. Some are given to some individuals, others to other individuals. No one charism is necessary for all Christians, even for them to excel in holiness. Paul dwells on the complementarity of charisms, comparing them to the various functions of the human body, whether in members such as hands and feet or in organs such as eyes and ears. In this respect he contrasts charisms, which are distributed selectively, to grace or charity, which is required of all.

(6) Charisms are given for a purpose, i.e., for the sake of some benefit that results from their use. Paul says that they are "for utility" *(pros to*

---

[3] Cf. Avery Dulles, "Earthen Vessels: Institution and Charism in the Church," Thomas E. Clarke, ed., *Above Every Name: The Lordship of Christ and Social Systems* (New York: Paulist, 1980) 155–87.

[4] Irenaeus, *Adversus haereses* 4.26.2.

[5] Vatican I, *Pastor aeternus*, chapter 4; *Enchiridion Symbolorum, Definitionum et Declarationum de Rebus Fidei et Morum* ("Manual of Creeds, Definitions and Declarations on Matters of Faith and Morals"), compiled by H. Denzinger (1854), continued by C. Bannwart and others to the present. §3071.

sympheron, 1 Cor 12:7). Taking this passage in conjunction with 1 Cor 14:4, 5, and 12, one may infer that charisms are given for the building up of the Church and for its unity. An ostensible charism that proves to be debilitating or divisive for the Church cannot be genuine.

(7) From this follows the seventh point, namely that charisms need to be discerned. There are pseudo-charisms, such as false prophecy, as is evident both from the Old Testament and from the New, not to mention the manifold deviations, beginning with Montanism in the second century, that are chronicled in church history. Paul lists the "discernment of spirits" as one of the charisms (1 Cor 12:10), without referring to any connection between discernment and office. Vatican II in its Pastoral Constitution on the Church in the Modern World teaches that the whole People of God, pastors and laity together, have the task of discerning the signs of the times (*GS* §44; cf. §4 and §11). But the Dogmatic Constitution on the Church maintains that the judgment about the genuineness of charisms rests with those who preside over the Church, i.e., with the pope and bishops (*LG* §12, referring to I Thess 5:12, 19-21).

(8) Charisms are supernatural. They differ from innate talents and from naturally acquired abilities. In their actual exercise, however, charisms and natural abilities are frequently found together. The Holy Spirit builds upon, and perfects, a person's natural capacities. In the words of Francis A. Sullivan,

> Just what kind of new capacity the charism will add to one's natural abilities will of course depend on the nature of the charismatic activities for which it is given. For instance, in a given case the charism for teaching may add little to a person's natural ability to teach, but it will at least add a new willingness to employ this capacity in the service of the people of God, and will probably also add a new effectiveness in teaching with conviction in matters of faith. Other charisms, such as healings and miracles, will obviously add a great deal to the natural capacities of the person who is used as the instrument of such gifts.[6]

(9) At the time of Vatican II, there was a division of opinion among Catholic theologians. Some held that charisms were rare and extraordinary gifts which had become practically extinct after the end of the apostolic age—a view represented on the council floor by Cardinal Ernesto Ruffini. The other school maintained that charisms need not be extraordinary; they were still given and were broadly disseminated among the faithful for the different tasks and ministries required of them in the Church. This latter view, espoused by Cardinal Suenens,

---

[6] Sullivan, *Charisms, opus cit.*, 13.

clearly prevailed, as is evident from the Council's description of charisms quoted above.

(10) My last comment is a question. Do all Christians receive charisms? This point is debated, and cannot, I think, be settled from Scripture, although texts such as 1 Cor 12:7 and 1 Pet 4:10 have sometimes been read as implying that all have charisms. It is certain that all the baptized receive the Holy Spirit, but it is not equally clear that all receive charisms in the technical sense we have been analyzing up to this point.

With this preliminary concept of charism I should like now to turn to our second question, what is the new evangelization?

First, it is evangelization. In the Greek Bible, the verb "evangelize" means to proclaim good news. The term occurs several times in the historical books of the Old Testament, in the Psalms, and most prominently in Deutero-Isaiah. This last work has a famous description of the herald who runs ahead of the people on their return from Babylon to Jerusalem. The message in this case is that YAHWEH is triumphing over the whole world and establishing his kingdom. The new age of salvation is being inaugurated:

> How beautiful upon the mountains
> are the feet of him who brings good tidings,
> who publishes peace, who brings good tidings of good,
> who publishes salvation,
> who says to Zion, "Your God reigns" (Isa 52:7).

In the New Testament the verb *evangelizesthai* frequently appears in Luke, Acts, and the Pauline corpus. Jesus is anointed to proclaim the Kingdom of God and bring the gospel to the poor (Luke 4:18 and 7:22). After the Ascension the apostles have the task of "evangelizing Jesus Christ" (Acts 5:42). With an implied reference to Deutero-Isaiah, Paul in Rom 10:15 exclaims: "How beautiful are the feet of those who preach the good news!" Paul is conscious of his call to be the apostle to the Gentiles (Rom 15:20; 2 Cor 10:16; Gal 1:16; 2:7). He uses the verb "evangelize" to describe his whole activity as an apostle (1 Cor 1:17)."[7] Conscious of standing under a divine constraint, he exclaims, "Woe to me if I do not evangelize!" (1 Cor 9:16).

In the New Testament sense, therefore, the verb "evangelize" means to proclaim with authority and power the good news of salvation in

---

[7] See G. Friedrich s.v. "evangelizomai, k.t.1." in Gerhard Kittel, ed., *Theological Dictionary of the New Testament* 2 (Grand Rapids, Mich.: Eerdmans, 1964) 707–37, at 719.

Jesus Christ. The word comes from God and arouses saving faith. The same message is proclaimed both to Jews and to Gentiles, both to unbelievers and to Christians (Rom 1:15, etc.).

The term "evangelist" (or, if you prefer, "evangelizer") occurs only three times in the New Testament. In Acts 21:8 Philip (one of the seven original "deacons" of Acts 6:5) is called an evangelist. In Eph 4:11 evangelists are listed as church officers along with apostles, prophets, pastors, and teachers. In 2 Tim 4:5, Timothy is exhorted to do the work of an evangelist. As a church officer, an evangelist seems to rank below an apostle and a prophet (Eph 4:11). Without being directly commissioned by the risen Lord, as were the apostles, the evangelists shared in one of the principal functions of an apostle, notably that of proclaiming the basic Christian message.

The teaching of Vatican II is fundamental to the concept of the "new evangelization." The Council describes evangelization as a task of the whole Church, which shares in the prophetic office of Christ the Lord (*LG* §12; cf. *Dignitatis humanae* §13). "Since the whole Church is missionary, and since the work of evangelization is a basic duty of the People of God, this sacred Synod summons all to a deep interior renewal" (*Ad gentes* §35). "Among the principal duties of bishops, the preaching of the gospel occupies an eminent place" (*LG* §25). But Christ continues to proclaim the Kingdom through the laity as well as through the ordained. "This evangelization [by lay people], that is, the announcing of Christ by a living testimony as well as by the spoken word, takes on a specific quality and a special force in that it is carried out in the ordinary surroundings of the world" (*LG* §35). "Every disciple of Christ," says the Decree on the Church's Missionary Activity, "has the obligation to do his or her part in spreading the faith" (*AG* §23).

The contemporary Catholic understanding of evangelization has been profoundly marked by the apostolic exhortation of Paul VI On Evangelization in the Modern World, issued in 1975, just ten years after the close of the Council. In a memorable passage this exhortation declares, "Evangelizing is in fact the grace and vocation proper to the Church, her deepest identity. She exists in order to evangelize, that is to say, in order to preach and teach, to be the channel of the gift of grace, to reconcile sinners with God, and to perpetuate Christ's sacrifice in the Mass, which is the memorial of his death and glorious resurrection" (*Evangelii nuntiandi* §14). The pope defines evangelization as a complex process that includes explicit proclamation, the witness of a committed life, and all that makes for full incorporation into the community of the Church. In a section that is of special relevance to the present symposium, Paul VI insists that the Holy Spirit is the principal agent of evangelization (*EN* §75).

Following in the footsteps of Paul VI, John Paul II has made himself, par excellence, the pope of worldwide evangelization. "The Lord and master of history and of our destinies," he said in 1990, "has wished my pontificate to be that of a pilgrim pope of evangelization, walking down the roads of the world, bringing to all peoples the message of salvation."[8] Since 1983 he has repeatedly called for a "new evangelization," new not in its content but in its ardor, its methods, and its expression.[9] In 1990 he devoted a major encyclical, *Redemptoris missio*, to the topic of missionary activity. In that encyclical he takes up the urgency of evangelizing new parts of the world and of reevangelizing regions that have ceased to be Christian except perhaps in a nominal way. The third chapter of *Redemptoris missio* bears the title "The Holy Spirit, Principal Agent of Mission."

By the "new evangelization" John Paul II does not mean some radical departure from the program of Vatican II as interpreted by Paul VI. On the contrary, he means a bold and consistent implementation of that program. The main characteristics of the new evangelization should be evident, therefore, from what I have already said. The following ten features may help to clarify its nature:

(1) It is *biblical*. In accord with the Vatican II program of *ressourcement* it takes its inspiration from the original orientation of the Christian communities as described in the New Testament.

(2) It is *christocentric*. The Gospel is by its very nature a proclamation of the good news about Jesus Christ.

(3) It is *comprehensive* because it includes not only the initial proclamation but the entire process from the advance preparation for explicit proclamation to the full transformation of individuals and societies in Jesus Christ.

(4) It is *sociocultural*. For the credibility of the Gospel and full transformation of individual persons, social structures and human cultures must be renewed through contact with Christian faith.

(5) It is *ecumenical*. It recognizes and respects the elements of the Gospel found in all Christian communities and also because it is seriously committed to the unity of all Christians in keeping with the high priestly prayer of Christ.

(6) It is *dialogic*. It respects the personal freedom and individuality of all who come to the faith. It is alert to detect "seeds of the Gospel" in

[8] Arrival speech in Mexico City, May 6, 1990; *L'Osservatore Romano* (English ed.) 7 May 1990, 1 and 12.

[9] John Paul II, "The Task of the Latin American Bishop," address to CELAM, March 9, 1983; English trans. in *Origins* 12 (March 24, 1983) 659–62, at 661.

peoples and cultures not yet formally evangelized. The good evangelizer, therefore, must not only speak but listen.

(7) It is directed in part *to Christians themselves* because it acknowledges that the battle between belief and unbelief is not a matter of
Christian self-assertion against other peoples. The struggle for faith is
continually being fought out in every human group and every human
heart. The Church itself is in constant need of being evangelized.

(8) While recognizing the need for dedicated full-time missionaries,
the new approach sees evangelization as a task for the *whole People of
God* and of every individual believer.

(9) While acknowledging the indispensability of personal testimony
through word and example, the new evangelization seeks to profit
from all the *new methods of communication* provided by contemporary
technology. Radio, television, and the Internet must not be allowed to
dictate the message but must be prudently employed in service of the
Gospel.

(10) The new evangelization relies less on human plans and projec-
tions than on the unforeseeable initiatives of the *Holy Spirit,* whom it
trusts as the principal agent of evangelization. The new evangelization,
I believe, takes on special urgency today in countries such as our own,
where religious affiliation is determined less by heredity than by personal choice. A Church that does not evangelize will rapidly shrink.
One that does evangelize will be able to attract many new and enthusiastic adherents.

Drawing on all that has been said, we may now turn to our third and
last question: How are charism and the new evangelization related to
each other?

In the New Testament evangelization is never explicitly designated
as a charism, but the list of ministries in Eph 4:11, which includes evangelization, would seem to correspond to what Paul elsewhere speaks of
as charisms (e.g., Rom 12 and 1 Cor 12). Thus we may say that the concept of evangelization as a charism does not lack a biblical foundation.

The New Testament likewise provides grounds for holding that the
charism of evangelization is operative in a variety of ministries. Paul
was an apostle-evangelist, Timothy a pastor-evangelist, and Philip a
deacon-evangelist. Because faith does not rest on human reasoning
alone, the charismatic element is essential for any fruitful proclamation
of the Gospel. In 1 Corinthians 2, Paul insists that he proclaimed the
crucified Christ not in plausible words of human wisdom but in
demonstration of the Spirit and of power. For faith—he goes on to
say—rests not on human argumentation but on the power of God (1
Cor 2:4-5). It remains true today that the Christian message cannot be

imparted by logical demonstration but only by words taught by the Holy Spirit. To speak in such Spirit-inspired words is to exercise a charismatic gift.

Paul VI and John Paul II, as already mentioned, agree in teaching that the Holy Spirit is the principal agent of evangelization (*EN* §75, *RM* §21, 30). Recognizing the fact, Paul VI maintains that all true evangelizers are such "thanks to the charisms of the Holy Spirit and to the mandate of the Church." Evangelization therefore has a double source. Both the institutional and the charismatic dimensions are necessary for it to be legitimate and fruitful (*EN* §74). To obtain the necessary guidance of the Spirit, all who are involved in evangelization must open themselves in prayer (*EN* §75).

For good reason Paul VI speaks of charisms of evangelization in the plural. For evangelization, as we have seen, is a complex reality. It consists of a diversity of services, and this diversity contributes to its richness and beauty (*EN* §66). Evangelization includes the whole process whereby individuals and societies are brought into contact with the Gospel and elevated and transformed by its power.

This comprehensive process, according to Paul VI, begins with pre-evangelization and even this, he says, "is already evangelization in the true sense," (*EN* §51). In saying this he means, perhaps, that only through the Gospel can people be suitably prepared for receiving the Gospel. At a second stage follows what Paul VI calls "proclamation to those who are afar" (*EN* §51). This step, which corresponds to the basic Christian *kerygma*, contains an explicit call for the acceptance of Christian faith. But the process of evangelization goes on even after Christian faith has been accepted. Work for unity among Christians is another aspect of the total process of evangelization (*EN* §77). So likewise are catechesis, advanced religious instruction, pastoral preaching, and the ministry of the sacraments and pastoral care. The social apostolate, insofar as it is truly Christian, must be viewed as integral to evangelization.

In Pope Paul VI's broad vision the term "evangelist" cannot be reserved to any one specific ministry. The evangelizers include believers of all ranks and conditions. In his chapter on "The Workers of Evangelization" (chapter VI), Paul VI distinguishes between the roles of the pope, the bishops, the presbyters, the religious, and the laity, all of whom need appropriate charisms. *Evangelii nuntiandi* declares, for example, that the laity today exercise a great variety of ministries according to the graces and charisms that the Lord is pleased to confer upon them (*EN* §73). Their field of evangelizing activity includes the complicated worlds of politics, society, and economics; the realms of culture, science, and the arts; the spheres of international relations and the mass media of communication. Lay people are primarily involved in professional and family life, but they also collaborate with the pastors in the service of the ecclesial community. Many of them exercise non-ordained ministries recognized by the Church, such as those of catechists, music directors, and eucharistic ministers. For all these activities serious preparation and formation are required.

John Paul II in his apostolic exhortation *Christifideles laici* (1988) speaks at some length of the variety of vocations, movements, and charisms that are required to fulfill the mission of the Church in the contemporary world. He urges the laity to be at the forefront of the great mission of re-evangelization, so challenging and so necessary in our day.[10]

In *Redemptoris missio* the present pope has a long and interesting section on new social phenomena, such as the migration to the new cities, the movement of refugees, and the new means of social communication. Each of these situations, he says, constitutes a new Areopagus, similar to that in which St. Paul proclaimed the Gospel when he arrived in Athens (*RM* §37).

Why, then, are charisms necessary for the new evangelization? Why is it not enough for evangelists to employ their natural talents and acquired skills, and to follow the directions of the institutional Church? They must surely use these means, but these means are not proportionate to the intended result. As Paul VI declares, all our human preparation and techniques will not be effective without the Holy Spirit.

In the New Testament it is evident that Jesus himself, beloved Son of the Father though he was, did not begin his career of evangelization until the Spirit descended upon him at his baptism. "The Spirit of the Lord is upon me," he proclaimed at Nazareth, "because he has anointed me to preach good news to the poor" (Luke 4:18). The apostles, even after their encounter with the risen Christ, were not in a position to evangelize until the Holy Spirit was bestowed on them at Pentecost.

John Paul II asserts very clearly, "Missionary dynamism is not born of the will of those who decide to become propagators of their faith. It is born of the Spirit, who moves the Church to expand, and it progresses through faith in God's love."[11]

Paul VI explains this relationship in greater detail: "The Holy Spirit places on the lips [of the evangelist] the words which he could not find

---

[10] John Paul II, Apostolic Exhortation on the Laity, *Christifideles laici*, text in *Origins* 18 (February 9, 1989) 561–95. He treats charisms in §24, 572–73, and evagelization in §§33–35, 576–78. In the conclusion (§64, 592) he brings charisms and evangelization together.

[11] John Paul II, address of February 12, 1988 to Italian bishops on Liturgical Course, *L'Osservatore Romano* (English ed.) 4 March 1988, 5.

by himself, and at the same time the Holy Spirit predisposes the soul of the hearer to be open and receptive to the Good News and to the Kingdom being proclaimed" (*EN* §75). This twofold operation of the Spirit, in the evangelizer and the evangelized respectively, merits some further consideration.

When Paul VI speaks of the Spirit placing words on the preacher's lips, he is probably alluding to the gift of speech, one of the charisms mentioned by Paul. Paul actually speaks of a double charism of speech: utterance of wisdom and utterance of knowledge (1 Cor 12:8). In the hymn *Veni Creator Spiritus* we invoke the Holy Spirit as the one who bestows speech (*"sermone ditans guttura"*).

This gift of speech is not separable from the light to the mind that comes from the Holy Spirit as the giver of wisdom, knowledge, understanding, and counsel. According to Paul VI the Spirit enables the proclaimer of the Gospel to discern the signs of the times (*EN* §75) and thus to perceive the apt means of evangelizing here and now. Contact with the living Spirit is needed for us to conceive of new ways to propose the unchanging message of the Gospel in new and unprecedented situations.

Besides giving light to the minds of those who herald the good news, the Spirit gives strength to their wills. He is the Spirit of fortitude, making them fearless in the face of hostility, ridicule, or persecution. The Acts of the Apostles uses the Greek term *parrēsia* to signify the apostolic boldness with which the early community and its members proclaimed the Christian message (Acts 2:29; 4:13, 29, 31, and many other texts in Acts, Paul, and John).

Still another manifestation of the Spirit's presence takes place in the heart of the evangelist. The Holy Spirit inflames the apostles with a pure and ardent love that manifests itself in all their activities. Without this inner union with God sealed by love, their words would be empty. Love transforms the heralds into living witnesses who testify not only by their words but by all that they do and are.

Another charism that has at times accompanied evangelization is the performance of deeds of power. From the canonical ending of Mark (16:17-18) and the account of the expansion of the Church in Acts it is evident that signs and wonders played an important role. Paul regarded such deeds as the very signs of his apostleship (Rom 15:18-19; 2 Cor 12:12). Miracles and sudden healings are of course beyond the capacity of any one of us to produce, and for this very reason they attest to the active presence of the Holy Spirit.

Like the gifts of speech, those of miracles and healings are listed by Paul in 1 Cor 12. In this passage he mentions several other charisms I have not discussed, such as speaking in tongues and interpretation of tongues. In chapter 14 he explains that these gifts, exercised "decently and in order," can serve to build up the Church and to arouse faith in unbelievers, but he subordinates them to the gifts of prophecy, knowledge, and teaching (1 Cor 14:1-40). Not every evangelist needs to be equipped with every gift, but some measure of charismatic assistance is essential for effective evangelization. The Church as a whole draws upon the full range of charisms.

It is important not to overlook the work of the Spirit in the persons being evangelized, even though this work is not generally discussed under the rubric of charisms. For any true conversion the Holy Spirit must assist, as he assisted Lydia by opening her heart to what Paul had to say (Acts 16:14). John Paul II explains how the Holy Spirit arouses existential and religious questions in the hearts of all, preparing them for the Gospel (*RM* §28-29).

The Church has constantly taught that no one can achieve even the beginnings of faith without the illumination and inspiration of the Holy Spirit, which arouse what the Council of Orange calls the "inclination to believe" (*credulitatis affectum*, DS §375) and joy and ease in assenting to and believing the truth (*suavitatem in consentiendo et credendo veritati*, DS §377). This inner movement includes both an enlightenment of the mind and a loving inclination of the heart. The Holy Spirit is celebrated in Christian hymnody as the blessed light that fills the depths of the heart. In the *Veni Sancte Spiritus* we sing: "O *lux beatissima, Reple cordis intima, Tuorum fidelium*." Without some intimations of love, unbelievers could not find the path to faith.

The missionary dynamism of the Church began with the descent of the Holy Spirit at Pentecost. "It was not by chance," says Paul VI, "that the great inauguration of evangelization took place on the morning of Pentecost, under the inspiration of the Spirit" (*EN* §75). The grace of Pentecost remains the powerful source of evangelization. As Francis Sullivan has said, "The power received at Pentecost was power to witness to Christ, and therefore a movement that is authentically Pentecostal must carry on this witness in the world."[12] Sullivan therefore expresses the hope that those involved in the charismatic renewal will engage ever more fully and effectively in the ministry of evangelization.

Granted that charisms are necessary for the Church to fulfill its mandate to carry the Gospel to the ends of the earth, some will press the question: how can these charisms be obtained? There is no way in which we, as earth-bound mortals, can steal fire from heaven. Charisms are distributed according to the divine pleasure, when and as the Spirit

---

[12] Sullivan, *Charisms, opus cit.*, 85.

wills. But we can and must pray. In the nine days between Ascension Thursday and Pentecost the apostles prayed together with Mary, the Mother of Jesus, and the other holy women in the upper room at Jerusalem. Those who aspire to participate in a new Pentecost and to renew the Church in our day must follow the same course. Only by insistent prayer can we as individuals and as Church dispose ourselves to receive whatever charisms the Holy Spirit may deem it fitting to confer.

4 Anointed and Sent: The Charism of Preaching

■ *Mary Catherine Hilkert, O.P.*

When John XXIII opened Vatican II he expressed the hope that it would be for the Church "a new Pentecost," a title which Cardinal Suenens adopted for his own book a decade later. Convinced that Vatican II had been a turning point in the history of the Church and that the Holy Spirit was revealing new dimensions of the mystery of death and resurrection to the Christian community, Cardinal Suenens offered an exhortation to those who had begun to grow discouraged. His reminder is perhaps even more needed twenty-five years later: "Now is the time to listen, in silence, with all our heart to what the Spirit is saying to the Churches" (Rev 2, 29).[1]

In Cardinal Suenens' judgment, the Spirit at the time of the Council was calling for a necessary institutional "overhaul" at every level, but at the same time inaugurating a "spiritual renewal of exceptional richness,"[2] both of which needed further development a decade later. Both that spiritual renewal and that institutional "overhaul" are profoundly connected to the preaching mission of the Church since in a very real sense, the mission of the Church *is* the preaching of the Gospel. Thus as Stanley Marrow has observed, "the crisis of the Church in any age is, ultimately, a crisis of preaching."[3] "Crisis" carries here, of course, the twofold connotation of "danger" and "opportunity."

[1] Leon Joseph Cardinal Suenens, *A New Pentecost?* trans. Francis Martin (New York: The Seabury Press, 1975) xii.

[2] *Ibid.*

[3] Stanley Marrow, S.J., "Vatican II: Scripture and Preaching," *Vatican II: The Unfinished Agenda—A Look at the Future*, eds. Lucien Richard, Daniel J. Harrington, and John W. O'Malley (New York: Paulist Press, 1987) 82–92 at 83.

As described in the Acts of the Apostles, the Pentecost event often referred to as the birthday of the Church might also be designated as "the birth of the preaching ministry of the Church." Disciples of Jesus, both women and men, were gathered in one place when suddenly they "all were filled with the Holy Spirit." Luke depicts the event with images of a "strong driving wind" and "tongues as of fire [that] came to rest on them." The effect of this powerful experience of the Spirit was that those who had lost hope and direction now began to "make bold proclamations as the Spirit prompted them" (Acts 2: 1-3). Even more important than the experience of the preachers was the experience of the hearers of the Word. The miracle of that first Pentecost was that all gathered in Jerusalem from every nation under heaven heard in a tongue that he or she could understand "about the marvels God had accomplished." That kind of preaching is possible only in the power of the Spirit and carries, as experiences of the Spirit characteristically do, a number of surprises, including who is anointed and sent to preach, who hears and in what language, and what "the marvels" are which God has accomplished. In the text, Peter describes this Pentecost event as an experience of the charism of prophecy:

> [I]t is what the prophet Joel spoke of:
> It shall come to pass in the last days, says God,
> that I will pour out a portion of my spirit on all humankind:
> Your sons and daughters shall prophesy,
> the young shall see visions
> and the old shall dream dreams.
> Yes, even on my servants and handmaids
> I will pour out a portion of my spirit in those days,
> and they shall prophesy (Acts 2:16-18).

If, thirty years after the Council, we are to continue to pray as Pope John XXIII exhorted us to before the Council, "Renew your wonders in this our day; give us a new Pentecost,"[4] then among the things we can expect are new manifestations of the charism of prophecy and the renewal of the preaching ministry in the Church, including whatever "institutional overhaul" is necessary to foster that ministry.

This chapter will explore how we might describe the charism of preaching and its relation to the charisms of prophecy and "wisdom in discourse" (1 Cor 12:8). Then in light of Cardinal Suenens' contributions to the nature and mission of the Church and the charism of all the baptized, we will turn to the question of who is anointed and sent to

---

[4] *A New Pentecost?* x.

proclaim the word of God and in what context. The final section suggests that the cardinal's assessment of the "signs of the times" both within and outside the Church is still pertinent today, as the spirituality he exhorted believers to embrace then is more needed now than ever.

The Charism of Preaching

In the Jewish tradition the prophets were the interpreters of where God was to be found in the history of their people; they are often described as the Jewish preachers par excellence.[5] Their task was to call to memory God's fidelity in Israel's past, to call for trust in God's presence with them in the present moment, and to stir up hope rooted in God's promise to be with them no matter what their future. Announcing the word of God meant proclaiming "God's dreams for Israel" in spite of dashed hopes, the destruction of the temple, or exile. The prophet announced a future when wounds would be healed, enemies reconciled, prisoners set free, and the land restored, precisely by recalling memories of the past when the God of the Exodus and of all creation had always been faithful, but often in unexpected ways.

The prophet Isaiah described the future reign of God in words that the Gospel of Luke presents as the text for the preaching event in which Jesus claims his own prophetic mission:

> The spirit of the Lord is upon me,
> because God has anointed me;
> sent me to bring glad tidings to the lowly,
> to heal the broken-hearted.
> To proclaim liberty to the captives and
> release to the prisoners.
> To announce a year of favor from the Lord and
> a day of vindication by our God (Luke 4: 16-21, cf. Isa 61: 1-2).

Christians see Jesus in the long line of Jewish prophets who announced the good news of the reign of God opening up a new and different future, a future full of hope. But the Christian community also believes that Jesus was more than a prophet. He not only proclaimed the future reign of God; he embodied it. In his person and his actions,

---

[5] See Gerhard von Rad, *The Message of the Prophets* (New York: Harper and Row, 1962); Abraham Heschel, *The Prophets*, vols. 1 and 2 (New York: Harper and Row, 1962) and Walter Brueggemann, *The Prophetic Imagination* (Philadelphia: Fortress, 1978).

as well as in his words, he announced the good news of salvation. Jesus not only preached salvation; he enfleshed it. Jesus preached God's reconciling mercy not only by words of forgiveness, but also by sharing a table with sinners. He announced God's healing power by touching lepers. He challenged the limited social roles and restrictions of his time by talking with Samaritans, entering into friendships with women, choosing a tax collector as a disciple, and curing the sick on the Sabbath. His whole life announced that God willed well-being and happiness for all people—universal salvation. Jesus did not just speak God's word of compassion, he *was* God's compassion in the flesh.

The Pentecost narrative reminds us that communities of believers, who claim to be followers of Jesus, are called and empowered to do the same. As the powerful preaching discourses in the Acts of the Apostles disclose, those entrusted with the name of Jesus are enabled by his Spirit to announce boldly the new age that the resurrection has inaugurated. Like the proclamation of Jesus, however, the preaching of his followers involves more than words; the witness of the lives of the Christian community is the most basic mode of announcing the Gospel. If in the words of the Gospel of John, "The Word became flesh and pitched a tent among us" (John 1:14), so, too, the preaching ministry of the Christian Church in every age involves pitching a tent wherever human beings or God's beloved creation are in need.

The 1971 Synod of Bishops' statement *Justice in the World* highlighted even more clearly than did the documents of Vatican II that the social ministries of the Church are an essential aspect of the church's preaching mission: "Activity on behalf of justice is a constitutive part of preaching the Gospel."[6] It is only from a stance of solidarity with the people of God and God's creation that the Christian community can come to understand the meaning of the opening lines of the Pastoral Constitution on the Church in the Modern World: "The joys and the hopes, the griefs and the anxieties of [those] of this age, especially those who are poor or in any way afflicted, these too are the joys and hopes, the griefs and anxieties of the followers of Christ. Indeed nothing genuinely human fails to raise an echo in their hearts."[7]

But the Christian community attends to the experience of humanity and the cries of the earth while listening for another echo—the echo of the Gospel. Jesus not only shared the experience of all of creation; he

---

[6] *Justice in the World* (Washington, D.C.: United States Catholic Conference, 1971) 34.

[7] *Gaudium et spes*, par. 1. All references to the documents of Vatican II are taken from Walter M. Abbott, S.J. (ed.), *The Documents of Vatican II* (New York: America Press, 1966). Translations have been adapted for inclusivity.

transformed it through his presence, words, and person; he redeemed it through his life, death, and resurrection. As the ongoing body of Christ in the world, the Church is entrusted with the mission to announce the good news of the death and resurrection of Jesus in ways that continue to transform and redeem humanity and the earth. Proclaiming that Gospel involves making connections between the human story, the story of the earth, and the story of God enfleshed in Jesus. Like Jesus and all the prophets before him, contemporary preachers are called to "name grace,"[8] to identify where the presence and power of God are to be found in ordinary human life and in today's world. Within the context of the broader prophetic witness of the Christian community that is the most basic form of preaching the Gospel, the charism of preaching is fundamentally the gift of the Spirit that enables Christians to announce the source of their life and convictions. Even in the midst of suffering, we are called to give account of the hope that is within us, to proclaim the good news of salvation in and through the death and resurrection of Jesus. Both "in season" and "out of season" the Christian community is called to "give account of the hope that is within [them]" (1 Pet 3:15), to proclaim the good news of salvation in and through the death and resurrection of Jesus the Christ.

To preach that good news in a way that it can be heard, however, involves more than retelling the story of salvation as recorded in the scriptures. Highlighting the role of the Spirit in bringing the word to life, Cardinal Suenens explained: "[The Spirit] calls to mind the word of God, giving to it a freshness and power to shed light on what is happening at this very moment. [The Spirit] does not repeat himself: each time his teaching of the Word has a new resonance, a new urgency."[9] This power of the Spirit to illuminate the present moment in light of the word of God should be evident in all forms of preaching, especially the liturgical homily. It would be interesting to interview believers who have listened for years to Christian preaching about their understanding of the preacher's task. Even those who have been formed by good preaching might say that the preacher is supposed to explain the Scriptures. But as the United States Bishops Conference's document on the Sunday homily, *Fulfilled in Your Hearing*, states, that is not enough. Rather:

---

[8] I have developed this notion of preaching as the art of "naming grace" more fully in "Naming Grace: A Theology of Proclamation," *Worship* 60 (1986) 434–49, and *Naming Grace: Preaching and the Sacramental Imagination* (New York: Continuum, 1997).

[9] *A New Pentecost?* 229.

Since the purpose of the homily is to enable the gathered congregation to celebrate the liturgy with faith, the preacher does not so much attempt to explain the Scriptures as to interpret the human situation through the Scriptures. In other words, the goal of the liturgical preacher is not to interpret a text of the Bible (as would be the case in teaching a Scripture class) as much as to draw on the texts of the Bible as they are presented in the lectionary to interpret people's lives in such a way that they will be able to celebrate Eucharist—or be reconciled with God and one another, or be baptized into the Body of Christ, depending on the particular liturgy that is being celebrated.[10]

It is precisely the prophetic charism that is needed if preachers are to interpret events in the community, to announce what God is saying here and now. The charism of prophecy enables Christian communities as well as individual preachers to see the connections between the story of God's fidelity in the past, the call of God in the present moment, and God's promise of a "future full of hope" (Jer 29:11). Effective preaching moves the hearers of the word to genuine conversion of heart and life, which is why Yves Congar could make the startling claim soon after the Council ended: "If in one country Mass were celebrated for 30 years without preaching and in another there was preaching for 30 years without the Mass, the people would be more Christian in the country where there was preaching."[11]

If that is indeed the case, we have to ask ourselves, what has happened to the charism of preaching in our day? As Paul VI questioned in his Apostolic Exhortation on Evangelization published ten years after the Council: "In our day, what has happened to that hidden energy of the good news which is able to have such a powerful effect on the human conscience? To what extent and in what way is that evangelical force capable of really transforming people of this century?"[12]

This question of what has happened to the "hidden energy of the good news" is directly related to the question of to whom the charism for preaching the word has been entrusted. In *A New Pentecost?* Cardi-

---

[10] *Fulfilled in Your Hearing: The Homily in the Sunday Assembly* (Washington, D.C.: United States Catholic Conference, 1982) 20–21.

[11] Yves Congar, "Sacramental Worship and Preaching," *The Renewal of Preaching: Theory and Practice,* Concilium 33 (New York: Paulist, 1968) 62. See also the description of the motivation for all Christian testimony in Vatican II's *Dei Verbum,* which draws on the words of St. Augustine: "so that by hearing the message of salvation the whole world may believe; by believing, it may hope; and by hoping, it may love." Augustine, *De Catechizandis Rudibus,* C. IV, 8: PL 40, 316, as quoted in *Dei Verbum,* Prologue, no. 1.

[12] Paul VI, *Evangelii Nuntiandi,* December 8, 1975, no. 4.

nal Suenens quotes an earlier address of Paul VI to the College of Cardinals in which the Pope asserted that: "the fresh breath of the Spirit . . . has come to awaken latent energies within the Church, to stir up dormant charisms, and to infuse a sense of vitality and joy."[13] In terms of preaching, we might ask: if good preaching engenders a sense of vitality and joy among those who hear it, can the frustrations expressed when good preaching is lacking in the Church also be interpreted as the work of the Spirit prompting a hunger for the word of God among believers and stirring up dormant charisms that are not yet fully recognized and exercised in the Church? What is the effect on the preaching mission of the whole Church if the "hidden energy of the good news" remains "latent" among the majority of baptized believers? This raises the question of who is anointed and sent to proclaim the Gospel and in what context.

Who Is Sent to Preach the Gospel?

Until recently allusions to preachers being "anointed" or "sent" to preach the Gospel were usually presumed to refer to ordained ministers.[14] Vatican II did place a much-needed emphasis on the centrality of preaching in the ministry of both bishop and priest.[15] The charism of the ordained is publicly recognized and celebrated by the Church, and the responsibilities that flow from the mandate of bishop and priest to preach the Gospel are clear. But the preaching mission of the Church is not limited to the preaching of the ordained. The basic anointing from which all ministry including that of the ordained, derives is the anointing of baptism and confirmation. Cardinal Suenens played a central role in two decisive debates at the Council that have direct bearing here. In the development of *Lumen gentium* it was Suenens who proposed that the chapter on hierarchy should be placed after the chapter

---

[13] Quoted in *A New Pentecost?* 89.

[14] See Mary Collins, "The Baptismal Roots of the Preaching Ministry," *Worship: Renewal to Practice* (Washington, D.C.: The Pastoral Press, 1987) 175–95. Collins argues that the Church's liturgical tradition illustrates that the language of "anointing by the Holy Spirit" so as to be formed for a share in the mission of Christ was primarily the language of Christian baptism in the early church, but in later practice was transferred to refer primarily to the ordained. Note especially Collin's discussion of the "break with tradition" in the revision of the Chrism Mass in the Roman Pontifical of 1970. See also Frank Henderson, "The Chrism Mass of Holy Thursday," *Worship* 51 (1977) 149–58.

[15] See *Lumen gentium*, 25; *Decree on the Bishops' Pastoral Office in the Church, Christus Dominus*, 12; and *Decree on the Ministry and life of Priests, Presbyterorum Ordinis*, 4.

on the People of God, and in the debates on "charisms" Suenens insisted that charisms are not extraordinary endowments of a few within
the Christian community, nor the prerogative of the ordained or of religious institutes. Rather, the gifts of the Spirit are lavishly bestowed on
all the baptized. Suenens was firmly convinced that, as he said, "[at]
baptism we all receive the fullness of the Holy Spirit, the lay[person] as
well as the priest, bishop, or pope. The Holy Spirit cannot be received
more or less, any more than a host is more or less consecrated."[16] In disputes with Cardinal Ruffini who relegated charisms to the early
Church and warned that an emphasis on charisms could endanger the
institutional Church, Suenens challenged his brother bishops to consider their pastoral experience:

> Does not each one of us know lay people, both men and women, in his
> own diocese who are truly called by God? These people have received
> various different charisms from the Spirit, for catechesis, evangelization,
> apostolic action of various types . . . Without these charisms, the ministry
> of the Church would be impoverished and sterile.[17]

Further, Suenens' conviction that charisms were entrusted to women as
well as to men led to the plea that women be somehow represented at
the Council. Suenens was the one to raise the question: "Why are we
even discussing the reality of the Church when half the Church is not
even represented here?"[18]

Although not fully developed in any one document, a renewed appreciation of the meaning of Christian baptism is at the center of Vatican II's theology of Church and ministry. In a foundational shift of
horizons beyond a previous theology that spoke of the "lay apostolate"
as a share in the ministry of the ordained, Vatican II proclaimed that by
virtue of their baptism and confirmation the laity share in the priestly,
prophetic, and royal mission of Christ (*LG*, 31; *AA*, 2, 3). That mission
carries with it a share in the responsibility of the entire Church to witness to the Gospel and announce the good news.[19] Both the blessing of
the water and the consecration of the chrism in the Easter Vigil high-

---

[16] *A New Pentecost?* 86.

[17] As quoted by Albert Vanhoye, S.J., "The Biblical Question of 'Charisms' After
Vatican II," in *Vatican II: Assessment and Perspectives Twenty-Five Years after (1962–87)*
vol I, ed. Rene Latourelle (New York): Paulist, 1988) 439–68 at 442–43.

[18] Quoted by Mary Luke Tobin, S.L., in "Women in the Church: Vatican II and After,"
The Ecumenical Review 37 (1985) 295–305 at 295. See also Carmel Elizabeth McEnroy,
Guests in Their Own House: The Women of Vatican II (New York: Crossroad, 1996).

[19] *Decree on the Church's Missionary Activity, Ad Gentes Divinitus*, #35.

light that the baptized are not passive hearers of the word, but active ministers called to preach the Gospel. The Blessing of the Water (Form C) proclaims: "You call those who have been baptized to announce the Good News of Jesus Christ to the people everywhere." And the Consecratory Prayer over the Chrism says: "Through that anointing you transform them into the likeness of Christ your Son and give them a share in his royal, priestly and prophetic work" (Easter 1, Preface 1). This is not to deny that there is a distinct role for the ordained, an office of discernment and a responsibility for ordering charisms specifically entrusted to the bishop, or an Order of men and women in the Church whose precise charism is "the preaching of the Gospel." But each of those claims is cast in a new light by the more fundamental emphases of the Council that all the baptized share in the mission of the Church by virtue of their baptism and that the Word of God is entrusted to the entire Church, not solely to the magisterium (*DV*, 10).

The insight that the power and responsibility to preach the Gospel is rooted in baptism and confirmation finds support not only in the liturgical tradition of the Church,[20] but even in the theology of Thomas Aquinas, who maintained that the one who has been baptized and confirmed "receives the power publicly, and as it were *ex officio*, to profess faith in Christ in speech."[21]

This conviction, that all those who have been baptized and confirmed are commissioned to preach the Gospel is the broad context from which to focus on a distinct charism for preaching that is given to specific members within the body of Christ for the building up of the

---

[20] See Collins, "The Baptismal Roots of the Preaching Ministry" (note 13).

[21] *Summa Theologiae*, III, q. 72, a. 5, ad. 2. See also Yves Congar, *I Believe in the Holy Spirit*, vol. III, trans. David Smith (New York: Seabury Press, 1983) 221–27. For Aquinas, this power is given to women as well as men. He explicitly addressed the objection to women's participation in the sacrament of confirmation. According to the interpretation of the time, confirmation was the sacrament in which "a person receives power for engaging in spiritual battle against the enemies of the faith" (ST III, q. 72, reply). Pope Melchiades had argued that "women are not suited for fighting because of the frailty of their sex. Consequently, neither should confirmation be given to women" (ST III, q. 72, a. 8, obj. 3). In responding to that argument Aquinas, however, quoted John Chrysostom: "As Chrysostom says, 'In worldly contexts fitness of age, physique and rank is required and so entrance is denied to slaves, women, the old and the young. In the heavenly contests, however, the stadium is open to every person and age without regard to sex.' He also says, 'Before God even women do battle for many women have fought with manly courage. Some have been the equal of men in bravery in the struggles of martyrdom; others indeed have been stronger than men.' Therefore, confirmation should be conferred on women" (ST III, q. 72, a. 8, ad. 3).

whole body. As *Lumen gentium* notes, the Spirit "distributes special graces among the faithful of every rank. By these gifts [the Spirit] makes them fit and ready to undertake various tasks and offices for the renewal and building of the Church" (*LG*, 12). The document is building, of course, on Paul's insight in 1 Corinthians 12: "To each the manifestation of the Spirit is given for the common good." In the larger context of that passage, Paul refers specifically to two gifts directly related to preaching: the gift of prophecy (v. 10), and the gift of "wisdom in discourse" (v. 8).

Important connections between preaching and prophecy were explored earlier in the chapter. Aquinas' description of what Paul called "wisdom in discourse" in terms of "the charism of speech" *(gratia sermonis)*[22] might be used even today to measure whether one has a charism for preaching. The "grace of speech" as Aquinas presents it includes the ability

(1) to teach in such a way that one instructs the intellect,

(2) to delight one's audience and move the affections, so that a person willingly hears the Word of God, and

(3) to move the hearers so that they may love what is signified by the words and want to fulfill what is urged.[23]

In more contemporary terms we might say that the preacher's gift and responsibility, in this more specific sense, is to draw others more deeply into the mystery of God. The preacher does this by connecting the human story with the story of Jesus as retold in the Scriptures and celebrated in the liturgy in such a way that the hearers of the word are moved to "go and do likewise."

This "charism of speech" is not given equally to all members of the community, but neither is it a grace reserved to orders. In his struggle over how to deal with what he judged as clear evidence from Scripture and human experience that both the grace of prophecy and the grace of speech are given to women as well as men, Aquinas addressed a dilemma that has important significance for any discussion of charisms. After quoting the First Letter to Peter, "As each has received a gift, employ it for one another" (4:10), Aquinas pondered, "But certain women receive the grace of wisdom and knowledge, which they cannot ad-

---

[22] Aquinas explicitly connects his discussion of the charism of speech with Paul's reference to "the utterance of wisdom" and "the utterance of knowledge" in 1 Cor 12:8. See ST II-II, q. 177, introduction.

[23] ST II-II, q. 177, a. 1, reply.

minister to others except by the grace of speech." Given the medieval conviction that women were by nature and divine creation intended to be subordinated socially to men, Aquinas concluded that women should exercise their gift for speech in the private, rather than the public, realm.[24] More important for the discussion at hand, however, is his conviction that a charism must be exercised; there is a dynamism to the grace of charism. Those who are given a "charism for preaching" have the responsibility to find ways to exercise that gift for the building up of the entire body of Christ. As Vatican II's Decree on the Apostolate of the Laity *(Apostolicam Actuositatem)* asserts: "From the reception of these charisms or gifts . . . there arise for each believer the right and duty to use them in the Church and in the world for the good of [humankind] and for the upbuilding of the Church" *(AA,* 3).[25]

For many, this raises the question of the restriction of women and all lay persons from preaching the homily at Eucharist. As important as that concern is, it would be a mistake to focus all of our attention on the "charism of preaching," on preaching at the Eucharist, or even preaching within the broader liturgical context. Most of the people in our world who hunger for the good news of salvation or liberation are not to be found in our churches. Further, as a layman in his own religious tradition, Jesus announced the reign of God in ways that were not limited to events of public teaching or preaching, and that rarely took place in a liturgical setting.

This reminds us that all of the activities and relationships in which the baptized promote the reign of God are part of the preaching mission of the Church. The ministries of those who keep vigil in prisons or in hospitals, those who provide shelter for battered women and abused children, or those involved in legal advocacy or political lobbying on behalf of the poor are all part of the action on behalf of justice which is a "constitutive part of preaching the Gospel." Further, an increasing number of pastoral ministers who have not been ordained are involved in explicit ministries of the word including spiritual direction, teaching, theologizing, pastoral counseling, and the leadership of parish communities. Both women and men who are not ordained are now involved in ministries very explicitly identified as preaching the Gospel: evangelization and missionary work, members of itinerant preaching

---

[24] ST II-II, q. 177, a. 2, ad. 3.

[25] See the new code of Canon Law (1983), Canon 759: "In virtue of their baptism and confirmation lay members of the Christian faithful are witnesses of the gospel message by word and by example of a Christian life." See also Canon 225 in which the baptized are not only encouraged to proclaim the Gospel, but also told that it is their responsibility to do so.

teams, pastoral associates, leaders of faith-sharing groups based on the Scriptures. These preachers direct retreats and days of recollection, preside at morning and evening prayer and services of the word, and form the faith of the Church as catechists involved in the Rites of Christian Initiation. All of this would be dismissed somehow if we were to restrict our understanding of preaching to the pulpit or liturgical context.

At the same time, it is precisely out of the richness of the experience of the many charisms entrusted to the community as expressed in these multiple ministries of preaching that Christian communities have begun to question the restriction of the preeminent preaching of the Church, the eucharistic homily, to ordained males. While the argument usually made is the canonical one that the homily is "part of the liturgy itself" and necessarily reserved to a bishop, priest, or deacon,[26] the German bishops over twenty years ago proposed an alternate theological and liturgical reading of the value of lay preaching, even at Eucharist. They proposed:

> Since the church teaches that the entire community preaches the gospel and celebrates the liturgy, the responsibility for maintaining the office of preaching should not be given to the priest alone. Lay preaching is a way of making visible the different charisms, services and offices which exist in the Christian community without detracting from the unity of its mission.[27]

[26] See Canon 767.1, and commentaries by John Burke and Thomas P. Doyle, *The Homilist's Guide to Scripture, Theology, and Canon Law* (New York: Pueblo, 1986), and Joseph Fox, "The Homily and the Authentic Interpretation of Canon 767.1, *Apollinaris* 62 (1989) 123–69. For discussion of the possibility of lay preaching at Eucharist that occurs after the gospel but is not referred to as the "homily," see James H. Provost, "Canon Law in a Time of Transition," *Preaching and the Non-Ordained*, ed. Nadine Foley (Collegeville: The Liturgical Press, 1983) 134–58; idem., "Canon 766" in *Roman Replies and CLSA Advisory Opinions 1986*, eds. William A. Schumacher and J. James Cuneo (Washington, D.C.: Canon Law Society of America, 1986) 71–73; idem, "Brought Together by the Word of the Living God (Canons 762–72), "*Studia Canonica* 23 (1989) 345–71; J. A. Coriden, "The Preaching of the Word of God (cc. 762–72)," in J. A. Coriden, T. J. Green, and D. E. Heintschel (eds.), *The Code of Canon Law: A Text and Commentary*, commissioned by the Canon Law Society of America (Mahwah, N.J.: Paulist Press, 1985) 551–55; and John M. Huels, "The Law on Lay Preaching: Interpretation and Implementation," *Proceedings of the Canon Law Society of America* 52 (1990) 61–79; idem, *Disputed Questions in the Liturgy Today* (Chicago: Liturgy Training Publications, 1988) 17–25.

[27] "*Die Beteiligung der Laien an derVerkundigung*," 2, 33, trans. William Skudlarek, Appendix III in "Assertion Without Knowledge?" This was part of the argument of the West German bishops in their 1973 request to the Congregation for the Clergy for authorized lay preaching at Eucharist. In their request, which was granted for

The *Directory of Masses for Children,* published by the Congregation for Divine Worship in 1973 and still in effect, offers another pastoral rationale for lay preaching at Eucharist when it states that "one of the adults may speak after the gospel, especially if the priest finds it hard to adapt himself to the mentality of the children."[28] The central pastoral concern here is clear: Whoever can most effectively communicate God's word to the community of gathered children should preach at the Eucharist. Again there is a clear recognition that the charism of preaching, even in the context of Eucharist, is not restricted to the ordained. Further there is the experience of Christian communities around the world where catechists or delegates of the word are the primary preachers or the Gospel or where the presider regularly invites the testimony of other believers as part of the preaching of the Gospel at Eucharist.[29] In the early 1970s Carlo Molari described what he called the "taking over of the word" in the Church by the Christian community as a "sign of the times," a sign of the Spirit's activity bringing the Church to fuller truth. Speaking specifically about the liturgical context, he argued:

> [T]he fact that only the priest comments on the scripture readings and
> unveils their present-day meaning is not sufficient for the authentic
> proclamation of the Word of God today. The fact that all the people take

eight years, the bishops allude to the shortage of clergy, the number of theologically literate lay persons in Germany, and finally, their most basic concern: more effective preaching. For the authorization, see letter of Cardinal J. Wright, Prefect of the Congregation for the Clergy, to Cardinal J. Döpfner, president of the German Bishops' Conference, 20 November 1973, in *Archiv für katholisches Kirchenrecht* 142 (1973) 480–82 and in DOL, doc. 344, nos. 2953–63, 914–16. Similar permissions were granted the Swiss, Austrian, and East German bishops. See H. Mussinghoff, "Predigt des Wortes Gottes," in K. Lüdicke (ed.), *Münsterischer Kommentar zum Codex iuris canonici,* Essen, Ludgerus Verlag, 1987, at c. 766, 1–2 as cited by Provost, "Brought Together by the Word of the Living God," 358, n. 42.

[28] Directory of Masses for Children, #24, ICEL translation in *Documents on the Liturgy 1963–1979* (Collegeville: The Liturgical Press, 1982) 682.

[29] See "Lay Preachers," in Pro Mundi Vita, *Ministries and Communities* 17 (July 1978) 12–13; J. Frank Henderson, "When Lay People Preside at Sunday Worship," *Worship* 58 (1984) 108–17 at 113; idem., "Sunday Celebrations Animated by Lay People: Current Practices around the World," unpublished report, 1980, 29–39; Congregation pour le Culte divin, "Directoire pour les célébrations dominicales en l'absence de prêtre," 2 Juin 1988 (Paris: Les Éditions du Cerf, 1988); F. Lobinger, *Leading the Community Service, Training for Leading the Community Service in the Absence of an Ordained Minister,* prepared by Lumko Missiological Institute, South Africa (London: Collins Liturgical Publications, 1978); Brian J. Pierce, "Delegates of the Word: Lay Preaching in Honduras," *America,* April 6, 1996, 14–17.

up the Word is not a fashionable innovation: it is a fundamental theological demand that today our culture permit all or at least the great majority of our faithful to publicly express some reflections on their own experience of faith. It would be truly strange that at this time, when two women are proclaimed doctors of the Church, lay people should be prohibited from expressing before the whole community gathered in remembrance of the redemption wrought by Christ, the meaning which it has for their own lives, when this is one of the fundamental conditions for the present-day meaning of the Gospel message to be discovered. On the other hand, anyone who has even the least experience of such participation knows how much benefit the priest himself derives, since he cannot himself achieve in his own life all the aspects of the Christian existence.[30]

In any of these cases the unity of word and sacrament remains an important liturgical concern and a primary focus of the ministry of the one who presides at the liturgy, but that does not mean that only the ordained can or should preach. Rather, as Mary Collins proposes, if Eucharist is the act of the whole Church and if the ordained is one who presides within, not over, the community of believers, then "[e]cclesial experience confirms that it is possible for one who presides within the liturgical assembly to engage another believer to lead them all together into deep communion with the mystery of Christ by the power of the word, and this collaborative ordering does not fracture the sacrament of unity."[31]

Even this brief discussion of lay preaching in the context of Eucharist raises questions about the distinction of the ministerial priesthood from the common priesthood, the relationship between charism and office, the role of the local church and in particular the bishop in discerning, testing, and ordering charisms, and the value, if not necessity, of liturgical commissioning of the ministry of preaching. These concerns go beyond the scope of this chapter, but that is not to dismiss them. Rather, it is to suggest that if we take "charisms" as the starting point for discussions of the ministry of preaching, or of any ministry, we will

---

[30] Carlo Molari, *La Fede e il suo linguaggio* (Assisi: Cittadella Editrice, 1972) 280–84. Translation by John Dunn. Molari states further: "Numerous episodes in recent years provide us with much food for thought, but for me they all converge upon this fact: the people of God are asking to speak the Word. It would be a tragic error not to let them do so . . . A new division in the Church would arise and through our own fault. A division which yet again would find in the Eucharist its own pain and its own condemnation."

[31] Mary Collins, "Baptismal Roots of the Preaching Ministry," 130.

find ourselves confronted with new theological questions and perspectives.

Cardinal Suenens spoke specifically about this shift in his address on the ministerial priesthood in a changing world at a symposium of European bishops in Chur, Switzerland, in 1969. There he noted that while a previous hierarchical vision of Church made the definition and role of the lay person in the Church unclear, Vatican II's focus on the Church as the people of God and the ministries of all the baptized called for a genuine rethinking of the theology of ministerial priesthood. Stressing that the proper ministries of the hierarchy can be discovered only in the larger context of the Church as the "ensemble of the baptized," he remarked: "The ministerial priesthood is distinct from the general priesthood though directed toward the latter." Fundamentally he insisted that "the ministerial priesthood, for the bishop as well as the priest, is secondary to the status and mission of these people as baptized."[32]

In response to the question of who is anointed and sent to proclaim the Gospel, the most fundamental response of Vatican II is "the Church —the People of God." All the baptized share the mission of the Church to announce the good news of salvation through witness of life, action on behalf of justice, and "giving account" of the Christian hope.[33] Some within the community are entrusted with a specific charism for preaching—a gift for perceiving and announcing the present activity of the Spirit of God in the community and in the world in light of the faith of the Church proclaimed in the Scriptures and liturgy. While this charism for preaching is not restricted to the ordained, it is a charism that is at the heart of presbyteral and episcopal office. As Vatican II emphasized, the proclamation of the Gospel is preeminent among the tasks of the

---

[32] *The Suenens Dossier,* 107. In his Pastoral Letter on Pentecost, 1970, Suenens commented, "We cannot enhance the priesthood of the faithful without looking with new eyes at the ministerial priesthood—which though irreplaceable—must be lived differently." L.-J. Cardinal Suenens, *Memories and Hopes,* trans. Elena French (Dublin: Veritas, 1992) 153.

[33] The "Decree on the Apostolate of the Laity" *Apostolicam Actuositatem* notes that the apostolate of all members of the Church is "to manifest Christ's message by words and deeds and to communicate His grace to the world." The decree states specifically that the "lay apostolate" does not consist only in the witness of one's way of life; a true apostle looks for opportunities to announce Christ by words addressed either to non-believers with a view to leading them to faith, or to believers with a view to instructing and strengthening them, and motivating them toward a more fervent life. "'For the love of Christ impels us" (2 Cor 5:14). And the words of the Apostle should echo in every Christian heart: "For woe to me if I do not preach the gospel" (1 Cor 9:16) (AA, #6).

bishop as pastor of a local church (*LG*, §25; and *CD*, §12) and the primary duty of priests as co-workers with their bishops (*PO*, §4). As overseer of the community charged with preserving both the authentic tradition and the unity of the body of Christ, the bishop is entrusted with the responsibility for recognizing and ordering the many diverse charisms of all the baptized within the local Church. That is why in *A New Pentecost?* Suenens makes reference to the episcopal office as "the charism of discerning charisms."[34] In a unique way the bishop bears the responsibility of Paul's mandate in the First Letter to the Thessalonians: "Test everything; retain what is good" (5:21), but the charge cannot be separated from the verses that precede it: "Do not stifle the Spirit. Do not despise prophecies" (5:19-20).

Announcing the Hope of the Gospel

Cardinal Suenens offered no explicit criteria for determining whether the Gospel has been authentically proclaimed, whether by ordained or other baptized ministers, but all of his writings suggest that one clear sign of the presence of the Spirit of God is the virtue of hope. In reflecting on the "signs of the times" in the late 1960s, just years after the closing of the Council, Cardinal Suenens detected pessimism and a sense of defeat, both within the Church and in the broader society. He even confessed to his own "dark night of hope" during what the called the "winter of the post-Council era."[35] But he also reminded all Christians who would preach and live the Gospel that it is precisely in situations that appear hopeless that genuine hope, which is sheer gift of the Spirit, is born. When we have no human reasons for hoping, Cardinal Suenens observed, we have only the promise of God to go on—and we are called to nourish our hope at its source—the word of God.[36]

There is a way in which a "dark night of hope," whether in the world, in the Church or in both, is a painful kind of blessing for preachers of the Gospel who are called to be rooted in the word of God and to preach authentically from their own experience. The bold preachers of the Pentecost event in the Acts of the Apostles are described in John's Gospel as gathered behind locked doors for fear. Mary Magdalene, the first preacher of the Gospel, remembered in the tradition as the "apostle to the apostles," is pictured in John 20 as standing beside an empty tomb weeping. Before Mary Magdalene or Peter or Paul could announce the hope of the resurrection, each one had to experience its

---

[34] *A New Pentecost?* 91.
[35] *A New Pentecost?* 213.
[36] *Ibid.*, xi–xii.

power in her or his own unique life. Each knew from experience that only the Spirit can empower human beings to announce the mystery of God, transforming even the most desperate of human situations.

When asked about the source of his own hope in 1974, Cardinal Suenens responded: "I am a man of hope, not for human reasons nor from any natural optimism, but because I believe the Holy Spirit is at work in the Church and in the world." He concluded a poetic letter that he wrote on Pentecost in 1974 with the question: "Who would dare to say that the love and imagination of God were exhausted?"[37] Cardinal Suenens intentionally ended the title of his *A New Pentecost?* with a question mark.[38] Thirty years later both questions still confront us. The renewal Suenens envisioned included an "institutional overhaul at every level," and at the same time "a spiritual renewal of exceptional richness." The contemporary resurgence of the preaching charism among the baptized, both as preachers and hearers of the word, carries an energy for institutional reform as well as the possibility for profound spiritual revitalization within the Church. Whether that "New Pentecost" will flourish in our day or whether at the level of both institutional and personal conversion we will "quench the Spirit" remains to be seen.

In 1987 Cardinal Suenens stated frankly, "If you were to ask me whether Vatican II was indeed a new Pentecost," I would say "yes"—in terms of grace that was offered—and "yes and no" in terms of grace received."[39] Nevertheless, when asked his hopes for the year 2000, he replied "that we should rediscover the secret of Pentecost, which is a mystery of conversion *(ad intra)* and of apostolate *(ad extra)*. And that we should not be afraid of the symbols of the wind which shakes the house—without uprooting it!—and of the flames which kindle from a spark."[40] The approach of that new millennium summons preachers and all the baptized to embrace and work toward Cardinal Suenens' hope that we might rediscover the secret of Pentecost and, with it, the charism of preaching.

---

[37] Suenens, *A New Pentecost?* xiii.
[38] *Memories and Hopes,* 280.
[39] *Memories and Hopes,* 372.
[40] *Ibid.,* 377.

5

The Charism of the Exegete: Unleashing the Power of the Word

■ *Barbara E. Reid, O.P.*

There is a story in our tradition of how a young man named Joseph was given the charism of exegesis. In his case, what he interpreted were not texts, but dreams. Using his gift around his siblings earned him a stay in the bottom of a cistern and bondage to Midianite traders (Genesis 37); but with Pharaoh it won him great favor (41). You take your chances when you exercise the charism of exegesis.

Not one to be daunted by the controversies and difficulties that he faced in his work of reinterpretation and revisioning for a renewed Church, Cardinal Suenens was a model for exegetes. We remember him with deep gratitude for his role in Vatican II in fostering the renewal in biblical studies and emphasizing anew the centrality of the Bible. It is notable how frequently Cardinal Suenens quoted Scripture and drew on biblical images and stories in his writings. He was truly a man steeped in Scripture. Grateful for Cardinal Suenens' visionary leadership, I offer these reflections.

Roman Catholics and the Bible—Then

There was a time, not so long ago, when the charism of the exegete was though to be a gift entrusted to a very select few. The image one had was of an aging, stoop-shouldered, bespectacled scholar, poring over dusty tomes, deciphering minute jots and tiddles of Hebrew, Aramaic, Syriac, Ugaritic, Greek, and Coptic manuscripts. Lost in an ancient world, an exegete might surface only rarely from his lofty intellectual pursuits. His students would assiduously copy his brilliant insights, hoping to be able to give them back by rote on the exam, without asking the question: "So what does this have to do with real life now?" Only his colleagues, fellow biblical scholars, truly understood the importance of the grammatical subtleties and methodological refinements that captivated him (I use masculine pronouns here deliberately; the surge in the number of women biblical scholars has occurred only in the last two decades).

Outside the academic setting, a typical Catholic family owned a family Bible—a big, coffee-table display Bible, with leather binding, giltedges, and Jesus' words printed in red ink. It would be opened only to record births, marriages, and deaths. It was not for just anyone to pick up and read or pray with—that was for Protestants. It was not that we were completely biblically illiterate, but what most of us knew of the Bible were popularized versions of biblical stories, told from memory. Multiple accounts of the same gospel episodes would be harmonized into one coherent story, often embellished with imaginative interpretation. When it came to prayer, we were much more likely each to have our own rosary than our own Bible.

Roman Catholics and the Bible—Now

Then came Vatican Council II and Catholic biblical scholars were encouraged to use modern methods of historical critical exegesis (*Dei Verbum* §12).[1] Recent discoveries from archaeological excavations, advances in linguistic understanding from newly found manuscripts at Qumran, Nag Hammadi, Amarna, Ugarit, and other sites made this an exciting endeavor! Translations of the Bible in the vernacular were now to be based on the original Hebrew and Greek texts, no longer on the Latin Vulgate (*Dei Verbum* §22). Preachers were now urged to make the Scriptures the foundation for their liturgical homilies (*Dei Verbum* §24). And finally, all the Christian faithful were exhorted to frequent reading of the Bible and prayer from Scripture (*Dei Verbum* §25). Scripture was well on its way to becoming, once again, "the soul of theology."[2]

And so today we see the burgeoning of interest in the Bible with its popular use in parish Renew groups, the Charismatic movement, *comunidades de base*, and Bible study groups. Today the charism of the

---

[1] Of course, use of such critical interpretive methods was not the innovation of Vatican II. See Joseph A. Fitzmyer, *Scripture, The Soul of Theology* (Mahwah, N.J.: Paulist, 1994) 5–38, for a description of the roots of the historical critical method in the Alexandrian School of interpretation in late Hellenistic times and its development to the present day.

[2] This phrase of Pope Leo XIII, from his encyclical *Providentissimus Deus,* was repeated in *Dei Verbum* § 24.

exegete is exercised not only by biblical scholars, but is, in some measure, a gift entrusted to every Christian. It is from the ranks of those who would formerly not have dared approach the sacred text (i.e., those who would least fit our opening stereotyped description of an exegete) that some of the most exciting developments in biblical studies have come forth in our day.

Liberation Approaches to Biblical Interpretation

One such development is the explosion of liberation approaches in the last three decades. Born in Latin America, with the work of people like Gustavo Gutiérrez, Carlos Mesters, Leonardo and Clodovis Boff, and many others,[3] a liberation approach begins with the insight that the principal objective of reading the Bible is not to interpret the Bible but to interpret life with the help of the Bible.[4] And so the starting point is not the text, but experience.

In Latin America the experience of the majority of the people is one of poverty. From this experience one moves to critical analysis of the social and political factors that cause poverty and oppression. This is accompanied by a critical reading of the biblical story, that underscores how in every part of the Scriptures, God's bias is always for the poor.[5] The biblical accounts, from the Exodus through the crucifixion of Jesus, tell again and again of God always being concerned with liberation for those oppressed. Finally, a liberation approach does not end with reflection on the Scriptures, but moves to action that will try to make the reign of God more fully incarnate in this world, here and now. This action involves not only personal conversion, but the concerted action of communities of believers to confront and dismantle oppressive systems.

This approach has revolutionized biblical interpretation. It has moved far beyond Latin America, as marginalized people everywhere have begun to ask the critical question, "Whose experience counts?" Through

[3] See Gustavo Gutiérrez, *A Theology of Liberation* (Maryknoll, N.Y.: Orbis, 1973); Carlos Mesters, *Defenseless Flower: A New Reading of the Bible* (Maryknoll, N.Y.: Orbis, 1989); Leonardo and Clodovis Boff, *Introducing Liberation Theology* (Maryknoll, N.Y.: Orbis, 1987); Ernesto Cardenal, *The Gospel in Solentiname.* 4 vols. (Maryknoll, N.Y.: Orbis, 1975, 1976, 1977, 1978); Christopher Rowland and Mark Corner, *Liberating Exegesis. The Challenge of Liberation Theology to Biblical Studies* (Louisville: Westminster/John Knox, 1989).

[4] Carlos Mesters, "Como se faz Teologia hoje no Brasil?" *Estudos Biblicos* I (1985) 10.

[5] See Clodovis Boff and Jorge Pixley, *The Bible, the Church, and the Poor.* Theology and Liberation Series (Maryknoll, N.Y.: Orbis, 1989).

whose lenses have the biblical stories been formulated and whose perspectives have shaped the centuries of biblical interpretation? Women,
African Americans, Hispanics, Asians, and many other previously
unheard voices are challenging traditional interpretations of white,
middle class, European, male exegetes.[6] The result has engendered
great hope for the former, while causing great upheaval for the latter.

There are many other new methods of biblical interpretation that
have developed since Vatican II: literary approaches, narrative criticism,
rhetorical analysis, canonical criticism, semiotic approaches, refinements in historical critical methods, and studies that engage tools from
sociology, psychology, and cultural anthropology. Like keys on a ring,
each opens a new door to understanding the biblical text more fully.[7]

---

[6] The works by feminist biblical scholars in recent years are myriad. Premier
among Roman Catholic women are Elisabeth Schüssler Fiorenza, *In Memory of Her.
A Feminist Theological Reconstruction of Christian Origins* (New York: Crossroad,
1984); *Bread Not Stone: The Challenge of Feminist Biblical Interpretation* (Boston: Beacon, 1984); *But She Said: Feminist Practices of Biblical Interpretation* (Boston: Beacon,
1992); *Jesus. Miriam's Child; Sophia's Prophet* (New York: Continuum, 1994); *Searching
the Scriptures,* 2 vols. (New York: Crossroad, 1993, 1994) and Sandra Schneiders *Beyond Patching* (New York: Paulist, 1991); *The Revelatory Text* (HarperSanFrancisco,
1991); *Women and the Word* (Paulist, 1986). For African American perspectives see:
Cain Hope Felder, *Stony the Road We Trod. African American Biblical Interpretation*
(Minneapolis: Fortress, 1991); *Troubling Biblical Waters, Race, Class, and Family* (Mary-
knoll, N.Y.: Orbis, 1989); Renita J. Weems, *Just a Sister Away: A Womanist Vision of
Women's Relationships in the Bible* (San Diego: LuraMedia, 1988); Vincent Wimbush,
"Biblical-Historical Study as Liberation: Toward an Afro-Christian Hermeneutic,"
The Journal of Religious Thought 42/2 (1985–1986) 9–21. For work by Hispanic schol-
ars, see: Justo Gonzalez, *Santa Biblia: The Bible Through Hispanic Eyes* (Nashville:
Abingdon, 1996); Ada María Isasi-Díaz, "The Bible and *Mujerista* Theology," *Lift
Every Voice. Constructing Christian Theologies from the Underside,* eds. Susan Brooks
Thistlethwaite and Mary Potter Engel (San Francisco: Harper, 1990) 262–65; Fer-
nando F. Segovia, "The Text as Other: Towards a Hispanic American Hermeneutic,"
We Are a People! Initiatives in Hispanic American Theology (Minneapolis: Fortress,
1992) 12–16; Elsa Tamez, *Bible of the Oppressed* (Maryknoll, N.Y.: Orbis, 1992);
Through Her Eyes: Women's Theology from Latin America (Maryknoll, N.Y.: Orbis,
1989). Works by Asian scholars include: Virginia Fabella and S.A.L. Park, eds. *We
Dare to Dream. Doing Theology as Asian Women* (Maryknoll, N.Y.: Orbis, 1990); V.
Fabella and Mercy Amba Oduyoye, eds. *With Passion and Compassion: Third World
Women Doing Theology* (Maryknoll, N.Y.: Orbis, 1988). A collection of essays from
authors world-wide is *Voices from the Margin. Interpreting the Bible in the Third World,*
ed. R. S. Sugirtharajah (Maryknoll, N.Y.: Orbis, 1995).

[7] For a description and evaluation of these new methods see the recent document
by the Pontifical Biblical Commission, "The Interpretation of the Bible in the Church,"
Origins 23/29 (January 6, 1994) 498–524.

A Sample of Liberation Exegesis: Luke 7:36-50[8]

I would like to concentrate on liberation exegesis for the remainder of my paper, and to give an example of it at work. More particularly, following will be an exercise in biblical interpretation from a feminist liberationist approach, using the text of Luke 7:36-50. It is the story of a woman who approaches Jesus at a dinner at the home of Simon the Pharisee. Although all four Gospels recount a similar episode, that of Luke is distinct. We will focus here solely on the details of the Lucan account.[9]

Setting the Scene

Setting the scene for the encounter between Jesus and Simon, the preceding episode in Luke tells of the messengers of the imprisoned John the Baptist coming to Jesus and asking, "Are you the one who is to come, or should we look for another?" (Luke 7:20). Jesus' reply is not a simple "Yes" or "No," but he points them to what they have seen and heard, "the blind regain their sight, the lame walk, lepers are cleansed, the deaf hear, the dead are raised, the poor have the good news proclaimed to them" (Luke 7:22). The unspoken question hangs in the air, "So what do you see in this?" One who has been reading the previous chapters of Luke knows that some have followed Jesus and glorified God for what they have seen,[10] while others have challenged and rejected him.[11]

---

[8] See also my article, "'Do you see this Woman?' Luke 7:36-50 as a Paradigm for Feminist Hermeneutics," *Biblical Research* 40 (1995) 37–49 and chapter 8, "The Woman Who Showed Great Love," in *Choosing the Better Part? Women in the Gospel of Luke* (Collegeville: The Liturgical Press, 1996).

[9] For a detailed comparison of the similarities and differences between Mark 14:3-9; Matt 26:6-13; Luke 7:36-50; and John 12:1-8 see B. Reid, *Choosing The Better Part? Women in the Gospel of Luke* (Collegeville: The Liturgical Press, 1996) 108–9. Most probably there are two strands of tradition: one tells of a woman who entered a dinner gathering in Galilee, at which Jesus was a guest. She had experienced forgiveness from Jesus and wept over his feet and dried them with her hair. The other strand relates that a woman at a dinner in Bethany anointed Jesus' head with costly perfume shortly before his passion. Whether the two strands of tradition represent two separate incidents in the life of Jesus or only one that has been variously preserved is impossible to determine. Because the two had many points of similarity, they became intertwined, and details from one passed over to the other in the oral retelling. Each evangelist has further shaped the episode to his own theological purposes.

[10] E.g., Luke 4:22, 36-37, 39; 5:11, 15, 25-26, 28; 6:12-16, 17-19; 7:6-9, 16.

[11] E.g., Luke 4:28-29; 5:21-24, 30, 33; 6:2, 7, 11.

Divided Responses

The next verses describe the divided response to John the Baptist: "All the people who listened, including the tax collectors, and who were baptized with the baptism of John, acknowledged the righteousness of God; but the Pharisees and scholars of the law, who were not baptized by him, rejected the plan of God for themselves" (Luke 7:29-30). Jesus asks the crowds three times, "What did you go out to the desert to see?" (Luke 7:24, 25, 26). And the section concludes with the observation, "John the Baptist came neither eating food nor drinking wine, and you said, 'He is possessed by a demon.' The Son of Humanity came eating and drinking and you said, 'Look, he is a glutton and a drunkard, a friend of tax collectors and sinners'" (Luke 7:33-34). In other words, people see what they want to see. Or they see what they expect to see.

At Simon's Home

With this as the backdrop, the episode at Simon's house begins, "A Pharisee invited Jesus to dine with him, and he entered the Pharisee's house and reclined at table. And a woman in the city, who was a sinner, having learned that he was eating in the Pharisee's house, brought an alabaster jar of ointment. She stood behind him at his feet, weeping, and began to bathe his feet with her tears and to dry them with her hair. Then she continued kissing his feet and anointing them with the ointment" (Luke 7:36-38).

These first three verses describe an episode that both Jesus and Simon witness. They see the same actions, but interpret them very differently. The point of the story is found not in the interaction between Jesus and the woman, but in the exchange between Jesus and Simon.[12] In the context of Luke 7, Simon exemplifies one who sees what he expects to see. The question that this episode poses is: can Simon ever see differently?

What Simon Sees

Verse 39 gives us Simon's initial judgment, "Now when the Pharisee who had invited him saw it, he said to himself, 'If this man were a prophet, he would have known who and what kind of woman this is who is touching him—that she is a sinner.'" Notice that two perceptions are intimately related: what Simon sees in the woman and her

---

[12] Contrary to Evelyn R. Thibeaux, "'Known to be a Sinner': The Narrative Rhetoric of Luke 7:36-50," *Biblical Theology Bulletin* 23/4 (1993) 152.

interaction with Jesus determines how Simon sees Jesus. Simon is clear about what he sees: she is a sinner and Jesus is not a prophet. Now it becomes apparent that Simon's ability to see differently not only concerns his attitude toward the woman, but also his relationship with Jesus.

A Parable

The story continues, "Jesus spoke up and said to him, 'Simon, I have something to say to you.' 'Teacher,' he replied, 'Speak'" (Luke 7:40). As most often in this Gospel, it is through parables that Jesus tries to help people see God's realm as he does. And so, Jesus tells Simon a parable:

> A certain creditor had two debtors; one owed five hundred denarii, and the other fifty. When they could not pay, he canceled the debts for both of them. Now which of them will love him more?" Simon answered, "I suppose the one for whom he canceled the greater debt." And Jesus said to him, "You have judged rightly" (7:41-43).

It's easy for Simon to "get" it in story form. But now comes the real test: will Simon "get" it when confronted with the real-life woman? And so the text continues,

> "Then turning toward the woman, Jesus said to Simon, 'Do you see this woman? I entered your house; you gave me no water for my feet, but she has bathed my feet with her tears and dried them with her hair. You gave me no kiss, but from the time I came in she has not stopped kissing my feet. You did not anoint my head with oil, but she has anointed my feet with ointment'" (7:44-46).

The purpose of this recitation is not so much pointed at what Simon did not do.[13] The focus is: "Do you see this woman?" (v. 44). Does Simon persist in seeing her as a sinner, or is he able to reinterpret her actions?

What Jesus Sees

If Simon is still not forthcoming with a different evaluation of what he saw, Jesus articulates his own conclusion, with the hope that Simon can be persuaded to see as he sees:

---

[13] See, e.g., Kenneth E. Bailey, *Poet and Peasant* and *Through Peasant Eyes*, 2 vols. in 1 (Grand Rapids, Mich.: Eerdmans, 1976) 2.11, who explores why Simon would have invited Jesus and then deliberately snub him. This is not the point.

"'Therefore, I tell you, her sins, which were many, have been forgiven; hence she has shown great love. But the one to whom little is forgiven, loves little.' Then he said to her, 'Your sins are forgiven.'" (7:47-48).

Verse 47 makes it utterly clear that the woman's sins had already been forgiven before this dinner party. The perfect tense of the verb ἀφέωνται, "have been forgiven," expresses a past action whose effects endure into the present. How or when the woman's sins were forgiven is not narrated. Jesus' words to the woman in verse 48, "Your sins are forgiven," are a reaffirmation to her of what has already occurred. One thing is very clear: the woman is not forgiven because of her lavish demonstrations of love; rather, the loving actions follow from her experience of having been forgiven. The parable in verses 41-43 and the conclusion of verse 47c make the same point: much love follows much forgiveness.[14]

Is Simon persuaded to adopt this perspective? Can he let go of seeing the woman as a sinner and see, rather, her great love? Can he see Jesus as a prophet and a special agent of God's forgiving love? Can he see himself as one in need of forgiveness as well? We don't know. Like all good parables, the story is open-ended. It remains for us to finish.[15] It invites us to take up the challenge presented to Simon and to be converted to Jesus' way of seeing.

[14] The Greek phrase ὅτι ἠγάπησεν πολύ allows the meaning "because she loves much," taking the conjunction ὅτι in a consecutive sense. However, the conclusion in v. 47c, "But the one to whom little is forgiven, loves little," and the parable in vv. 41-43 have the opposite point: that the love follows the forgiveness. In this context it is clear that ὅτι must be understood in the causal sense, pointing not to the reason why the fact *is* so, but whereby it is *known* to be so. The translation of the *Revised English Bible* makes this the clearest: "So I tell you, her great love proves that her many sins have been forgiven; where little has been forgiven, little love is shown." See further Joseph A. Fitzmyer, *The Gospel According to Luke I-IX* (AB28; Garden City, N.Y.: Doubleday, 1981) 687. This interpretation also makes an important theological point: divine forgiveness is not dependent on a person's demonstrations of love; the remittance of sin is prior.

[15] The concluding verses: "Then he said to her, 'Your sins are forgiven.' But those who were at the table with him began to say among themselves, 'Who is this who even forgives sins?' And he said to the woman, 'Your faith has saved you; go in peace'" (7:48-50) append sayings found in other Lucan stories that have only a loose connection to 7:36-47. In the story of the man who had been paralyzed (Luke 5:17-26) Jesus also says, "Your sins are forgiven" (5:20). The scribes and Pharisees react by asking themselves, "Who is this who speaks blasphemies? Who but God alone can forgive sins?" (5:21). Simon's asking himself about Jesus' identity in 7:39 recalls 5:20-21 and prompts Luke to end the episode in chapter 7 with the same statement, "Your sins are forgiven" (7:48) and the same question, "Who is this?" (7:49). The

Look Again

This text can likewise serve as a challenge to modern believers and exegetes to take another look at what we see when we approach a familiar text. If we ask the question of ourselves, "Do you see this woman?" what is it that we see? Has our vision been colored by past interpretations that tend to reinforce Simon's initial perception and never move beyond that? It is startling to see how many commentators and translators do precisely that.

Titles

First, a sampling of titles given to the passage by modern scholars is revealing.[16] The *New American Bible* (with revised New Testament, 1986) entitles it: "The Pardon of a Sinful Woman." The *New Jerusalem Bible* (rev. 1985) and the *New Revised Standard Version* (1989) call it: "The Woman Who Was a Sinner." *Harper Collins Study Bible* (1993) has, "A Sinful Woman Forgiven." *La Nueva Biblia Latinoamericana* (1972) confuses matters entirely by making her *La mujer pecadora de Magdala* ("The sinful woman from Magdala")! *The Christian Community Bible* (1988) is noncommittal: "Jesus, the Woman and the Pharisee."

In five out of these six titles, the sinfulness of the woman is the focus. Two mistakenly lead the reader to believe that the pardon of her sins takes place in this episode. It is remarkable that none has thought to

---

central point of the episode in 7:36-50, however, does not concern Jesus' ability to forgive sins, but rather Simon's misperception of a forgiven sinner. The effect of Jesus' statement in 7:48 is that it reaffirms to the woman the forgiveness she has already experienced. The question in 7:49 indicates that Jesus is the agent of the forgiveness, although the verb ἀφέωνται, "have been forgiven" (v. 47) may be understood as a theological passive, i.e., the forgiving has been done by God. In context, the effect of v. 49 is that Simon's companions are shown as contradicting Jesus' attempt to move Simon to a different perception of the woman. The reader is left wondering who will win out: Jesus or Simon's cronies?

The concluding verse, "Your faith has saved you; go in peace" (7:50) is identical to the closing line of the healing of the woman with a hemorrhage (8:43-48). In the latter story, faith is at the heart of the message; in 7:36-50 faith only appears in the final verse, and is not the point of the episode. The similarities of the two narratives, in which a woman thought to be unclean approaches Jesus without his bidding, and touches him, followed by objections from a character named Simon, causes Luke to append 7:50 to the story of the woman who loved greatly, giving the two episodes identical endings.

[16] There are no subtitles in the Greek manuscripts of the Gospel. Although these additions by modern translators may help the reader to find his or her place in the text, they also interpret the passage—often in a mistaken direction.

point the reader to the way Jesus perceives her (v. 47) by entitling it: "A Woman who Shows Great Love."

Mistranslations

In addition to titles that direct attention to the woman's sinfulness, there are mistranslations of verse 47. The 1970 edition of the *New American Bible* translates: "I tell you, that is why her many sins are for-given—because of her great love. Little is forgiven one whose love is small." Similarly, the 1971 edition of the *Revised Standard Version* has, "Therefore, I tell you, her sins, which are many, are forgiven, for she loved much; but he[17] who is forgiven little, loves little." Both of these wrongly make the woman's forgiveness a consequence of her actions. Note that the *RSV* reverses the direction in the second half of the verse, correctly rendering that little forgiveness results in little love.[18] Happily, the revised versions of the *NAB* (1986) and *NRSV* (1989) have corrected these mistranslations.

Finally, the rendering of verse 37 in some translations also serves to reinforce the woman's sinfulness. The text clearly says that the woman was a sinner, but the verb tense in verse 37 is imperfect, which has the connotation, "used to be." In other words, she was a sinner, but is no longer, as is also clear from verse 47. That the woman was a sinner in the past is completely obscured in the translation of the *NAB*, "Now there was a sinful woman in the city." Moreover, this translation juxta-poses "sinful" and "woman," making it all the more difficult to ever eradicate the equation of the two. The *NRSV* is far preferable and trans-lates the Greek more literally, "And a woman in the city, who was a sinner . . ."

A Prostitute?

What about the kinds of sins this woman committed? It is curious that, although the text does not say what sort of sins she had commit-

---

[17] The relative pronoun ᾧ is rendered inclusively, "the one to whom," in the newly revised version.

[18] The same is true of the translation of the *New Jerusalem Bible*, "For this reason I tell you that her sins, many as they are, have been forgiven her, because she has shown such great love. It is someone who is forgiven little who shows little love," *La Nueva Biblia Latinoamericana*, "Por esto te digo que sus pecados, sus numerosos pecados, le quedan perdonados, por el mucho amor que demostró. Pero aquel a quien se le perdona poco, demuestra poco amor" and the *Christian Community Bible*, "This is why, I tell you, her sins, her many sins, are forgiven, because she loved much. But the one who is forgiven little, returns little love."

ted, much attention is given to speculation on the nature of her sinful past. By contrast, commentators never discuss what might be the type of sins Simon Peter has committed when he says he is "a sinful man" in the story of his call (Luke 5:7). The usual presumption is that the woman in 7:36-50 was a prostitute.[19] In verse 47 Jesus acknowledges that her sins had been many, and Luke hints in verse 37 that the whole city also knows this. But does that warrant the conclusion that she is a prostitute?

In a first-century Galilean city everyone knows everyone else's business. This woman need only have been ill, disabled, or have contact with Gentiles to be considered a sinner by all Jews in the city.[20] Simon's remark in verse 39 implies that the woman's sinfulness is not immediately apparent to a stranger. A possible scenario is that the woman is employed in work that brings her into frequent contact with Gentiles,[21] perhaps midwifery. Or her work may be in one of the trades considered unclean, such as dyeing.[22] Everyone in the city would know her occupation and would consider her sinful from her association with the unclean. Simon, unaware of any prior contact between her and Jesus, remarks to himself that if Jesus were, indeed, a prophet, he, too, would know that she is a sinner.

---

[19] E.g., Kathleen Corley, *Private Women, Public Meals* (Peabody: Hendrickson, 1993) 124; J.D.M. Derrett, *Law in the New Testament* (London: Darton, Longman & Todd, 1970) 167–68; Elisabeth Moltmann Wendel, *The Women Around Jesus* (New York: Crossroad, 1993) 65; A. Plummer, *The Gospel According to S. Luke* (5th ed. ICC. Edinburgh: T. & T. Clark, 1981) 210; E. Schweizer, *The Good News According to Luke* (Atlanta: John Knox, 1984) 139; B. Witherington III, *Women and the Genesis of Christianity* (New York: Cambridge University, 1990) 66. Fitzmyer dissents: "No hint is given of the kind of sins that she has committed" (*Luke*, 1.689). M. Black (*An Aramaic Approach to the Gospels and Acts* [3rd ed.; Oxford: Clarendon, 1967] 181–83) thinks that the Lucan text is playing on the Aramaic word for "sinner," *hayyābtāʾ*, "debtor," and is thus providing a connection between the pronouncement-story and the parable.

[20] That sickness and disability were equated with sinfulness in Jesus' day is evident from the question of Jesus' disciples in John 9:2, "Rabbi, who sinned, this man or his parents, that he was born blind?" Jesus' reply is, "Neither this man nor his parents sinned; it is so that the works of God might be made visible through him" (John 9:3). The equation of gentile with "sinner" can be seen in 1 Macc 2:44; Gal 2:15, and is implied in Luke 6:32-33; 24:7.

[21] The phrase αἱ ἁμαρτίαι αὐτῆς αἱ πολλαί, "her many sins," in v. 47 indicates that her sinfulness came from numerous acts.

[22] See J. Jeremias, "Despised Trades," *Jerusalem in the Time of Jesus* (Philadelphia: Fortress, 1969) 303–12.

Women at Banquets

Her mere presence[23] at the banquet does open her up to the accusation of being a prostitute. In antiquity women who attended banquets were prostitutes who were there to enhance the pleasure of men. Although in the Roman period respectable women became more liberated and were beginning to attend banquets with men, the pervasive attitude was that such actions made a woman sexually suspect.

But the woman who comes to Simon's house is not a participant in the banquet. Nor does she do any of the things that banquet courtesans were known to do: engage in witty conversation or discussion with the banqueters, drink with them, recline beside them, dance, act, play the flute or harp, or in any way entertain.[24] Nor is she named by any of the known terms for such women: πόρνη, "prostitute, whore," κοινή, "common," i.e., "shared by all," γύναι πάγκοινε, "public woman," πιλάσωτος, "wanton" or ἑταῖρα, "companion to men," the term for the highest class prostitutes.[25]

Loose Hair = Loose Woman?

Nonetheless, some find in Luke 7:36-50 proof of the woman's prostitution in the details of her loosening her hair, possessing an expensive alabaster flask of perfume, and emptying it out on Jesus' feet. First the hair. It is true that in Leviticus and Numbers there are references to di-

---

[23] John Koenig (*New Testament Hospitality* [Overtures to Biblical Theology 17; Philadelphia: Fortress, 1985]) notes that rabbinic texts (*Abot.* 1:5; *Tos. Ber.* 4:8; *Ta'an* 20.b) speak of virtuous Jews who were known to open their houses to the needy, particularly for Sabbath eve supper. This explains how the woman could have gained access to a Pharisee's meal.

[24] See such descriptions of banquet courtesans in Corley, *Public Meals*, 38–48; see also Sarah Pomeroy, *Goddesses, Whores, Wives, and Slaves. Women in Classical Antiquity* (New York: Dorset, 1975) 88–92.

[25] Furthermore, it is not known whether any of the women who responded positively to Jesus were prostitutes. Such speculation is based on one lone saying unique to Matthew. It occurs on the lips of Jesus at the end of the parable of the two sons. He says to the chief priests and elders, "Amen, I say to you, tax collectors and prostitutes are entering the kingdom of God before you. When John came to you in the way of righteousness, you did not believe him; but tax collectors and prostitutes did. Yet even when you saw that, you did not later change your minds and believe him" (Matt 21:31-32). The saying serves as a warning to the religious leaders, who think themselves upright, but who in fact, may not be. It contrasts their negative response to Jesus with that of those least expected to be upright: tax collectors and prostitutes. It is a warning to the leaders, set forth in polemical terms, not a historical attestation on the makeup of Jesus' itinerant band of followers.

sheveled hair as a sign of mourning, uncleanness, and shame.[26] Numbers 5:18 prescribes as part of the ordeal for a woman suspected of adultery, that the priest have the woman come forward and stand before the Lord; he would dishevel her hair, and place in her hands the cereal offering of her appeal. The disheveled hair was a sign of uncleanness and shame. However, there is no indication in Luke 7:36-50 that this woman's loosened hair connotes adultery, shame, or uncleanness.[27] The narrative does not say that she entered with her hair disheveled, or that it was already loosened. In fact, had she been a prostitute, her hair would have been beautifully groomed.

J. F. Coakley[28] lists rabbinic texts that show that a *married* woman was not to let down her hair in the presence of other men (*t. Sota* 5.a; *y. Git.* 9.50d, etc.). But he observes that "none of these passages touches the question of what an unmarried woman might decently do in a neighbor's house among friends." He cites *m. Ketub.* 2.1 as seeming to assume that a woman did not bind up her hair until her marriage. He asks further, why, if letting down her hair in public was such a gross act of immodesty, the woman, supposed to be penitent, went out of her way to shock, and why no one commented on the offensiveness of her action.[29] In fact the Pharisee host says to himself (v. 39) that Jesus would have to be a prophet to realize what sort of woman this is![30]

There are other meanings associated with loose, flowing hair. In the Song of Songs (4:1; 6:5) among the charms extolled by the bridegroom-

---

[26] In Lev 13:45 the instructions for a person with a leprous disease include wearing torn clothes and letting their hair be disheveled as a sign of their uncleanness. In Lev 10:6, 21:10 are directions that priests were not to perform the mourning observances, including disheveling their hair, since they were to maintain themselves in a state of ritual purity.

[27] Alfred Plummer (*The Gospel According to S. Luke* [ICC; Edinburgh: T. & T. Clark, 1981] 211) asserts that among Jews it was shameful for a woman to let her hair down in public, but he interprets the woman's action as a sacrifice she makes in order to minister to Jesus.

[28] "The Anointing at Bethany and the Priority of John," *JBL* 107 (1988) 241–56.

[29] Louise Schotroff, in "Through German and Feminist Eyes: A Liberationist Reading of Luke 7:36-50," a paper presented at the AAR/SBL in Chicago, November 21, 1994, resolves the tension in the opposite direction: the woman is a whore but not repentant. She argues that because of economic necessity the woman remains a prostitute, but has experienced and has given love. She believes the story is not about prostitution that can be overcome by Christian repentance. Rather, the issue is mercy and respect toward prostitutes exhibited by Jesus contrasted with prejudice against them shown by Simon. Schotroff states that it is the moralizing tendency of Christians that prevents us from accepting such an interpretation.

[30] Coakley, "Anointing," 250.

to-be of his beloved is her beautiful hair that is "like a flock of goats, streaming down the mountains of Gilead." Her dark, flowing hair evokes in him awe and love; there is nothing of shame or uncleanness. As in the Song of Songs, the flowing hair of the woman in Luke 7:38 evokes an image of beauty. Like the bridegroom of the Song of Songs, Jesus sees this woman as lovely and loving and attempts to get his host to perceive the same.[31]

A Wealthy Woman

What of the expensive alabaster flask of ointment? That the woman possessed such attests to her wealth.[32] But prostitution was not the only source of wealth for women in antiquity. According to Num 27:8 an unmarried woman without brothers could inherit money and property from her father.[33] A woman could also acquire money by working, either on her own, or by sharing in her husband's work. From Acts 16:14, for example, we know of Lydia of Thyatira, who was a dealer in purple goods, luxury items. Acts 18:3 tells of Prisca working together with her husband Aquila at tentmaking. Inscriptions that Bernadette Brooten has examined from Jewish women who were donors to synagogues show that at least some Greco-roman women had money or property and the power to donate it.[34]

---

[31] Another suggestion by I. Howard Marshall (*Commentary on Luke* [New International Greek Testament Commentary; Grand Rapids: Eerdmans, 1978] 308–9) is that in Luke 7:36-50 the woman's gesture of wiping Jesus' feet with her hair simply signifies that her tears were not premeditated and that, lacking a towel, her hair was the only means at hand for drying Jesus' feet. Or, taking another tack, J. F. Coakley remarks that "the woman's tears can surely not have been so copious as to need wiping up at all!" ("Anointing," 250). This detail, he suggests, derives not from factual reporting, but from "quasi-poetic hyperbole," such as found in Ps 6:6, "every night I flood my bed with weeping; I drench my couch with my tears."

[32] In antiquity alabaster was quarried only in Egypt, and so, was a luxury item, as was perfume. See J. L. McKenzie, "Alabaster," *Dictionary of the Bible* (New York: MacMillan, 1965) 19. It is interesting that although the anonymous women who anoint Jesus in Mark 14:3-9 and Matt 26:6-13 also use alabaster flasks of very expensive ointment commentators never conclude that they are prostitutes. Nor is such a slur directed at Mary of Bethany, who anoints Jesus with a pound of costly ointment of pure nard in John 12:1-8.

[33] See Moshe Meiselman, *Jewish Woman in Jewish Law* (New York: KTAV, 1978) 84–95, for information on inheritance by women in rabbinic tradition. He also demonstrates Jewish women's financial independence by entering into contracts to acquire and dispose of property (81–83).

[34] B. Brooten, *Women Leaders in the Ancient Synagogue: Inscriptional Evidence and Background Issues* (Brown Judaic Studies 36. Chico, Calif.: Scholars Press, 1982) studies

Even the action of pouring out the ointment from the alabaster flask has been interpreted as the action of a prostitute who disposes of a tool of her trade now that she has been forgiven. Kenneth Bailey, for example, notes that women were known to wear a flask with perfume around the neck that hung down below the breast, used to sweeten the breath and perfume the person. He then remarks that "it does not take much imagination to understand how important such a flask would be to a prostitute."[35] If one is predisposed to see this woman as a prostitute, then he is right, one's imagination would not have to be pressed far.

An Image of Christ

But if one were predisposed to see in a female figure a potential disciple, or one who could prefigure the Christ, it is possible to envision the symbolic action in another direction. Does not her pouring out of the expensive ointment out of love prefigure Jesus' pouring out of his precious life-blood on behalf of those whom he loves (Luke 22:20)? In fact, this story has a number of thematic connections to the death of Jesus.[36] This woman is assured salvation in 7:50, just as is the repentant criminal in 23:41-42; her tears stand in contrast to those of Peter, who weeps bitterly after denying Jesus (22:62); her kisses contrast to the betraying kiss of Judas (22:47); and her position at Jesus' feet is the stance of a servant, the stance which Jesus instructs his disciples to take at the last supper (22:26-27).

The woman in 7:36-50, then, exemplifies one who responds properly to Jesus, and whose actions mirror his own. The key question her story poses, not only to Simon, but to the modern exegete is, "Do you see this woman?" In the narrative, not to see the woman and her actions properly is not to perceive Jesus and his identity correctly. The story is open-ended: there is yet hope that Simon's vision can be corrected. What about ours?

---

forty-three such inscriptions. See also Richard Atwood, *Mary Magdalene in the New Testament Gospels and Early Tradition* (European University Studies. Series 23, Band 457. Bern: Peter Lang, 1993) 17, n. 23 for examples of women who gave monetary aid and property to rabbis. B. Witherington, "On the Road with Mary Magdalen, Joanna, Susanna, and Other Disciples—Luke 8:1-3," *ZNW* 70 (1979) 244, n. 9 lists rabbinic texts that refer to women offering support to rabbis and their disciples in the form of money, property, or foodstuffs.

[35] Kenneth E. Bailey, *Poet & Peasant* and *Through Peasant Eyes,* 2 vols. in 1 (Grand Rapids: Eerdmans, 1976) 2.8.

[36] Corley, *Private Women,* 128.

The Consequences of Liberationist Exegesis

Feminist liberationist exegesis unmasks the gender biases that have shaped both the text and our interpretations of it. Such an approach challenges us to look again with new eyes and to be converted from misperceptions, prejudgments, and stereotyped views of women that can blind us to the full identity of Jesus. It is not earthshattering to reflect on a woman being forgiven by Jesus, nor even that women were disciples of Jesus. But to assert that a woman fully images the Christ has profound theological and christological consequences, not to mention implications for ministerial roles.

These kinds of results from biblical exegesis are bringing new hope and vision to many. To others they are very disturbing as they challenge the underpinnings of whole systems of patriarchal practice. This upheaval is not unlike that faced by Cardinal Suenens as he worked tirelessly for renewal in the Church from the inception of Vatican II forward. His words and example can encourage us to continue on this path with bold faithfulness.

The Power of the Spirit

One of the most evident characteristics of Cardinal Suenens was his unwavering belief in the power of the Spirit to guide the Church in the task of renewal. He insisted that the Spirit would open our eyes to the meaning of the Scriptures, just as the risen Christ did with the two disciples on the road to Emmaus.[37] He explained that, "In this renewal in the Church today we have a new awareness of the full spectrum of the gifts of the Holy Spirit. We must not be afraid to accept the Spirit with all its manifestations, just as we find them in the Gospels and St. Paul." His prayer was, "Come Holy Spirit with *all* Your manifestations (emphasis original). We are ready to receive them even if they are disturbing."[38]

Charisms Shared by All

One of the startling things about the manifestations of the gifts of the Spirit is that they fall on whomever God pleases to give them. Today the charism of the exegete is being exercised by women as well as men, and by scholars from all corners of the earth. In this age of global communication, voices from those on the margins are reaching the ears of those in dominant Western cultures, bringing new perspectives to the work of biblical interpretation.

---

[37] *Come Holy Spirit* (New York: Morehouse-Barlow, 1976) 61.
[38] *Ibid.*, 56–57.

Moreover, the charism of the exegete is not given only to biblical scholars, but to all believers in some measure. Cardinal Suenens insisted that Jesus' command, "Go preach the Gospel" was meant for every Christian.[39] This implies that every Christian must then know the Gospel through prayer and study. Cardinal Suenens stressed that all believers listen to the Word of God daily. To open the lectionary in a spirit of faith each day, he said, was to "keep an appointment" with the Holy Spirit.[40] He advised that hearing God's word from the pages of the Old and New Testaments was like receiving the letter of a friend who shares all our cares, fears, and hopes, who walks at our side, showing us the way.[41]

Cardinal Suenens understood his mandate as a bishop to be authentic interpreter of the Word. But he also asserted that all receive a similar mandate at baptism; that all are servants of the word and bearers of its message. He considered it a sign of hope that so many were newly engaged in study of the word.[42]

One further consequence of an increased biblical literacy among believers in general is that more careful attention than ever before will need to be given to the use of Scripture in official Church documents and pronouncements. The use of biblical citations as proof-texts for previously decided conclusions will not be accepted by believers who become more conversant with contradictory traditions in the Scriptures and with methods that yield new possibilities of interpretation. A case in point is the use of New Testament texts in Vatican pronouncements to illustrate the inability of the church to ordain women after the Pontifical Biblical Commission concluded that no obstacle is presented from the biblical texts.[43]

The Special Charism of the Biblical Scholar

Cardinal Suenens was also clear that the gifts of the Spirit are diverse and not given in equal measure to all.[44] That Roman Catholic believers

---

[39] *The Gospel to Every Creature* (Westminster: Newman, 1964) 94, 156; *The Future of the Christian Church* (New York: Morehouse-Barlow, 1970) 73–94.

[40] *A New Pentecost?* (New York: Seabury, 1975) 38.

[41] *Ibid.*, 38.

[42] *Ibid.*, 39.

[43] Pontifical Biblical Commission, "Report on the Role of Women in the Bible with a View to the Question of Women's Ordination," *Origins* 6 (1976) 92–96. See also Catholic Biblical Association of America, "Women and Priestly Ministry: The New Testament Evidence," *Catholic Biblical Quarterly* 41 (1979) 608–13.

[44] *The Church in Dialogue* (Notre Dame: Fides, 1965) 14–16.

on the whole are more biblically literate makes all the more essential the particular charism of the biblical scholar. There is greater need than ever for those who embrace the disciplined, detailed research and technical study of the biblical languages and scientific methodologies that lead to ever greater understanding of the texts. Far from being a dry study of dead civilizations, the task of the biblical scholar is an exciting one. Like one who drops a pebble into a lake, the scholar's love of the word ripples outward, instilling in others a thirst to know God more and drawing them to the Scriptures.

The scholar does not set forth once and for all what the texts mean, but as Jesus did in telling parables, she or he incites the imagination and creativity of others, particularly those with the charism of preaching. Like a midwife who draws forth new life from existing life, the exegete aids the believing community in bringing forth ever new life from the biblical tradition, impelling us forward to renewed life in an ever changing world.[45]

Exegesis and Social Action

Cardinal Suenens was no armchair theologian. As an influential drafter of *Gaudium et spes,* his commitment to faith in action is most evident. In his *Dialogue* with Dom Helder Camara, Cardinal Suenens clearly embraced liberation theology and called all believers to come to a clearer awareness of institutionalized structures of sin. He insisted that Christians have the responsibility to work against all oppression and flagrant inequalities, in whatever domain: cultural, economic, and political. He saw this impetus from liberation theology as a present-day incarnation of the protests of the Old Testament prophets.[46] Continuing in this vein, it is incumbent on the exegete today to keep a hyper-sensitive ear tuned to the cries of those most disadvantaged in our world and to engage the Scriptures as a clarion for justice and peace-making. The rampant violence and disregard for life in our society make it urgent for interpreters of the Bible to bring to the fore most insistently the message of God's liberating word for the poor and Jesus' unwavering message of non-violence.

A critical task of exegetes is to evaluate varying interpretations of the Gospel; for we all know that the Bible can be used by anyone to advo-

---

[45] Cardinal Suenens speaks of "Living Tradition" in *Essays on Renewal* (Ann Arbor, Mich.: Servant Books, 1977) 60–64.

[46] Cardinal Suenens and Dom Helder Camara, *Charismatic Renewal and Social Action: A Dialogue* (Malines Document 3; Ann Arbor, Mich.: Servant Books, 1979) 90–91.

cate whatever position desired. Warring parties have always quoted the Bible to show that God is on their side. As the new millennium approaches, one alarming trend in biblical interpretation is the rise in apocalyptic fundamentalism. This approach goes exactly counter to liberationist methods we have been describing.

Apocalypticists work from a dangerous dualistic framework that constructs a world of "us and them," absolute good against absolute evil, God against Satan. Rather than work to prevent the destruction of life in our world, they are cheered by it. They see violence directed against others with whom they do not identify as evidence of divine punishment, while violence against themselves is persecution of the righteous. Both forms of violence are proofs for them that the "last things" are happening and that their own deliverance is at hand.[47]

In the face of misdirected interpretations of the Bible, exegetes must keep these questions before us: From whose perspective is the text told? Through whose eyes comes this particular interpretation? Who benefits by it? A simple question to help us know if we are following the lead of the Spirit, faithful to the way of Jesus, is: Does this interpretation bring fullness of life for all (John 10:10)? Does it reflect that all are created equally in God's image (Gen 1:27), equally redeemed by Christ (John 3:17), and equally endowed with the Spirit (Acts 2:4)?

One example of an issue of social action about which Cardinal Suenens was quite prophetic was his attention to women. He insisted that charisms had been bestowed on women as well as men. He advocated the inclusion of women, if only as observers, at the Council.[48] In several of his books he wrote frankly about how changing roles of women in society demand new thinking about women's roles in the Church.[49] I was startled to see "Christianity and Feminism" as a subheading in chapter 2 of *The Nun in the World*.[50] More than three decades ago Cardinal Suenens spoke of how the teachings of Jesus are the basis for "fundamental equality of the sexes" and he saw the Church as a constant advocate for "the emancipation of women so that they should be accorded equal rights with men in the organization of their lives and the enjoyment of their freedom."[51] Though many today would find him a little over-optimistic in this last statement about Church praxis, the in-

---

[47] Rosemary Radford Ruether, *Gaia and God* (San Francisco: Harper, 1992) 81–84. See also the issue of *Chicago Studies* devoted to the topic, "The Second Coming. The Biblical Roots of Fundamentalism," vol. 34, no. 3 (December 1995).

[48] *A New Pentecost?* 30.

[49] E.g., *The Gospel to Every Creature*, 85–86.

[50] (Westminster: The Newman Press, 1962) 10–16.

[51] *Ibid.*, 10.

sight is quite on target that the Gospel and the practice of the Church are to be about liberated, full life for all.

Ecumenism

Cardinal Suenens was also a tireless advocate for greater union among Christians.[52] As Roman Catholic biblical scholars joined their colleagues from other denominations in the use of historical critical tools, exegetes from varying traditions found that what we have in common is far greater than what divides us. Biblical interpretation is still a very fertile ground for ecumenical exchange toward greater union.

Open Horizons

In conclusion, the new juncture at which we find ourselves today is not unlike the position of Jesus' first disciples. Having witnessed the death of the Jesus they had come to love, the women believers entered the open space of the empty tomb, which impelled them forward to unimaginable new horizons. Everything they thought they understood and believed about their Scriptures and tradition demanded a radical reinterpretation in the face of the empty tomb. Their terror at this prospect soon dissolved as they experienced Christ alive again and as the Spirit unleashed in them uncontrollable joy and zeal for spreading the gospel. Like those first women evangelists, Cardinal Suenens' wise, joyful, and dauntlessly hope-filled spirit can be a beacon for us as we embark on new exegetical roads. From the open space of the empty tomb the way of life lies open before us.

---

[52] *The Church in Dialogue,* 27–34, 53–56; *The Future of the Christian Church,* 113–27; *Ecumenism and Charismatic Renewal Theological and Pastoral Orientations* (Malines Document 2; Ann Arbor, Mich.: Servant Books, 1978).

6 | The Charism of Parenting

■ *Wendy M. Wright*

The day I began the actual composition of this essay, I received a gift that surprised and moved me. For almost a year, since I first received the invitation to address the topic "The Charism of Parenting" at this symposium, I had become especially attentive to theological and scriptural references to the Spirit and to the ways we traditionally and in common parlance allude to the workings of the Spirit in our lives, Church and world. Amid the busyness of preparing lectures on church history, grocery shopping, singing at liturgical celebrations, carpooling to my middle child's ballet lessons and sitting in the bleachers at my youngest child's baseball games, I had been notetaking, ruminating and asking questions about that rushing, leaping, breathing, living Spirit of God that is at the center of our reflections at this gathering in honor of Cardinal Suenens.

The day I sat down to begin to transform my sheaf of notes into a narrative text, I received a most wonderful gift in the mail. It was from a former colleague of mine at the University of Nebraska, a professor of philosophy and a practicing Zen Buddhist who, incidentally, knew nothing about my interest in charisms or the movement of the Spirit. Inside a brown-wrapped package I found two tapes of recorded music that, my friend wrote, he found "deeply moving" and hoped I would too. The tapes were of symphonic and choral pieces composed between 1984 and 1992 by Estonian composer Arvo Pärt. Most of the choral texts were in Latin, modern settings of the traditional parts of the Mass: the *Te Deum, Magnificat*, and *Miserere*. The compositions had been variously commissioned by German and Scandanavian patrons, performed by Estonian musicians, recorded in Finland and published in

Vienna, Austria. The liner notes, written in French, German and English, began with a quotation from the Gospel of John 3:8. The English version read:

> The wind bloweth where it listeth and thou hearest the sound thereof but canst not tell whence it cometh and whither it goeth.

I sat for some time with the liner notes unfolded on my lap, considering this evocation of the Spirit's unbounded mercy couched in King James English come to me by way of medieval Latin Christendom, Austria, Finland, Estonia, Germany, and my Zen Buddhist philosopher friend in the heartland of America. Indeed, the Spirit moves where it pleases. And I trust that its movements will guide both my insights and what occurs among us during this symposium with the same wonderful circuitousness yet sureness and fittingness with which John, chapter 3:8 was placed in my lap a month ago today.

Parenting as a Charism

I have been asked to speak about parenting as a charism for the Church in the twenty-first century. Because this is a topic which, as far as I am aware, has never been addressed in quite this way, I want first to clarify my use of the phrase, the "charism of parenting." I will then explore some of the qualities and characteristics of this charism as discovered through the experience of those who parent. And finally, I will suggest how this charism might truly be a spirit-prompted gift for the entire Church.

First, how am I using the phrase "the charism of parenting"?

I consider this spiritual gift to be a distinctive form of love, the greatest of all the *charismata* poured out by the Spirit.[1] I see it as a generative form of love. Sent for the nurturance and raising up of the new generation. Sent for the spring-greening of the community, for the unfolding of new life. Sent for the judicious preservation of past wisdom, the conservation of the soil out of which new life grows. It is a charism exercised by the mature, the mothers and the fathers, so that the fullness of God's promises might continue to germinate in the body of Christ.

I would assert that the gratuitous charism of parenting may be bestowed on anyone within the Christian community who is called to do this essential nurturing work. It might be discovered among religious educators, high-school or grade-school teachers, among bishops or

---

[1] I am taking Paul at face value and treating love as a charism, not as the chief of the theological virtues that can be distinguished from charisms.

members of sodalities, among spiritual directors or parish council presidents, among laity who attend weekly bible study or clergy who work among the poor, among grandmothers or youths who parent those younger than themselves. The charismata are poured out prodigally, coming through diverse members, given to the Church to nurture and raise up the next generation, through the wisdom of the Spirit, when and where needed to whomever the Spirit chooses.

Yet at the same time I will assert that it is accurate to say that the *distilled* experience of parental love is discovered and cultivated most explicitly among those who raise children. So it is to the actual experience of parents that we must look to truly understand the charism. The Spirit's varied expressions are never generic, but concrete, embodied, and particular. The charism of parenting is not an abstract ideal to which to aspire but a lived reality, an encounter with the animating life of God. Not all persons who parent, however, would seem to "have" the charism in its fullness. It might be more accurate to affirm that the charism is given as potential gift to those who actually raise children. As such it is a spirit-filled experience into which one is invited to grow. The lived experience of being a parent can provide opportunities for the heart to stretch and contour to the shape of this mature, generative love. Parenthetically, I think it is important to note that the capacity for such a love cannot be seen as the exclusive possession of the two-parent household. It certainly might be argued that such a family structure creates conditions that alleviate some of the obstacles that stand in the way of response to the gift. But single parents, stepparents, extended family members or others who parent may exercise the charism as authentically as a biological or adoptive mother and father couple.

In considering the charism of parenting in this manner—as a generative form of the gift of love which may be bestowed in its fullness on anyone within the communuty but which is offered in a particular way as a potential gift to those who actually raise children—I am taking my inspiration from St. Paul's description of the gifts of the Holy Spirit found in 1 Corinthians 12–14. In Paul, the marvelously diverse gifts of the Spirit are seen to be poured out on all within the body of Christ. Powerful, transformative energies, the gifts are given not for individual enhancement or prestige but for the building up of the whole body of Christ. The Spirit's gifts appear to be given irrespective of considerations such as life circumstances, occupation, institutional role, gender, class or ethnicity. Their power, if it is not to be divisive, must be exercised under the aegis of the greatest gift of all, love.

Certainly Paul does not specifically name the charism of parenting (it would be anachronistic to think that he might), but he does speak of the gift of love, and tradition has given us reason to think of love not simply as sentiment or as one undifferentiated reality but as a reality with a variety of modalities whose unity lies in their one source. In general, these modalities have been considered four or five: *agape* (the sacrificial love of God for humans evidenced most in the redeeming love of Jesus Christ as well as the grace-given, selfless love we have for God and one another); *philia* (the mutual and equal love of friendship); *eros* (the passionate desire to be united with the beloved or with truth, beauty and goodness); *epithemia* (lust or the drive toward the satisfaction of desire); and *storge* (affection or familial love, which, incidentally, has been either ignored or downplayed as a "lower" or "instinctual" form of love).[2] Although strands of the spiritual tradition have viewed the supernatural love of agape as the antithesis of the other "natural" loves, deep in the tradition is the affirmation that all the loves are interconnected, proceeding from and orienting toward God who is Love itself. The loves, however, are differently experienced and articulated.[3]

I would describe parental love as a powerful, generative form of love which, like friendship, involves a certain intense mutuality between parent and child yet, unlike friendship, is not characterized by equality. Parents and their children are bound together in intimate ties that span a lifetime and connect them at depths of which they are often only dimly aware, but they love one another differently. Deeply, yes. But differently. A parent "holds" a child in a way that a child does not a parent. In the womb, in arms, in the heart, in memory, in hope, a parent holds the story of the child's earliest beginnings, all the steps along the way, all the promise of the future. This is a unique way to love. As we cultivate in our hearts the capacity for such a love, we live into the great dignity and hope for which we were created, we live into our identity as creatures created in the image and likeness of the God of Love.

The Qualities of a Parent's Love

Parenting as a modality of love, the greatest charism of them all, has specific characteristics. While I certainly do not pretend that I can ex-

---

[2] C. S. Lewis in his *The Four Loves* (New York: Harcourt, Brace, 1960) includes storge but relegates it to a sort of "animal" love which is based on need, like the fully uddered cow that "loves" its offspring because of its own overflowing pain.

[3] In this latter approach I follow St. Francis de Sales. Human beings, in the saint's view, most clearly reflect the image of God in their capacity for love, in the "heart" as he puts it. God's "heart" overflows, breathes out, and draws back, breathes in, in love. So too human hearts, in inspiration and aspiration, breath in rhythm with God's heart as they love both God and others. All love ultimately flows from and returns to God.

haustively name all of those characteristics, I can attempt to name a number of them. I will draw upon my own experience as a parent as well as upon the experience that many other parents have shared with me. The characteristics I will explore are: the capacity to welcome and let go, the capacity for flexibility, for discernment, for empowerment and for reconciliation. These experiences are not simply a matter of theory, they are matters of the heart.

> Boston, Massachusetts. 1985
>
> I sit on the edge of my son's bed. His face is smooth with sleep. The glow of the night-light stands vigil against the "monsters" that he worries lurk beneath his changing table. In the warm dark of the room, the two rhythms of our breathing punctuate the silence. As I stand up to leave, I feel my heart, utterly self-contained a moment before, pulled out of my breast, stretched to span the widening distance between us. A presence, palpable in its intensity, connects us. Before he was born, I did not know how I could ever let him in. Now that I have, I don't know how I will ever let him go.[4]

Parenting is many things. It involves, in part, the acceptance of adult responsibility, nurturing and guiding the helpless and unformed, and passing on the living fund of culture, knowledge and wisdom from one generation to the next. But being a parent as a spirited undertaking is, I think, a matter of the heart. And that involves the reformation of the core of our beings, a radical expanding of the established contours of our hearts to include others in a permanent and life-altering way.

Any genuine experience of love alters the heart and creates it anew. It gentles us. For authentic love is not a transient emotion but a spiritual dynamic of immense power that we as Christians know to be stronger than anything else, even death. To love at the deepest level of our beings is to participate in the life of our God who is love. This is not a simple matter. Parenting is an especially demanding discipline of loving because, in a heightened way, it calls for an increased capacity of the heart to love a person who is totally other and to love enough to let go. The great and twin dynamics of the charism of parenting are, I think, welcoming and letting go. These are matters of the heart.

Any parent knows what it means to welcome a child. The entry of new life does not call for a polite if celebrative ritual and then a return to business as usual. Nor does it mean that you just schedule this per-

---

[4] This story and several of the others used in this piece also appear in variant forms in my *Sacred Dwelling: A Spirituality of Family Life* (Leavenworth, Kans.: Forest of Peace Books, 1994).

son into your established routine like an appointment or meeting. You don't make a little space in your day or share a little concern and then wish an infant Godspeed. To welcome a child is to accept responsibility for another person twenty-four hours a day, seven days a week, for a good many years. Ultimately, it is to welcome the unfolding mystery of an entire lifetime's joys and pains as your own. To welcome a child is to give priority to the unpredictability of another life, to tend it in sickness, no matter what you had otherwise planned, to allow your plans and dreams to be altered, even set aside, because of another's need. To welcome a child is to learn to think and speak in response to a different and constantly changing worldview, to be outside of your own frame of reference. It is to learn patience and judgment and be confronted with your own very real and heretofore untested limitations. To welcome a child is to recognize the surprising expansiveness of your own capacity to love and to confront the shattering truth of your own violence and self-centeredness.

To welcome a child is to have your heart stretched, made capable of loving in a new and unrepeatable way. To love in this way is quite different from the love elicited by a beloved, a spouse, or a friend. Each of these loves too has its heart-stretching capacity, but they tend more to equality and mutuality, to the alignment of interest and point of view. They involve companionship, partnership, and the convergence of experiences. A parent's love is different. It opens places in the heart that have never been exposed before. It awakens inexpressible tenderness, the awareness of the extraordinary beauty and terrifying fragility of human life. It calls forth hope, the almost giddy consciousness of the promise of what might be.

To watch each child unfold the mysterious uniqueness of his or her life is to have your deepest longings called forth. One need only be in a room full of parents as they witness their children's First Communion or sing at the Christmas pagent with the kindergarten class or cross over some developmental threshold, to sense how deeply, how poignantly, the hope flows. Yet to see the wonder of each life little by little stunted, crippled, wounded by bitter encounters with the harshness of social realities, by illness and accident, by inborn limitations is to risk the loss of hope. To welcome a child is to have the doors of the heart flung wide open to embrace the fullness of life, both at its sweetest and at its most bitter. To love with the welcoming embrace of a parent stretches to the furthest extent the contours of the heart.

The twin capacity of a parent's wide-opened, welcoming heart is the capacity to let go. Letting go does not consist of ceasing to love, or detaching oneself from the affection one feels, but in loving more. Letting go involves radical faith. It means entrusting what you most love to the expansive care and protection of God. I do not mean that if you pray hard enough God will keep all the awful things that could happen from happening to your child. Nor that every evil, even evil perpetrated on the innocent, is somehow "all in God's plan." But that somehow God's presence is available to us even in the mysteries of human suffering and death. Our trust is in a God whose presence accompanies us in every facet of human experience, a God who celebrates, laughs, plays, weeps, wonders and is seared with pain just as we are. This kind of radical trust in an accompanying God is what allows us to let go. We let go not only so that our children can become independent adults guiding their own lives, but also so that God may parent them and that we all may know ourselves as children of God.

Omaha, Nebraska. 1996

Catholic Omaha, where I live at present, has the feel of a big smalltown. One senses the reverberations from various quarters, no matter how directly connected you are to the people involved. And in the last two months, the hearts of Omaha's parents have been sorely exercised in the heart-discipline of letting go. Two funerals, both untimely, have stretched hearts so that they might dare to trust in a God whose mercy must be greater than our capacity to comprehend, whose providential view must be more expansive than our present vision. The first funeral was for the sixteen-year-old son of a political science professor at Creighton University where I teach. The young man, a genius of a computer whiz, with a quirky sense of humor and a future that should have had him following his big brother to Cal Tech on a science scholarship, complained of stomach pains. Two months later, after a wrenching series of chemotherapy treatments designed to treat the fast growing colon cancer, he died of complications from the treatments. The second funeral was for an eighteen-year-old, a soon-to-be-graduate of Omaha's Catholic boy's prep school who, having finished his exams, was spending the interim weeks before the graduation ceremony, like most of the rest of Omaha's senior classes, attending open houses and parties celebrating the transition from the old life of high school and home to college and a wonderful new life. On the eve of Mother's Day he caught a ride home from a party with a friend, both of them too buoyant, too invincible in their celebrating. As curfew approached, the friend speeded up, went over a speed bump and lost control of the car. His passenger was killed. The driver, a young man with no previous record, was charged with homicide.

Not all parental letting go requires the heart to stretch so far, love so generously, continue to trust so uncompromisingly as did these two untimely deaths. Most of it is more mundane—children growing up, not being the student or the athlete one expected, leaving home, following a career you never would have dreamed, marrying who they will, choosing lives you never would have chosen. But by all of this the heart can be made pliant, wide, capable of bearing paradox and ambiguity, capable of a trust that transcends life's ability to provide trustworthy results.

If the chief characteristics of a parental heart are these capacities to welcome and to let go, another related quality I might name is flexibility. Perhaps this might also be called developmental sensitivity. Parenting over the course of a lifetime is not one monochromatic experience. Different moments in the developmental cycle call forth different responses. An infant requires different love from a parent than a toddler or a grade school child or an adolescent or a young adult or an adult offspring. Anyone who teaches knows that certain teachers have a knack and a liking for certain ages—that, for instance, a superb kindergarten teacher might really flounder in a junior-high classroom, or that a gifted professor of graduate students might be totally inept with a class of fifth graders. Yet parents are called upon to develop a love that is capable of growing and changing in response to the different developmental phases of their children's lives. The same kind of twenty-four-hour-a-day physical proximity and labor-intensive nurturance that is appropriate for a four-week-old infant is utterly inappropriate for an adult child of forty years. Yet the same person who was the parent to the four week old is also, years later, the parent of the forty-year-old.

Parental love also requires that one cultivate the ability to love and nurture a variety of differing personalities. Any parent of more than one child will tell you how unique each of their children is, how you could never interact with each of them in the same way. A timid, retiring child calls forth a different response than a boisterous, self-assertive child. To love a child is to take her best interests to heart, to concern yourself with his special problems. Parental love is manifold, changing, boldly adaptable in response to the individuality of each child. What I am suggesting is that there is an art, liken it to a delicate dance if you will, to staying flexible and adventurous enough to continue to love in the myriad ways that being a parent calls forth.

A flexible heart, like the one I am describing, is also a heart that is discerning. What do I mean by this? I mean that a discerning heart is a heart constantly attentive to the emergence of the new moment, constantly responsive to the changing demands of parenthood at each phase. Discernment—in the classical sense of the term—involves paying attention to the Spirit of God moving in and among us and distinguishing that Spirit from the vast array of other outer and inner movements that vie for our attention. To adequately discern we must be aware on many levels: consult Scripture, seek the advise of trusted advisors, heed the teaching of the Church as it emerges on many levels, read widely and deeply the best of ancient and contemporary thinking, pray, attend to the prick of conscience and the yearnings of our hearts. Watch, wait, and listen. Discernment is about discriminating: sifting through and evaluating the evidence of our focused attention. It is not simply a question of problem-solving. Nor is it an attempt to find, once and for all, the one, correct answer. Discernment is about feeling textures, assessing weight, watching the plumb line, listening for overtones, searching for shards, feeling the quickening, surrendering to love. It is being grasped in the Spirit's arms and led in the rhythms of a new dance.

1:00 a.m. Winter. Omaha, Nebraska. 1995

I lie awake in the darkened bedroom, my husband's somnambulant breathing accompanied on and off by the onrush of sound from the forced air heating ducts. I press my ear to the air space between these two respirations where I hear the click of the key in the downstairs lock that signals my teenaged daughter's curfewed arrival home. I read her step, cautious, or self-assured, fatigued or energized? I note the tone of her response to my verbal welcome—hearty, irritated, ringing with contentment or tense and preoccupied?

It has been a roller coaster year. Not atypical, others keep assuring me. But painful nonetheless. Pressing all the buttons and boundaries that have been in place for some time. Her bedroom door snaps smartly shut behind her. An audible symbol of the unique emergent psychic space she is structuring for herself. I stare into the dark void above the bed, aware now of my own breath, a light cadence like a descant above my sleeping spouse's airway melody and the furnace's punctuating bass.

In the last year there have been many decisions to make about how to respond to the vigorous stretching of adolescent wings. We have received advice about tough love, and about unconditional acceptance, admonitions to stand firm and to make space. We've muddled through on the level of "how to" and "what's best" and problem solving. But the level on which it has been perhaps the most challenging has been the level of spiritual discernment. By this I do not mean "what would God want the perfect family to look like?" or "What are the proper roles that daughter, father, mother and son are supposed to play there?" No, the spiritual discernment has been more akin to the sort of groping, confused reorientation I experienced as a first-time mother when the call was to recast myself as a parent, to learn, painfully by trial and error, not only the new psychological identity but the new spiritual challenges to which that identity called me.

The plumb-line question that has emerged in this recent process is "Where does love lie?" I have learned a lot about myself (which, the spiritual masters say, is the beginning of knowing God). How, while all along I thought I was cultivating a certain simplicity of person, I discover myself in fact to be a person very preoccupied with unfavorable appearances. Continually, I am forced back to the question "Where does love lie?" The depth to which the question falls—the level of the Spirit's dancing—says, "Looking good is not the point. The point is you don't earn belovedness. You receive it. It descends like a dove, unbidden, and you open your ears and heart and life and receive."

I have learned too that my cowardice—my fear of not being loved in return—can masquerade as maternal solicitude, that my inability to love the real wounds, the real out-of-boundness in myself—because they seem unlovable, is, in fact, a kind of spiritual pride, a closing in on myself. I have groped about asking "Where does love lie, and for whom and when and how?" The hundreds of half answers to the questions emerge only in the groping, only in the process of feeling texture, assessing weight, listening for overtones, feeling the quickening, surrendering to love.[5]

Such a discerning heart is truly parental. So too is the heart that seeks the empowerment of the child. To be a parent is to exercise power, to hold authority. So it should be. But parental power, I believe, is not exercised simply for its own sake, not simply to continue its dominance. Parental power seeks the empowerment of those over whom authority is exercised; it seeks to empower the child. And this is where that capacity for flexibility, for developmental sensitivity, comes clearly to the fore. A mother carries an infant, closely held, across a busy street because the infant cannot walk. A father clasps a toddler firmly by the hand as they cross because the toddler does not yet have the judgment or the motor control to cross safely by herself. A mother verbally instructs her six year old in the procedures for safe conduct as they stand side by side and prepare together to cross the street. A father reminds his ten-year-old son to observe pedestrian safety as the child leaves the house by himself to walk to school. Power and authority are exercised with appropriate firmness not so that power is retained but in order for the child to become empowered.

Analogously, parents pass on the fund of wisdom they have gained, not simply for the sake of preserving the wisdom itself but for the sake of imparting it to the child. So that the child might flourish, might have roots planted deeply enough that flourishing can continue for a life-

---

[5] This story appears in longer form in "Passing Angels: The Arts of Spiritual Discernment" in *Weavings,* "Discerning the Spirits," vol. X, no. 6, (November–December, 1995).

time. Parental empowerment consist not only of providing children with the information and skills they need to safely negotiate life's busy boulevards, it consists also of providing a history, a story, an identity for the child. It consists of vision-questing, of living into a vision that is wide and generous enough to sustain the deepest yearnings of the human heart. Most parents I know want their children to have deep roots in a story that can powerfully sustain them. They want them to "be believers," to "have faith," to "live by a set of values," or to "know who they are." In part this "knowing who you are" comes from knowing one's unique family history—where your people come from, what they did, what they stood for. Whether they were Irish immigrants who worked as laborers when they came to the new world or whether they were from the literati of Latin America, whether your grandmother had a deep devotion to the rosary or worked assiduously so that women might have the vote, whether your uncle was a Jesuit priest, or your nephew was healed of cancer through charismatic prayer—all of this is part of your story, part of knowing who you are.

Parents pass on this identity to their children. They also pass on a deeper identity, a knowledge of themselves as beloved children of God. This they do in part by immersion in a community of faith that continues to tell the great, primal stories of our creation and redemption by God. In part they impart this identity by living faithfully themselves, witnessing to the depth of the faith they embrace, unleashing its truths in their lives. This sort of empowerment, this giving children roots, a place to stand, a story, is essential. It is characteristic of parental love. Yet, to reiterate, a parent does not provide a story so that the story might be frozen in time. It is not told simply for archeological interest. The story is told so that it can continue to unfold, have new chapters, more character development, and live on in the next generation. The delicate dance of parental empowerment straddles the line between past and future, gathering up the fund of past wisdom that can sustain, yet willing to let that wisdom emerge in new forms to respond creatively to the demands of present and future times. A heart so shaped indeed parents with expansive, generative love.

Spring, 1988

One Saturday, my husband, whose work is in social justice ministry, was filled with a desire to do something about a pile of limbs and logs that lay at the far end of our garden. After a particularly frustrating week at the office, he decided to rent a chainsaw and go to work on the fallen tree debris. He wanted to saw something and relished the thought of bearing down on that wood with fervor. Catharsis that was needed. The logs would provide it. But the announcement of his impending plans provoked cries of alarm from our two girls. Those fallen logs had been their fairyland. They had set up games there. There was no other "secret place" in our yard for them to play. This was their sacred place (yes, they called it that). He could not cut the logs.

He was headed in too straight a line to pay much attention to them. "The logs are an eyesore!" he declared and set off to the equipment rental store for the chainsaw. The girls were not to be dissuaded. "He can't do that to our fairyland," they wailed in tears. The younger became belligerent, "I'll put on war paint and beat him up when he gets home!" she fumed. Her older sister had another plan. "No," she stated, "We will stage a nonviolent demonstration. We will protest the injustice of what he is doing!"

They ran off into the house. I was in the garden pulling weeds from the vegetable patch and decided to remain neutral and just observe what happened. Pretty soon they came out again. With them now was their little brother. Each was wearing a tee shirt on which the words "Save the Logs" had been printed in crayola on front and back. They were carrying cardboard signs scotchtaped onto twigs on which were scrawled these slogans: "Save Nature—Leave the Logs Alone," "Nature Knows Best," "Nature Did It First," "If God Put Them Here, God Must Want Them Here," "Please Reconsider," "Decide on Compromise." My middle daughter (who was just learning to read and write) held the sign she had made herself: "No. No. No. No. No. No. No. No. No."

They sat down on the logs and planned their strategy. "We must be calm and firm," my eldest instructed the demonstrators. "We must appeal to his conscience." She began to teach them the song she had written for the occasion:

[Refrain] "Please reconsider. This is nature at its best. 'Save Nature, Save Nature.'"

[Verse 1] "Don't act like a big corporation. Please understand. We'll try to make a compromise. We'll help you through."

[Refrain] "Please reconsider. . . ."

[Verse 2] "If God didn't want it there then why is it there? Please understand. Save Nature."

[Refrain] "Please reconsider. . . ."

They practiced diligently. They practiced singing "We Shall Overcome." Then came a failure of nerve. The waiting was getting tedious. "He won't pay any attention." "He'll just do what he wants." Then came what to my ears sounded like a succinct analysis of the temptations of power and authority. "He'll just say this is his. He owns it and can do what he wants with it." "But what about us? Maybe we don't own it but we have a right to say what's done to it!"

They were almost giving up when the car rolled into the driveway. They galvanized for action. Up went their signs. Little bodies were seated indignantly between their sacred space and the advancing chainsaw. "We shall overcome. We shall overcome," they quavered. My husband, in a mood to brook no opposition, arrived at the tiny demonstration. They began their song, "Please reconsider." I'm not sure he was amused. He needed to saw something. Those eyesore logs had been grating on him all winter. He had just spent twenty dollars renting a chainsaw to get rid of them.

They offered him a compromise. He could saw the log near the mulberry tree. But he had to leave alone the circle of logs they had designed as their space. I cannot claim that this demonstration ended in a triumphant celebration of the power of nonviolent resistance, but it did save the logs. Daddy, irked, sawed away at the lone log by the mulberry, too frustrated to be gracious or charmed by their witness. Yet he sawed only the one log and a large pile of tree branches. The wood turned out to be so hard that the sawing of just that amount of kindling took him all afternoon and produced the physical catharsis he needed. The girls were not sufficiently aware of their "victory." They were so worn out and ready to be on to other things by that time that I'm not sure they savored the fruits of their labors. I did.

I savored the fact that somewhere in their vision of what the world can be is a sense that there are alternatives to the way things are generally done. Somehow they know that the voices of the small and the dispossessed must rightfully be heard. Somehow they know that to appeal to conscience, to speak truth, to witness to that in action is a legitimate response to the "evils" of the world.

The final quality of parental love I would name as essential is the quality of reconciliation. The deeply painful yet redemptive work of forgiving, healing, reconciling, spanning differences, coming half way, finding common ground: this is at the core of parental love. It is also, if I am not mistaken, at the core of the Christian understanding of the God of Love.

The work of reconciliation is not one-sided, of course; it generally requires that estranged parties both agree to seek reconciliation. But there is, in a mature understanding of the nature of love, some initiative that must be generated, some first step that must be taken, some far-sighted choice to seek the healing of breaches that must occur. The heart of a parent, I believe, is capable of such initiative, and longs, above all, to realize the fullness of relationship. The desire for union, for a conjoining of hearts, is intrinsic to all forms of love. A lover seeks to embrace his beloved, a friend longs to stand side by side in mutual harmony with her friend, the one who loves altruistically strives for the other to

experience love bestowed. So too a parental heart aches for love's fullness to become manifest with each child.

This is an especially delicate art, for the exercise of parental love also
calls for boundary-setting, guidance, and discipline that might appear
to the child as unloving or divisive of relationship. Further, as parents
and children negotiate the changing terrain of their relationships over
the years, they encounter many obstacles to the realization of their
shared love. Generational gaps, personality differences, cultural conflicts, clashes of values, divisive economic realities, misunderstandings
of a thousand sorts conspire to divide us. Yet struggle toward reconciliation we must. A parent's heart holds tight to the hope that the love of
parent and child, as unequal as it is, will gradually achieve its potential.
Yet the love of a parent is always, as it were, situated in a slightly different vantage point, somewhat "ahead." Riper, more aware of past
failures, wiser in retrospect, conscious of the short sightedness of the
child's love.

One of my favorite images of the reconciling heart of a parent is
found in the final scenes of the film adaption of Jewish author Chaim
Potok's *The Chosen,* which tells the story of an Hasidic rabbi in New
York during World War II whose eldest son forsakes the spiritual inheritance to which he is heir. The brilliant young man, destined to take
over the role of *rebbe* or spiritual mentor to his father's community,
finds himself more and more drawn to the developing secular field of
psychology, more and more assimilated in his thinking, less and less
bounded by the particular thought world of the devout but sectarian
religiosity of his father. The father knows the brilliance of his son's
mind yet fears that intellectual brilliance overshadows the boy's heart.

The father knows to be a *tzaddick,* a charismatic spiritual leader, one
must have not merely a mind, but a soul: one must have heart, righteousness, compassion, mercy, strength to suffer and carry pain. Against
all odds, the father struggles to instill these qualities in his son, knowing all the while that the son will go his own way, to the secular world
drawn by the lure of knowledge. His methods of teaching are severe.
For years he instructs his son through the medium of stony silence. He
does this that his son might obtain a heart that can reverberate with the
suffering of the world. Yet the father also allows his brilliant son eventually to chose his own path; with anguish he gives his paternal blessing to his son's entry into the secular university, though it means the
abandonment of many of the sectarian practices of the Hasidic community.

At the end of the film version of *The Chosen,* the son, shorn of his distinctive earlocks and without his Hasidic dress, is shown departing for
his new life. A voice-over narrates these words: "There is a a story in

the Talmud about a king who had a son who had gone astray from his father. The son was told, 'Return to your father.' The son said, 'I cannot.' Then the father sent a messenger to say, 'Return as far as you can and I will come to you the rest of the way.'"

Flung wide open in welcome, stretched to the point of breaking in its willingness to let go, generous in its flexibility, plumbed to the depths by its discernment, seeking empowerment and reconciliation even amid painful paradox and ambiguity: these are the qualities of parental love. Those describe the parent's heart, formed by the Spirit's indwelling, the gift bestowed.

Parenting as a Charism for the Entire Church

Women and men who raise children are cracked open to the possibility of learning the arts of parental love. The gift of a child can indeed confer the charism of parental love. And it is especially to those whose experience teaches and forms them in this charism that we must look for wisdom. They offer us, the entire church community, an experience of love that gives us a specific kind of insight into Love itself, into the very nature of God. But the gift of parental love cannot be restricted to the family. Parents show us a quality of heart that truly can nurture the entire Church, and provide the essential leavening for the rest of the charisms so that they do not become clanging symbols. The gift of parental love might well be discovered, the Spirit willing, in many places in the Church. When it is given it is recognized by the qualities I have suggested above. It is a gift that is not identical to but which complements the other charisms.

Cardinal Suenens has been remembered these last few weeks, in most of the accounts that I read, as a man who straddled the extremes in the Church. A man with a passion for passing on the rich foundations of faith yet readily open to the freely moving Spirit that blows among us, he was familiar with the arts of welcoming and letting go. Deeply discerning and wonderfully flexible, he exercised power for the sake of empowerment. In his ecumenism, and in his openness to co-responsiblity in the Church, he was a man of reconciliation. In many ways, the late cardinal possessed the charism of parenting. He danced the delicate dance between fidelity to the past and fidelity to the future. He was fearless enough, profoundly trusting enough to believe that the Church could be animated by the Spirit, that what was essential must and would be carried into the future.

In a very real sense, all of us in the Church who are of the age to mother and father, are invited to live into the charism of parenting. We are asked to welcome the next generation, love them with hearts flung so wide that we are willing to let go. We must never forget that we are not God. It does not all depend on us. We must exercise discernment, asking ourselves "where does love lie?" We must be flexible enough to parent the next generation to know that the Church is composed of adult children as well as teenagers and toddlers, that sometimes we must carry, sometimes verbally instruct and sometimes simply listen to the stories, listen to the experience, listen to the newly unfolding wisdom of those whom we nurture. We must not simply teach the younger generation to say their prayers. We must empower them to become mature practioners of deep, Spirit-responsive prayer. We must not conceive of our role as supplying the "right" answers. We must dare to enable them to live into the questions. We must dare to live into them with them. Always we must be willing to say "Return as far as you can and I will come to you the rest of the way."

I will close with a story of a parent's heart. It is a story about coming to know the heart of God.

March, 1986

Sometimes my eldest daughter and I collide. I with the single focused trajectory of a steel arrow, may be trying to herd children out the door or into bed. She, with the equally impressive dynamic of a monumental boulder, may have other plans. Sometimes we can manage to metamorphosize ourselves, becoming, say, two circus clowns who can laugh at their own quarrelsome antics, or two whitewater rapids whose currents merge into a tumultuous but one-directional stream. Other times, frustration, fatigue, and anger catch us in their nets. I become a mechanized earth mover, ruthlessly clearing all objects from my path. She becomes the obstacles to be unearthed. At times like these there are tears and sometimes the anguished cry, "I want mommy!" The first time she cried out in this way I remember shouting out in exasperation, "I'm here!" "No, you're not! You're not my Mommy! I want my real Mommy!" she protested. "Is this a ploy, a power play?" I remember wondering. Is this an appeal to me to be what I cannot and do not want to be, some ever-smiling ideal mother like the ones depicted in baby lotion advertisements? Do I need to be firmer and more consistent in my discipline? Have I spoiled her? Is this a cry for help?

I have reflected for some time now on this curious exchange that we as mother and daughter from time to time used to enact.

I have come to see that my daughter's plea for her real mom is a religious intimation. It is a calling upon a presence that she sometimes feels coming through me—not when I am an "ideal" mom but when I am most deeply in touch with the source of unconditional love, when I begin to experience and to live out the reality that this love is indeed with us.

As my eldest daughter reached preteen years, her spoken demands for the appearance of her "real" mother decreased, but her need for me to embody those maternal qualities did not. I was at this life stage, when we were struggling with her incipient independent identity and readjusting who we were with each other, that my insights into who this "real" mother is became clear. Disharmony between us threw me back upon prayer. There, struggling with my own sense of inadequacy, of limited resources, of anger and pain, and reaching deep into the marrow of my prayer to discover a source of life and hope that could exorcise my demons of self-doubt, I discovered the warmth of the "real" mother's embrace.

It was a meditation on my own embrace of my children in its most gracious form that led me into those wider loving arms. I imagined my daughter, now fully grown, coming to me weary with the burdens and experiments of life, coming to be held, to be loved, to be nourished in the arms that had first given her some intimation of the foundational goodness of life. In my own embrace I discovered that there was nothing that she could bring, no experience, no pain, no excursion into the twisted labyrinth of human frailty that could separate her from the love I had for her. This entering into the consciousness of the "real" mother brought me into a realm of loving that was so expansive, so vast, that its parameters could expand to contain all the pain, the failure, the sinfulness that my daughter carried with her. The loving of the gracious mother did not pretend that the pain did not exist. All the weight of sadness and desolation that a parent feels for the suffering of a child was felt and borne in that deep embrace.

The knowledge of my own capacity to embrace in this way made me newly aware of the arms that open to me in this same manner. God's arms are those of the "real" mother.

They are arms always open. They reach out for us, God's children. We are the graced recipients of the nourishment we need to sustain life through the tender ministrations of arms that surround and support us, arms that tilt us gently to a food that comes directly out of the substance and the deepest resources of the maternal life itself. God feeds us like a nursing mother whose own flesh and blood are given to us for our life. God becomes bread and wine, blessed and broken for our eating and our drinking so that we in turn can be blessed and broken for each other.

7

The Stones Will Cry Out: The Charism of the Voiceless

■ *Mercy Amba Oduyoye*

While Vatican II was in session, I was a graduate student at Cambridge University in Great Britain doing readings for a Tripos Part III in Dogmatics. Of the ecclesiological issues associated with the Council, two have remained with me: the unity of the Church and the renewal of the Church. The latter had Roman Catholic Church connections for me specifically because I was to investigate *aggiornamento,* a term that emanated from the proceedings of the Council. It was like giving back to the Church the liberative voice it was meant to have. "Renewal of the Church" calls up a vision of God's mission of justice and compassion, so it comes as no surprise that Leon-Joseph Cardinal Suenens put such a passion into that theme. For the poor and the vulnerable, this ministry of compassion and solidarity in resistance and transformation calls for celebration. Personally, I am pleased to be part of that celebration through these pages which honor him.

Cardinal Suenens' ministry, including some thirty or more books, is a gift of God to all who would have otherwise been overlooked and marginalized by the "definition makers." Being a woman and an African and a theologian, I would be defined and, maybe, would have counted myself as one who is as powerless and irrelevant as they come, but for perspectives of people like Suenens who lift up for us God's empowering justice. That God uses the little ones, the foolish ones, the weak ones to accomplish great things is a lesson from the history of the Hebrew people and many African folktales that is often ignored by the mighty ones. Suenens' acknowledgment of difference opens doors for the marginalized of the world to offer their specific and special gifts to the global pool that nourishes our lives together on this planet.

As one who has inspired many to recognize their direct mission from the Spirit, Suenens is an agent for the liberation of those who have been rendered voiceless, because they have been robbed of their self-esteem. There is nobody who is a nobody in the plan of God. All have a special charism. All are empowered by the Holy Spirit and would know their call if only they would listen for the voice of God and not to the noisy disempowering din of those who define them as "voiceless."

Rendered Voiceless

"Who are the voiceless?" was the question Dr. Teresa Okure, S.H.C.J., from Nigeria once asked me. From our anthropocentric perspective the privileged are the only beings in this cosmos whose "speech" matters. We are the interpreters of the rest of creation, and we tell the times and the seasons as well as manipulate culture and nature to our benefit. The whole cosmos seems to be present to serve us. Seeing all as being at our disposal, we have seen ourselves as standing outside creation. We have become exploiters, the wicked shepherds who feed on the flock without tending the lambs. Today, however, we discern the language of nature loud and clear in what we have named the ecological crisis. Nature is not voiceless; it is just that we humans hear and hear but do not comprehend.

In our communities worldwide, ruling elites treat the ruled as if they have no voices until they rise up in a revolution, shouting out in anger and frustration at the oppression they have endured for generations. "The Voiceless" exercise their power to become "ungovernable" and to force those in power to rethink and remold what it means to exercise power. In our human communities worldwide, those who are poor—I mean those who often are without the basic necessities of food, clothing and shelter—are treated as voiceless. Not having economic power, i.e., capital, they also are not considered as having political power. They are not heard, they do not count for much even when they have "the power of the ballot," for it does not get them beyond choosing spokespersons from among the wealthy, who very often forget the promises made to the poor after the elections are over. Yet for those who have ears to hear, the very existence of the poor and the destitute, the homeless and the refugee, speaks volumes.

In our human communities worldwide, women are treated as voiceless. Their voices do not reach the ears of men in power. Yet women shed the tears of God as they protest patriarchy and all that brings death to humans and to nature. Even when women speak as they did recently at Beijing and in Huairou, what they ask for is still ignored by faith communities and by nation-states whose interests in gender-inequality is challenged by the women's vision of a just, participatory, and sustainable eco-community. The cosmic vision of women and their call for an end to the distorted relations among humans remain unheeded or challenged by obtuse traditionalism.

We often hear, "children are to be seen, not heard." All people of color are silenced in various degrees and in all structures because humanity's power-holders seem to prefer pale skins and fear the dark-skinned, or else equate being truly human with having economic power. Indigenous peoples everywhere have been marginalized and silenced by newer immigrants. All of these oppressed, exploited and marginalized peoples have been *rendered voiceless* by those sitting on the tops of the patriarchal pyramids. From the voiceless the cry for liberation continues to go up to the high heavens, and from their eyes flow the tears of God while with their whole being and the resilience of the gift of life they struggle for survival and for justice. God has given them the gift of life, and they are grateful for that and seek every occasion, however meager, to celebrate.

But there remains another category of the Voiceless Ones—the voiceless who make a deliberate choice, a form of resistance against justice and compassion. Humans who refuse to speak up on behalf of nature because they cannot afford to let go of their current life-style: men, voiceless over the oppression of women; human beings who have lost their voices because they are the ones violating children; the global economic elite, the "money-makers" and power-brokers, who do not understand the language of primary-producers, miners, factory workers, road-makers, all who are paid below the minimum wages of the nations they work in and for. Voiceless are those at the top of the structures that live on profit. Many are the voiceless whose silence speaks of the death of those below them in the patriarchal pyramid against the voiceless ones who cry to God daily for justice. Is not the silence of men and women a strategy of resistance? Since when did those who benefit from a system voluntarily criticize the system?

Who then are the voiceless ones who charisms we hope to uncover? Not the charism of those whose silence and whose voices speak of the death of others. They are the charisms that are yet to be fully tapped by humanity that we need to search for. Voiceless ones in this contribution are the stones along our path. What do they symbolize? What are they saying to us?

The Voice of the Voiceless

Stones do speak, or at any rate have been endowed with voices by human beings. Diamonds are "forever"; they are hard enough to cut through a lot of resistance. We have given meaning to rubies, agate and topaz and *bota*. And I am still intrigued by a saying attributed to Jesus of Nazareth: "the very stones would shout out" (Luke 19:40). What would the stones have to say about Jesus?

In Africa's mission history, there are many "actors" who have not made it to the books, but whose presence and actions shaped what the "history-makers" were able to achieve. They are the stones that went into the building of cathedrals and schools and hospitals and the accommodations for mission personnel, named "Mission Houses" by the Wesleyan Methodists who "labored" in Ghana. They are the stones that make up the statistics of converts and the anonymous contingent of local agents and catechists. These "stones" rarely speak out of the pages of books but they are at the foundations of the churches in Africa. They are the living stones whose living faith continues to speak to their posterity. The Bible is replete with talking stones.

Talking Stones

Stones are trodden under foot.
But when you hit your foot against
a stone, you know it is there.
Stones are missiles for execution.
But in the sling of a David a stone brings
Judgement to the oppressor.
Stones are piled up to mark our theophanies.
But they can be used to drown us when we
violate and hurt children.
Stones can be our pillow for the night.
But stones can prevent the seedling from flourishing.

Stone deaf, we say.
But we hear the sound of stone-breaking.
The African woman has to feed her family
and she has only her primordial strength
unaided by harnessed power.

The youthful poor resisting injustice
would arm themselves with stones
and will be gunned down by armed police,
custodians of law and order,
Agents of rulers who care little for the ruled.

Stones are majestic! Stones are heavy!
Stones are beautiful! Stones are hard!
Stones are precious! Stones are common!
A stone might cut a metal.
But other stones are vulnerable.

They crumble and turn to dust.
They are rolled along and
they are shaped by friction,
They are broken up by heating and by cooling.
They are dented by the constant and persistent
dripping of water.

With a rod from the hands of God
Stones become a source of living water.
Once a stone was used to seal a tomb.
The rolling away of that stone did speak.
And power-full was the word of the stone.
For what it said was
Death cannot conquer life.

Contemporary power structures, especially the economic, have put many into the category of people who are dispensable, stones to be trampled under foot and crumbled into dust. But those who live by faith know the Scripture that says:

The stone that the builders rejected
has become the cornerstone;
this was the Lord's doing.
And it is amazing in our eyes (Luke 20:17).

Then Jesus went on to say, "The one who falls on this stone will be broken to pieces; and it will crush anyone on whom it falls" (Luke 20:18)—a dynamic use of the Hebrew proverb "the pot falls on the stone, woe to the pot; the stone falls on the pot, woe to the pot." So then it is better to read what the stones say and to discern for what purpose the particular stone exists. What has shaped the stone? What can it become? Those whom the "definition-makers" have labeled voiceless have voices and charisms needed for the justice and peace that we so much yearn for. Maybe they are the carriers of the signs of the KIN-dom of God, the household of God, the living *oikoumene.*

Among the marginalized of humanity are the poor, i.e., women and men of little or no economic means beyond the life they hold precariously in their bodies. Children and all who have neither economic nor social standing, all who cannot vote or whose votes change nothing—these are the poor. Most women, producers of primary resources and miners; all who operate on assembly lines of mass-produced goods are deemed voiceless. All the "tail-less ones," whose only protector and defender is God, cry out with a deafening silence for God to drive away the flies from their backs. The very presence of the least of these people and their visibility is an indictment and a disturbance to the peace of the powers-that-be, the economic and political elites at the pinnacle of the patriarchal pyramid.

The very existence and resistance of Africans, especially African women and their children, is a testimony to the justice and compassion of God. Their very presence is and can become a vehicle for transformation. Like the tortoise and the snail, symbols of peace and deliberate measured pace, the mills of God grind slowly, but they also grind exceeding small. They are bound to touch every power and every structure. Shalom will arrive, however long it takes, is the message of the voiceless. There are around us symbols, signs, and events that speak to us by their very presence; they often make no sound and they are not announced by trumpets or flags and other insignia, but that they speak we can have no doubt. In this light even God may be said to be voiceless unless human beings are empowered to voice the "Will of God" and to declare God's intentions. The Christian religion and especially the Church has laid claim to being a vehicle for the voice of God. This "voice of God" which Christians affirm is crystallized in the Gospel of Jesus of Nazareth, the one whose very presence on earth is good news.

Voices from the Bible

See how the stones speak! The silence of a stone can bear a message. Not all the voices of the stones we have just heard carry a message we want to hear, but they are speaking of the everyday lives that we lead. They bring us pages from the "Book of Life" through which God speaks to us. We read life, we read the Bible, we hear God speak. So you see, even the stones can speak and do speak if only we have ears to hear. The silent screams of the voiceless reach beyond our hearing, but they do shape our world. At God's command and our obedient action, stones can yield living water. Stones can speak of the love of God.

In our holy book, the Bible of the Oppressed, there are voices that we have not heard or do not want to hear because they disturb us. The blood of Abel cries from all our war fields. The Canaanites whose walled cities were reduced to rubble cry out as the "conquest" of their land becomes the paradigm for divesting other people of land which is their root, mother, and source of life. We too often prefer to be voiceless when we meet uncomfortable events in our holy book. We are unable to utter a word that would appear to be in criticism of what another generation and people say are the words from God. We are afraid to own up to human hand, human interpretation, human culture, human ethnocentrism, in short, of admitting to the historical location of the holy book and the human communities' self-interests that dog its pages. We are afraid of throwing away the bath water for fear of losing the baby too. We own that the Bible continues and it is for us to retrieve God's voice from the many others that fill our ears when we hear the Bible speak.

What is the gift that the Bible brings to us? The contexts in which we read the Bible, and those in which the various books were written have become increasingly important because we are witnesses and often participants in the destruction that is going on around us. The destruction of hope among the poor brought about by the force of the market economy, the use of the Bible in Africa to keep the poor content with their lot or else to instill into them attitudes of self-blame and self-abasement make us increasingly aware of the importance of context. For the Bible to speak a message of love and hope, we need the faith and the charisma of the poor, of women, and of all who walk the paths of justice and compassion.

What Are Charisms

In the Greek Testament, Paul has put together lists of *charismata*. His letter to the Romans says "We have gifts that differ according to the grace given us," and he enumerates prophecy, ministry, teaching, exhorting, giving, leadership and compassion (cf. Rom 12:6-8). He then follows with a long list of what makes for harmonious community life and instructions on how to comport ourselves as Christians. In 1 Cor 12:27-29, the *charismata* are given to empower people to become apostles, prophets, teachers, people who perform deeds of power, gifts of healing, various forms of assistance, leadership and speaking in tongues. In chapter 13 Paul excels himself with description of three cardinal gifts—faith, hope and love—waxing eloquent on the latter. Paul speaks of all these traits, skills, and dispositions as spiritual gifts.

Another way of approaching charisms is to look at the fruits of the Spirit which appear in the letter to the Galatians 5:22-23 as love, joy, peace, patience, kindness, generosity, faithfulness, gentleness and self-control. But above all to speak of charism is to look at how Jesus of Nazareth lived this life with us. One event among many in the life of Jesus comes to my mind at this time to give a glimpse of charisms in operation. The event is the healing of the paralytic in Matt 9:2-8, wherein it is the response of the crowd that strikes me. Matthew reports as follows: "When the crowd saw it, they were filled with awe, and they glorified God, who had given such *authority to human beings*." The authority given to Jesus to demonstrate the love of God is seen by the world as authority given to human beings. We are endowed with charisms to do as God does. Jesus puts this in characteristic simplicity, "Be holy as God is holy." What of Paul's lists of charisms does the twenty-first century need and which is being offered by those rendered voiceless?

Retrieving Charisms

The charisms of the voiceless may be organized around the principles of gender, culture, race, age, nature and all those who are at the receiving end of globalization, the new name which we have coined to cover up the fact of colonization. Let us begin with issues that women raise, as they embody the voices of several voiceless ones. The central charism displayed by many women is that of being in touch with life at its core. They are no longer victims, but beings whose very existence is an indictment against patriarchy's gender injustice. Women's ability to unmask, analyze, and critique patriarchy is a gift to the human community. Patriarchy is more than the rule of the father, which is a gift to the human community. Patriarchy is more than the rule of the father, which is its primary reference. In the vocabulary of feminists, patriarchy is a social construct that operates hierarchies (which in the final analysis benefit no one, not even those who sit at the top of the pyramid), and which also sees and presents the world in dualistic form. In the patriarchal world there have been many voiceless women whose charisms have sustained and promoted their men, sons, husbands, lovers, bosses, colleagues and friends, and most of these women have gone uncelebrated. Rarely are they named and acknowledged, yet we know there were women who followed and who used their wealth to support the "Jesus school" and who became missionaries to their people and to their colleagues and collaborators—women who challenged Jesus to broaden his paradigms.

In our day some women have come away from being the power behind the throne and have offered to contribute directly to the shaping of human history.[1] They are the women I am describing with the term "feminists" and whose world view I believe the twenty-first century cannot afford to ignore, and whom a Church that wishes to pursue justice and compassion and to live it cannot marginalize. Whoever ignores what women say today does so at his or her own peril. Getting people to recognize the existence of patriarchy and to admit that it is not God-intended has been one of the tasks of Christian feminists.[2] Like other

---

[1] Leon-Joseph Suenens, *The Hidden Hand of God* (Dublin: Veritas, 1994). Suenens writes of Veronica O'Brien, international leader of the Legion of Mary movement and longtime collaborator with the Cardinal in his apostolic work and describes her as a "woman with theological acumen and ecclesial vision."

[2] Womanist theologian Delores Williams in her book *Sisters in the Wilderness* (Maryknoll, N.Y.: Orbis Books, 1993) traces the development of sexism and racism

feminists, women in Africa have tried to show how patriarchy shapes, molds, and conditions the experience of all. They have unveiled social-ization traditions and the justification of patriarchy by labels such as "natural" and "sacred traditions" and have called for a rebirth into a new humanity that dispenses with patriarchy.[3] All of humanity with the ecosystem has been warped by patriarchy. This is the "shared expe-rience" of all women who have a liberative consciousness. This daily experience of women may be shared by some men, but as the feminist Hyun Kyung Chung puts it, "Men are addicted to the crumbs from the patriarchal table,"[4] and this tends to render them voiceless in the face of gender inequality. Women are offering humanity the power of qualita-tive survival.

The oppressed stand at a vantage point from where they can see more clearly the oppression of others. For such as these, empathy and solidarity are not just slogans but a way of being. This is what has made feminists the spokespersons for social justice for all and sensitiv-ity to ecological exploitation. While many women and men are com-mitted to a positive transformation of current structures and attitudes, they often include women only as one of the many groups of the "voiceless" and the "powerless" without an adequate analysis of gen-der inequality and the effects of race and class within this. Women worldwide have specific hopes, such as the day when no woman will have to sell her body to support her family. Women confront militarism and misogynist religion as shared experiences that have negative influ-ences on daily life. African women have, in addition, to cope with hunger, disease, displacement, and a globalization geared towards cre-ating despair in Africa. In spite of all this, women hold before them the struggle for utopia of the Biblical vision of *shalom*, peace, well-being, healing, freedom, justice, an empowering, healing community, unity, and wholeness. For women, these are not just abstract principles, but matters of the moment, and of each and every day. The power to hold on to faith and to struggle to reach what we hope for is a gift the Church needs for the twenty-first century.

---

in the U.S.A. and in the fourth chapter illustrates how the Bible is used as an ideo-logical weapon for the subjugation and demonization of women and dark-skinned people, especially Blacks.

[3] See Mercy Amba Oduyoye and Musimbi R.A. Kanyoro (eds.) *The Will to Arise: Women, Tradition and the Church in Africa* (Maryknoll, N.Y.: Orbis Books, 1995 edi-tion) and Mercy Amba Oduyoye, *The Daughters of Anowa: African Women and Patri-archy* (Maryknoll, N.Y.: Orbis Books, 1995).

[4] Dialogue on "Women's Experience of the Sacred" organized by the Ecumenical Association of Third World Theologians (EATWOT) in New York, January 1996.

Of one thing I am certain, women's self-abasement, and their acquiescence to their own dehumanization are not virtues and therefore should not be carried by women into the twenty-first century—let alone be offered as a gift to the Church and to societal structures. Women offer the principle that gaining power in an oppressive structure is not liberative, so a distinction has to be made between opting out in order to seek a liberative alternative and coping with an oppressive system in order to attain the peace of the cemetery. Women who hold on to the Cross and to "living sacrifice" as a way of life give that as a gift to be emulated by all. They would desire that all would come to learn that taking on responsibility does not have to lead to self-aggrandizement, a disease that seems to afflict some African politicians and others. What it should do is enhance the life of the whole community.

The day-to-day lives of struggling women offer the world the view that the voiceless are worthy and that their situation calls for urgent and positive transformation. The voiceless matter, and God holds the Church accountable for their plight. We remember with sorrow that the Church has joined in demanding that women be voiceless. We remember how Paul's admonition, "Let the women keep quiet . . ." (1 Cor 14:34) has been used and misused a thousand times over. The questions raised by women's experience of daily life need to be reflected upon theologically, but the male power of definition has not recognized this to be the case, thus rendering women voiceless. Moving into the twenty-first century, it will be important to hear what women have to say about God through women's theology and women's source of meaning. It will be important to exercise the charism of empowerment, to raise consciousness about hunger, poverty, and other dehumanizing agencies, and to act more like beings who believe that there is a theistic foundation to life. The Womanist theologian Delores Williams writes: "The ideal aim of feminist/Womanist pioneers is to help evolve a world in which sexual, racial, class and caste oppression no longer exists . . . a world in which people live in peaceful and reciprocal relations with each other and with nature."[5]

From Third-World women theologians one discovers imagery of what it means to be empowered by one's faith in God and to be a source of empowerment to others. An Uruguayan woman loves the imagery of "making space for the development and well-being of others." A Kenyan woman describes women's penchant for enabling and making possible the existence of others in the words, "Women know how to ease over," and African American women "make a way where there is

---

[5] *Voices from the Third World,* The Ecumenical Association of Third World Theologians, June 1993. "Emerging Concerns of Third World Theology," 23–32.

no way." Women's patience, persistence and power are lodged firmly in hope. Generosity and sharing are what will hold creation together in the twenty-first century.

Gender is a relatively new cultural paradigm, the beginning of a profound cultural transformation of the human psyche, style of life, of thinking, and of relationships. It bears the marks of the source of a socio-cultural revolution, and that of course is scary. Women are not a homogeneous group. Women's solidarity as females does have a checkered history, marred by race and class as evidenced most dramatically in the history of the United States of America and in the Republic of South Africa. But our contemporary women's movement presents such a formidable profile because where sin is acknowledged, confessed, and repented, then reconciliation, solidarity and collaboration have been possible. Women call on others who participate in oppressive divisions to do the same. This is a pre-condition to a twenty-first century of justice and compassion.

Africa

Today there is a way of speaking about Africa that seems calculated to murder hope and to undermine the will to resist oppressive economic structures. Many who talk about Africa seem bent upon rendering people voiceless and hopeless. The "ethnocide" that began with slavery and colonialism is reaching a culmination in a globalization that deliberately excludes Africa's voices of hope and resistance of dehumanization. An African woman knows all this and more and yet continues to present herself and to labor as a life sustainer. Africa has been rendered voiceless in the push towards globalization that the world's powerful nations and economic powers are forcing on all. The people of the continent do not matter; the only thing that matters are the wars they generate to feed the arms industry. They have become like the earth, like women—it is what they can give that matters, not what they need to receive. Reciprocity in doing good has been murdered.

To ask what does Africa have that the twenty-first century needs is to ask, in my opinion, the wrong question, for it is Africa's readiness to give that has led her into the state of being an exploited continent with a people that is expendable. The rich nations of the world are building walls, putting up screens and fences to prevent them from hearing the voices of those they have rendered voiceless. The United Europe has become adept at splitting hairs. When Europeans migrated all over the world, how did they describe themselves—as explorers seeking adventure, merchants selling goods, colonizers stealing land? They were empire-builders, missionaries, refugees from religious oppression, and deportees of judicial systems. But were they not economic migrants when they went looking for land and wealth? Did some not return to colonies they had been forced to leave, when the economies of their own countries could not sustain them after devastating wars and political upheavals? For example, I have in mind the Dutch in Indonesia and the Portuguese in Mozambique. Did some not stay on, creating wealth and repatriating wealth when they had the opportunity? We have to be honest and to admit that slavery was never abolished; it was only transformed. See how diligently some sectors of America see to it that African-Americans remain visible by their poverty.[6]

The silence over the exploitation of Africa by Europeans and peoples of European descent has a long history. Remember how the League of Nations ignored African voices protesting against the processes of instituting apartheid in South Africa, the appropriation of land and cattle, expulsion, genocide, all deliberately programmed? In South Africa slavery never ended, it was only transformed. Remember how Dr. Verwored voiced the mind of Europeans: "There is no room for the Bantu in the European community above the level of certain forms of labor."[7] How very prophetic! Now it has become "there is no room for the *Bantu*, Black African humanity, period." Some would today delete completely the voices from Africa that demonstrate the effects of this history. They stop up their ears and they shout, "It is time to put all that behind you. You have been independent for forty years. Is it not time to do something for, with, and by yourselves?" Thus a historical position and blindness to the structures of global economic relations are calculated to render Africa mute.

But now has come the charism of the voiceless, the powerless, and those with the charism to see where true peace lies. Apartheid, South African style, has been dismantled. This is a gift, a charism in our hands against the evil philosophy of a hierarchy of races and colors, coupled with the oppression of the darker by the paler. The 1976 Soweto young peoples' resistance, their refusal to submit to discrimination and degradation was loudly reported to the conscience of the world through a simple photo, the body of eleven-year-old Hector Peterson borne in the arms of a seventeen-year-old with a bewildered sister running along.[8]

---

[6] See the historical review provided by Delores Williams in *Sisters in the Wilderness*, chapter 4. "Color Struck: A State of Mind," *op cit.*

[7] Francis "Woodie" Blackman, *Dame Nita: Caribbean Woman, World Citizen* (Kingston: Ian Randle Publishers, 1995) 129.

[8] Blackman, *op. cit.*, 130. This seventeen-year-old ended up in Nigeria and in Ibadan among a bus load of young people who had fled from the Republic of South

Meeting these young black South Africans gave me hope. So now I can say to all, "Rejoice, for you are living in days when the voiced can learn from the voiceless. The voiced will learn to read signs and symbols, they will put more into building relationships when they can no longer fill ears with words while the bread baskets remain empty."

For generations, the generosity of Africans has exposed the continent to exploitation by its neighbors—Arabs and Europeans. Acquiescence and collaboration dulled the voices of resistance, and history is written with Africa's voice absent from Africa's history. The same absence applies to the North American scene. Peace without justice is what promoted and sustained voicelessness in Africa. As Jeremiah would have said, they have treated the hurt of my people in an off-handed manner. They have dispensed cups full of words of reconciliation, where a pinch of confrontation would have rooted out the cancer in injustice. They have rendered my people voiceless in the assemblies of the nations, voiceless with astonishment at the obtuseness of Europeans and peoples of European descent. Voiceless because even when they shout, the ears of their oppressors are not tuned to the pitch of the voices that come from Africa. Africa is effectively voiceless. Her generosity has not been reciprocated. What has Africa to offer anyway, since the continent is no longer important to world trade? All "her" natural resources are now depleted, some would say with disdainful satisfaction. Africa is a forgotten continent, report the tabloids. Commentators on Africa point to Black-on-Black genocide in Rwanda, forgetting White-on-White genocide in Nazi Germany and parts of today's Europe. It came to me as a surprise to read the following words about Africa from a woman whose people know the meaning of bouncing back. Inga Gibel, identifying herself as a Jew, a Zionist, and a feminist, said at the final session of Forum 1985, speaking of the "cruelties which had been the expressed collective concern of thousands of women at the forum": "At the very base of the column of despair were poor, black women of South Africa, Uganda, and Ethiopa, where the only future foreseeable was painful death, the misery of watching one's children die, and the death of hope itself."[9] In place of this column of despair, I present the Africa that clings to the symbol that says Aye Nyama—accept God. The February 1990 release of Nelson Mandela and subsequent events in South Africa have put the lie to the death of hope in Africa. Only the struggle to be free continues. Will God give stones when we ask for bread?

Africa to Botswana following this Soweto event. They were being hosted by the Nigerian government. The seventeen-year-old was in my home with others.

[9] Blackman, *op. cit.*, 103–4.

Africa and Charism

Sometimes I wish it were true that Africa had been forgotten, especially by those who have milked her for generations! But alas! How can that be? Who can imagine the twenty-first century without Africa? Africa still has an abundance of natural resources. But who benefits from this, and how long will they last? Africa has wild life, plant life, animal life, and microscopic life in abundance, but how much of all of this will be saved? Africa has people, but do they really matter if they are not of European or Arabic descent? Unfortunately, one cannot speak of Africa without speaking of Black Africa, where the ideology of color-coding from the palest to the deepest is based on the exploitation of the deeper colors by the paler ones. Black Africans in this scheme are people who have been rendered voiceless; they are non-citizens in their own countries, merely a source of manual labor.

Did not the Akan proverb say *wopinkye asuo a na wote se okoto bo waw* ("If you get close to the river, you will hear the crab coughing")? Many who talk about Africa do not know Africans or else they only think they do. Many have neither slept in an African home nor even drunk water from her rivers. Some would never dream of learning an African language! Some never hear an African speak except with the borrowed tongue of the colonizer, yet we all know that language is not only a matter of culture but an issue of power. Black Africans were either enslaved in the "New World" or in quasi-slavery in their own countries. In both locations, they were silenced. Africa's refusal to accept all of this as "normal" or ordained of God is a charism offered to the human community. God does not ordain exploitation, degradation, and oppression; human beings impute this to God out of their own self-interest. The Church must learn to read the Bible from the perspective of those who do not fit into the conventional Christian "salvation history," for they too are children of God.

When Europeans spilled over into other lands, they made no attempt to create an atmosphere for dialogue. The legacy of conquest and of exploitation has not been edifying. What kind of human being succeeds? The power of the gun and trickery have taught that success in human life follows the law of the jungle. We know that Christ and the Church say something different. But will the style of holding on to life at its core be a charism that the rulers of this world would consider taking into the twenty-first century? Will the miracle of a Nelson Mandela, who refused to accept injustice, who grew angry at oppression, yet who remained dignified in negotiation, not count as a charism from the voiceless?

The Powerless

There are many more that human structures and attitudes have rendered voiceless—people whose cries we do not hear or who have cried so much they seem to have lost their voices: the indigenous and those who are landless because immigrants some five hundred years ago stole the land their ancestors depended upon, or because not so long ago they were forcibly removed from their homes in favor of "new developments" and/or "worthier people." The voiceless are children—boys and girls who live in the streets—or those sold to pornography and prostitution and drugs—who cannot talk because talking means death. They grow up, live aggressively or sullenly, and silently beg for life until they die from violence or grow old and die in our streets.[10] The phenomenon is becoming global. The presence of these voiceless ones tells us that it is not easy to die from "natural causes," because life resists death to the end. Of course it is easy to get killed, but it is not so easy for the death-wish to materialize. The struggle of the voiceless for life tells us life is precious, that life is sacred, and convicts us of our own carelessness concerning the quality of life of the other. The human being challenged to live with impaired mobility, sight, hearing, sense of smell and language confirms for those whose only challenge is how to use their senses and mobility to live well that full life is lived in community.

One could illustrate the courage and ingenuity that all these people demonstrate to refuse to accept dehumanization. The collaboration, solidarity, and team work that empowers them to survive the streets and the unease of those among whom they live, sends a clear message to all who have ears to hear. They demonstrate that there is no such thing as a "useless person." Those who work with severely challenged persons come away humbled. The right to be human includes the right to self-expression and to life-enhancing relationships. All strive for this, whatever their physical, mental, or economic status may be. Hope is reconstructed as we share with joy the paintings and writings of "disadvantaged" children—children with no hands! Hope is rekindled as people patiently research and experiment to collaborate in the will to live fully and creatively. We dare to re-imagine alternatives in other situations when we realize that feet and toes can function as hands and fingers. Resourcefulness is a charism the voiceless offer the twenty-first century.

---

[10] Bruce Ritter, *Sometimes God Has a Kid's Face* (New York: Covenant House, 1988). This "little" book is dedicated to "thousands of good, brave and beautiful bought and sold kids who never make it back because no one reached them in time. . . ." God forbid such in the twenty-first century!

The indices of voicelessness are all around us. The poverty-makers have globalized poverty; physical and mental challenges to life are everywhere, and God, the "Voiceless One," tells us, "those who have ears to hear, let them hear." It is the vocation of all to discern the voice of God and to communicate it in acts of love and compassion. The people who name themselves theologians have undertaken to craft as many varieties of theology as is needed for this task.

Theologians

We have a painful vocation as theologians. Often I have asked myself: 'Does anybody listen? Does anybody care what comes out of the minds of theologians, much less women theologians, and even less African women's theological discourse to the Church? Theologians are not "wordless." They fill shelves with their words, seemingly potent speech, but often impotent words that get nothing done. When they begin to speak by living out their theology among the poor, they are quickly disposed of, if not by the Church then by the state or whoever is the immediate powerful one whose self-interest is undermined by their words. Theologians call the Church to listen for what God is saying through other faith communities, but most of the Church is not ready to listen. Theologians point out how "the ancients" developed theologies relevant to the socio-political economic experience and language of their days, and they call on the Church to do the same for our generation. But the institution of the Church insists on ignoring our contemporary context and continues to serve the ancient dishes.

I studied theology, excited at the justice of God as interpreted by Amos, and by God's attention to the vulnerable. What do we say to the injustices around us? I have been disturbed by the ethnocentricity and misogyny of parts of the biblical account, yet bowled over by the acts of courage and self-giving in the same book. It makes me wonder whether we should not be reading the Bible with our world as a hermeneutical tool. I was ecstatic about the intensity of the debates in the early Church in hammering out exactly what we believe, and I was disquieted when we lost patience with each other and anathematized the other and called each other heretical and syncretistic. I never gave up our human attempt to talk about God, but I always felt we should do more to act out of love and compassion and justice, and so come a little closer to our affirmations that we are made in the image of God. As people who claim to be blessed, we need to "stand up with strength, to move away the stone that seals in life." Is the KIN-dom of God not in our hands?

We insist that God is our creator, that we come from God. We search for appropriate relational language to hitch ourselves closer to God. We call ourselves children of God—not as biological parent, mother or father, but one to whom we relate in love and care and mutual respect. We offer all this to the Church and world, but does anybody want to live by these approaches? Theologians become really "voiceless," especially when what we have to say bears no relation to the daily lives and experiences of people and to the quality of life they strive for. In many aspects of life theology is rendered mute.

And yet people seek meaning in life. Maybe we are voiceless because we really have nothing relevant to say. The challenge to the Church in the next century is that it become relevant to real life or else give way for a new creation. Contemporary theologians from Africa, Asia, Latin/South America, and among African Americans, people who have been voiceless in the shaping of Christian theology, have something to say. Their ability to direct attention to injustices in their history and their contemporary situations is a gift to be appreciated. The movement of women theologians, rereading the Bible and Christian history, naming the male biases of this traditional script and striving to understand God's ways, is a gift to the Church and to the twenty-first century. African American women showing us Hagar's God, and African women seeing the meaning of the Christ in the life of Jesus, call the Church to do as Jesus did—to heal broken persons and broken relations. These voiceless women have broken onto the theological stage bearing gifts from the Holy Spirit. Will the Church receive them into the twenty-first century?

Charisms That Transform

We are asking in this symposium to honor the justice-loving and compassionate Cardinal Suenens. So we ask: What charisms do we discover from living and relating to all who have been rendered voiceless? Can we refurbish, cultivate and encourage the charisms they possess, and can we augment these charisms in ourselves as individuals, communities and Church? Are we asking which gifts are most needed by the Church and society as we enter the twenty-first century? How do we activate those insights? How do we as Christians and the institutional churches we belong to become active in the pursuit of justice? We who have voices and platforms from which to reach the ears of the powerful have the responsibility to speak and to act. The question then is what acts will bring our life-sustaining and life-enhancing transformation? Can we craft an alternative ethic to the "law of the jungle" and "winner takes all?" Can we become avenues by which the Holy Spirit convicts the world of evil? What gifts are needed to do this as we enter the twenty-first century? What do we need to survive, even to flourish, in the twenty-first century? These are some of the challenges before us. We shall honor those to whom honor is due not only by "drinking together" our wisdom on these questions, but more so if we go away determined to break the silence around dehumanization and move to become human enough to hear the voices of the voiceless and to respond with life. Rejoice, for you are living in days when the voiced can learn from the voiceless, for they will learn to read signs and symbols. They will put more into building relationships when they can no longer fill ears with words while bread baskets stand empty.

What the voiceless are saying is that they exist as stumbling blocks to our common humanity. The more we struggle not to dash our foot against the stones placed to impede others, the slower our progress towards the plenty we seek. Generosity and sharing, turning stones into bread for others as for self, making the desert yield water, "Making a way where there is no way"[11] is what the voiceless present to the church, to society. The voiceless survive and struggle for an enhanced quality of life while they live the hope of the Kenyan proverb: "A time will come when the bean splits and will be shared equally." The voiceless have the power of survival because they live an active hope. The charism of an active hope must accompany us into the twenty-first century.

Women have identified the link between economy and ecology, for Church and society. Christianity should have made a more positive, clearer and more deliberate use of its teaching that creation belongs to God; it is God's *oikos*. We should have known that knowledge about the *oikos* should go together with God's management of it, the *oikonomia* of God; and that we who claim to mediate between God and the rest of creation should build our economy on the *oikonomia* of God. We should have known that religions other than Christianity, and cultures other than the Europeans, are also bearers of God's grace and channels of God's salvation. The voiceless of these locations demonstrate to us what we need to heed and to do. Their faith and lifestyle is a gift to the twenty-first century and to the Church.

The voiceless teach us to put human faces on our categories. They remind us of the style of Jesus who spoke not just of the poor and the neighbor and the stranger, but who showed who they are and said what you have done to each of them, you have done to Jesus himself. We do need studies and statistics, but behind them is flesh and blood crying silently. So the call is to open your eyes and attune your ears be-

---

[11] Williams, *op. cit., et passim.*

cause there is a voiceless one nearby. Perhaps it is a baby abandoned in the bush because its mother cannot bear to see it die. Be the image of God, the God who sees, and save that life, point the violated woman to resources that her dehumanized eyes are unable to see. Cry out with the voice of the voiceless, get involved with the salvific work of God, make a positive difference. Speak out as God is said to have spoken out numberless times with the voices of human beings in our Holy Book and act to save as God has shown us how. The voiceless teach us that each human being is worthy of life and of dignity.

Africans are not just sitting by the Nile and the Niger, the Congo and the Zambezi waiting to die. What the African resistance to death and dehumanization says to the twenty-first century is "come nearer, we are just as human. We love life, so we struggle to survive and we strive to improve our quality of life. We are just like you. All we ask for is that you accompany us as members of the one human race, and that we together cultivate the art of living in community." What the African brings to the twenty-first century is a call to all, to learn more about different cultures, to respect "the other" and not to presume to teach before we have learned, for dialogue shall be the creative process of relationships.

It is as one human community that we need to refurbish our flagging love for justice and to encourage in one another the charism of compassion and generosity. What we need is to work together in designing and crafting a global culture with a richness of diversity that will be worthy of celebration. Surely, it cannot be that God is present only in the economically rich cultures. Globalization has to be more than westernization. The courage and ingenuity of the homeless remind us of the infinite resources of brain power and skills with which God has imbued humanity, while at the same time convicting all who live rattling in mansions and houses of many rooms by themselves or in pairs while others cannot have shelter from the elements. In the twenty-first century could "we live simply, so that others may simply live?"

The Church of the Twenty-First Century

When we look towards the next century, we see faith communities other than our own, and we can consider them as allies in the journey towards a just and compassionate world. In this symposium, therefore, I have had in mind people of goodwill of all faith communities. But now the call is to those of us who call ourselves the Church, the body of Christ. The future Church has to be a continuation of the presence of Christ in the world. The rest is negotiable. How do we make this claim believable? What do we retrieve from the charisms of the voiceless to aid us in this task? We have been told what is good, "to do justly, to love compassion," and to walk with our hands in God's hand going where God goes and doing what God does.

The struggles and the survival of the voiceless tell us that if we keep quiet the stones will speak out. The stones may speak out to save, but they may also speak out to destroy. If there are hungry people, we must not send them away, we must feed them. If there are paralyzed on stretchers we cannot pass the buck. If we shall discover cheating and dishonesty in high places, even the "houses of God," we shall have to take the whip. Often the charism of the powerless is to show our complicity in their disempowerment or in coopting their voices, or taking them away completely when they refuse to be co-opted.

The history of the Church among the voiceless has wide patches of bleakness. South Americans, South Africans, and African Americans can all attest to this. The Church's recent involvement in solidarity with the voiceless has not been enough to redeem that history. Indeed the silence of many Christian communities vis-a-vis the greed of Western culture screams complicity. When churches speak, it is often to lay down rules concerning so called personal morality. Inside the Church some even question the full humanity of the female, claiming that only the male is of the divine image. What I hear the voiceless poor and the voiceless human females saying is that it is about time the Church became the vanguard of joy and beauty, putting back into human life the sacred and the mystery that will imbue us with the blissful charism of encountering God and walking with God in the cool of the evening. It is about time we cultivate the knowing heart that thrives on loving relationships, solidarity, generosity, power-sharing, and struggles against dualism, building each other up, accompanying one another in the struggle for fullness of life.

People who come to Church love and respect the Church. What they hear in Church should make them go out and be the Church, not just make them feel good about themselves. The poor and the voiceless who still come to Church, come seeking community, and the power to continue to live, and the opportunity for participation in the only place where they have been made to believe their humanity is honored. But should the Church not be the place from where they emerge with light to shine on the presence of God in the world and power to be the image of God to an ailing world? Should the Church not be the place from where they emerge with their gender-blindness cured and their racism and ethnocentrism exorcized? Should gender-justice not emanate from the Church? The Church should make itself vulnerable, it should be willing to engage this issue and be engaged by it as more and more women are willing to do in spite of threats of exclusion and ridicule.

Should the Church not stand in solidarity with women as they insist and as they demonstrate that gender-justice is an important dimension of social justice and the justice that God enjoins us to live by?

Even if it were not stated in the Bible, the principle of love as Jesus lived it should move us into privileging the poor and the oppressed on moral grounds. The Church has to continue to provide a voice for the voiceless in our words to the world and to be accountable to the communities of voiceless out of which we speak. The Church is called to accompany the voiceless as they erupt into the consciousness of the powerful. Where the voiceless still struggle to be heard, their efforts should move the Church to speak. Remember how the angel spoke to Mary and Joseph on behalf of the "voiceless" Christ Child, the baby Jesus? The Church of the twenty-first century should join the reconstruction of hope, to re-imagine alternatives to this exploitation-ridden world. The Church needs to re-read life and to re-read the Bible and history and to make audible the silenced voice of God.

■ *Mario Marazziti*

I would like to begin by recalling some historical facts and events which are of relevance when one comes to speak about the Community of San Egidio, but which may at first seem strange to the reader. I hope later on their relevance will become clear.

I begin with the high Middle Ages. In those days it was customary to divide Christians into two categories. The Decree of Gratian sealed the division of Christians into *spirituals* and *carnals*. The spirituals had the task and privilege of taking care of the things of God, while the carnals were to busy themselves with the things of the world. Thus the carnals came to be called *the laity* to distinguish them from the clerics.

As you well know, the word *lay* or *laity* comes from the Greek word *laos*, which means "the people." The word as such did not have a content of its own; it signified something that the layperson is not, namely not monastic, not clerical.

Indeed, in the high Middle Ages words tended to have a very concrete meaning. Then since theology was the concern of the monks and clerics, they went so far as to speak of the carnals as the *idiots*. However, some theologians, in search of a more positive definition, called the lay people *laicorum genus bestiale,* that is to say, "those beasts who are in fact the laity." They went further and sought to establish the right of lay people to speak by founding this right on the biblical story of Balaam's donkey, through whose jawbone the word of God was able to come forth. If the jawbone of a donkey could become the vehicle of the word of God, they argued, then the laity could surely speak.

But, as we all know, church thinking on the role of lay Christians has come a long way since those days. An effort has been made to see lay Christians as the salt of the earth and the leaven in the batch. The change was swift and it followed a biblical route. In fact, it went beyond the mentality of the times.

The change was very rapid when one thinks of how St. Francis of Assisi was a layperson and a poor friar. In the thirteen century he spent his intense, short life in preaching the Scriptures. In fact, his own life was his preaching, even to the point of his being physically conformed to the Jesus whom he loved. As we know, St. Francis sought and obtained permission from the pope and Lateran Council IV for both himself and his companions to preach the Gospel and to live in the company of Lady Poverty. It should be noted that he got this permission without having to become a cleric. In fact, St. Francis was a layperson for most of his life and, in any case, he never became a priest.

St. Francis' special empathy and friendship with his brothers and with the world came from the extraordinary intensity of his relationship with the crucified and risen Lord Jesus and from his relationship with the poor and the Scriptures, the word of God "without gloss." This even drove him at the height of the Crusades to cross the Mediterranean and to dialogue with the Sultan Melek el Kamal.

At this point I would like to recall another historical fact. Between the third and the seventh century ordinary men and women gave rise to the monastic experience in both the East and the West as they sought to be like the apostles and to change the world in the light of the Gospel. In the Western tradition this experience included prayer, the centrality of the word of God through the *lectio divina*, that is, the continuous reading and reflection on the Scriptures. It led to the creation of the monastic community as a place of hospitality. It required the monks to live by the work of their own hands. All these elements of monastic life were part of the life of ordinary men and women. I repeat, ordinary men and women who were monks or nuns but not clerics. In fact, when one reads the *Rule of Benedict,* one discovers that the priests who belonged to the monastic life were assigned places in the choir and in the community according to their seniority in the community. It was not at all linked to their status as clerics.

I have recalled this history as a background to my presentation of the San Egidio Community. As I speak about the community, I hope you will perceive the links between our present community life and those historical episodes. I am sure that you will have grasped already that in speaking of these things I was also speaking of how San Egidio is trying to live the Gospel in today's world and Church.

A layperson therefore is not simply one who is not a cleric. Neither is it simply one who is a specialist in secular affairs. In our understanding, the real challenge for lay Christians is to live in empathy and feeling for the world and for the women and men in it.

If we were to find a short definition of what it means to be a lay Christian today, one definition could be: "All that is human is of concern to me." Or if we look at it in biblical terms, we might recall the feelings that Jesus experienced when he saw the crowds like sheep without a shepherd or when he saw the faith of the poor people or when he met the widow of Nain or the woman who had had a hemorrhage of blood for a long time. These feelings of Jesus bring us very close to the heart of what it means to be a lay Christian.

But certainly, we believe, the fullest definition is to be found in the passion of Christ. This describes in all its depth and width what is the essence of being a lay Christian. Jesus in his passion loves his own to the very end. He gives his life once and for all for each one of them and for us—for those who understand little and for those who do not understand at all, for his persecutors and for those who do not know him but who nevertheless also have need to be loved and healed and saved.

It is highly significant that in the tradition of Eastern Christianity the rite of baptism is accompanied by the rite of tonsure. This highlights the total tension that exists at baptism, even to the point of rupture, with oneself and with the past. There is here a great similarity with the gestures that accompany the entry into the monastic order. The prayer in this latter rite says: "Blessed be your servant who has come to offer you the tonsure of the hairs of his head as the first fruits."

The lay person comes to understand himself or herself as "a monk" of the "interior monasticism," subject to the absolute demands of the Gospel. At the heart of the call of the lay Christian is the call to be faithful to the whole Gospel, to live with urgency a truly apostolic life, to live as the apostles lived. It is this "monasticism of the heart" that gives the lay Christian the courage to try to change the world through the weakness of the Gospel.

And now I will speak more directly of the San Egidio Community. First, the saint. San Egidio is not a famous saint in Italy. Indeed, in France and Great Britain he is called "St. Gilles" or "St. Giles." It is the name of an enclosed convent and adjacent little church in the heart of Rome, which the enclosed Carmelite nuns abandoned in the late 1960s after living there for over three centuries. In 1973, five years after we first began our meetings, we were given this church in the historic center of Rome, in the downtown neighborhood of Trastevere. This is close to the ancient port of Rome, which was also the port of the popes until the last century.

This area of Rome closely resembles the Latin Quarter of Paris or London's Piccadilly or New York City's Greenwich Village. In this ancient setting there are many tourists and restaurants and places of entertainment. From 1973 onward, the little Church of San Egidio has opened its doors for prayer every evening. Anyone who wishes can join the community in prayer there. Once, in the mid-70s also Cardinal Suenens joined us and more than once, I think, Cardinal Danneels, like many simple faithful.

We gather in this church in the evening at the end of our day's work and perhaps also after providing some service to the poor. For us it is a way to enter deeply into ourselves. We do not seek to cancel the noise of the city life; rather we seek to find again our priority centered on the word of God as found in the Scriptures.

Perhaps we come here after having accompanied some poor people in their difficult urban pilgrimage. They may be the homeless or the immigrants; they may live helpless lives in some old folks home; or they may live in shanty dwellings or in gypsy caravans. They may be terminally ill or have AIDS.

Our prayer is a way of coming face to face with Jesus and finding or refinding ourselves for what we truly are. For when we have done all that is asked of us, we are, as the Gospel says, mere useless servants. For us, this evening prayer has been and is the great antidote to the violent self-affirmation of oneself; it is the antidote to an ideological or merely sociological approach to the one who is poor. It is the great antidote to those fastidious forms of "proud humility" or the pathetic sense of superiority which can take root even among Christians.

We came to this place in 1973, and we took the name of this saint about whom very little is known. There is, of course, a portrait of San Egidio. It shows a monk, an abbot and therefore a man of the word of God. It shows him with an arrow through his hand—the hand that protects a doe. At a distance we see a king or a prince holding the bow from which the arrow has come. We count ourselves fortunate. For San Egidio is portrayed as the defender of the weak one against the strong, violent, powerful one. There is even a touch of ecological concern in the portrait! And, there is certainly an ecumenical element because San Egidio was a monk of the undivided Church, a monk at the time when the Churches of the East and the West were united. He came from Thessalonika in the East, and he died in France, in the West.

Today, in the lefthand aisle of the Church of San Egidio, you can see a wooden cross. We found it some time ago, thrown away by the roadside. One can hardly call it a cross because it lacks the transversal branch, the arms. Today, only the central body, the trunk, of the cross remains. It even conveys an expression of suffering. We call it "the Christ without arms," "the powerless Christ," "the Christ of weakness." For us it symbolizes the call to transform the world through the weakness of the cross, without resorting to powerful means.

All that I said early on about the laity is pertinent to the Community of San Egidio. In 1968 a group of young Roman high school students from the Virgilia Lyceum was gathered together by a fellow student, Andrea Riccardi. Andrea was then eighteen years old. They began to reflect together on the Gospel. It inspired them to come close to the poor and challenged them to try to change the world. They asked themselves the question, How can we become more than just people who reflect and think? How can we spend our lives for other people?

The community's founder, Andrea Riccardi, is today a professor of church history at Rome State University. He is a central reference point for the whole community even though he is no longer the president. Some years ago he was one of the official mediators who helped broker the peace accord and end the sixteen-year-long civil war in Mozambique. He did this together with Don Matteo Zuppi, Archbishop Goncalves, and a member of the Italian Parliament.

The San Egidio Community is in a certain sense both a child of Vatican II and of the 1968 student movement, with its strong push for authenticity and its indignation at the dramatic conditions of life of so many people.

The community is a child of Vatican II and of its teachings. Without Cardinal Suenens and without the royal priesthood of the faithful, San Egidio would not exist. It was through the Scriptures and *Dei Verbum* that we came to understand such teachings as the royal priesthood of the laity. As we read the Scriptures, we were particularly struck by the early Christian community as described in the Acts of the Apostles. We were also captivated by such stories as the good Samaritan, read together with the story of Martha and Mary—we read both without putting into opposition the "better part," that is prayer and contemplation, and "the service to the poor."

The community is also a child of 1968 in its radical desire for change and in its choice of a decisive relation with the Scriptures. The centrality given by the community to the word of God in the Scriptures has made the great difference to our life. It was the Scriptures that gave the community a great freedom from the prevailing ideologies. The Scriptures liberated us from the ideology which asserted that "everything is political," from the Marxist ideology, and from the ideology, where everyone withdrew from public life. Scriptures also set us free from the"yuppyism" which came later, and it frees us today from "consumerism" and the temptation to "group" or "ethnic" closure.

We took to heart the words of the famous Karl Barth that Christians should live with the Bible in one hand and a newspaper—now it could be the Internet?—in the other. It was the reflection on the Scriptures that inspired the community to work concretely first with the poor in Rome's shanty towns.

Over the years, the community also came to work with many more poor people in other parts of the world. We approach the poor in concrete friendship as brothers and sisters. We do so not as a protective and excluding umbrella, but as a concrete way to be less defenseless in the face of the great drives to different types of conformism. We see our service to the poor as "a bridge of friendship" to worlds that are different from those of our origins. It was in this way that the first San Egidio communities came into existence. First, communities of adults in the poor periphery of Rome, and then later they took root in other cities in Italy and elsewhere outside Italy.

From 1968 to the present day, the history of the San Egidio Community has been short and intense. The Holy See recognized the community as an international public association of lay people in 1986. In the decree in which it recognized the community, in accordance with the new Code of Canon Law, the Holy See identified these fundamental elements of the community: the primacy of evangelization; the service of the poor; fraternity as a form of common way of feeling and acting and as a friendly attitude to the world; the commitment to ecumenical and interreligious dialogue; the concrete service to peace.

As one can see, the specific charism of San Egidio is in reality almost a "noncharism," in the sense that it is what in reality every Christian woman and man are called to do as disciples of Jesus.

Today there are about fifteen thousand people in the San Egidio Community worldwide; they are women and men; young and not so young from every part of society. They are gathered together in small communities in more than twenty countries of the world. Every four years the community elects the leaders of the different communities. These leaders elect the international leaders. Then there is an international council of twenty members. A characteristic of the internal structure of the community is the habit of having wide consultation and as wide as possible discussion among those who are working in the same area. San Egidio is classified as a charity under Italian law and is for the most part based on volunteer work. It is, in fact, also a nonprofit association which has given birth to a nongovernmental organization that is active in the field of cooperation for development and in the area of peacemaking.

If one were to meet a member of the community somewhere around the world, what would one find? One would find him or her working with the poor of Rome, Genoa or Naples; one would meet him or her around the port of Antwerp in Belgium or active in the shanty towns of Boca, Buenos Aires, or with the children in the schools for peace in El Salvador, the Ivory Coast, and Mozambique. San Egidio tries to be what Pope John XXIII once called "The Church of all and particularly of the poor."

In more recent years the community has dedicated more and more of its time to the work for peace. This gained a new impetus from the success of the Mozambique peace effort, which ended sixteen years of terrible civil war. Some people who have seen San Egidio working with the poor, on hearing of the work for peace, began to wonder whether the community was abandoning its commitment to the poor to dedicate itself to informal diplomacy in the service of peace. This is simply not true.

The reality is in fact quite different. It is the community's fidelity to the poor and its attempt to live this in a commitment of friendship without borders that has led it to take up the sufferings of entire peoples who are poor. The community has come to understand that there is a poverty which is the mother of all poverties—it is the absence of peace. It is to have war as the one desperate companion of one's life.

After 1989 this desperate companion took on a crazy ethnic overtone, as we well know, in Rwanda and the former Yugoslavia. In this work for peace, San Egidio has gathered together people, friends of the poor and friends of peace, in the common effort, without any limits, of a radical fidelity to Gospel "without gloss," as St. Francis called it.

I see this relationship between San Egidio and the poor—indeed the relationship between every Christian and the poor—as fundamental to being Christian. I think of Matthew 25, which tells the story of the Last Judgment when the king will ask if we have given drink and food to the least of his brothers. And I wish to underline the fact that the word "brother" is used for the one who is poor, independent of his moral condition, only for the fact that he is poor. Moreover, the word "brother" is used in the Gospels for the disciples, for the members of the community, to identify the community itself.

In our eyes, the alliance, the friendship with the poor is then not just something more, a desirable sense of charity which the Christian should tend to have. On the contrary, we see it as a constituent element of being Christian. Moreover, we see the poor as not simply an important problem outside the Church; rather they are the decisive crossroads within every community and for the conscience of every Christian. I shall return to that point again before I conclude.

Today San Egidio is a church association which has lived this alliance with the poor for more than twenty years, linking its civil commitment and solidarity to prayer—the evening prayer in the little Church of San Egidio in Trastevere and in other places in Rome and outside Rome, and also linking it to personal prayer. For us, this has been the most effective way to avoid "spiritual flights" or the merely social and political reductions of one's being Christian. It has been the most effective way to remind each one of us, in the words of the Gospel, that when we have done all that is asked of us we are but "useless servants."

On returning home in the evening after perhaps a day of friendship and concrete struggle with the immigrants, seeking a more human horizon of life and a less-frightened and xenophobic society, one finds that the community evening prayer is the way to lay the table for another person—for the Lord Jesus, and not just for ourselves.

This evening prayer has over the years impacted profoundly the lives of very many people. It has been the great salvation from the temptation of ideology at the time of the great triumph of the ideological clash. It is today the great salvation from the temptation of antagonism or from the despising glance at a world which seems to have left little space for pity or solidarity.

The Community of San Egidio is today an attempt not to avoid the responsibilities of a life well rooted in the affairs of everyday life, without particular protections, without walls and without enemies. The prophet Isaiah speaks of the resurrection of Jerusalem as "the city of open gates" (Isaiah 60). In Zechariah the city without walls is the fruit of the true Pentecost. Frequently too, the walls which others raise up have bricks that have come from our own furnaces. We have to interrogate ourselves seriously on this point.

Indeed, while the community wishes to remain faithful to its own specific character or intuition, to its own history, this does not mean that it wishes to raise walls. Certainly not. In this regard I have always been struck by how Pope John Paul II grasped the true, profound character of the San Egidio Community when he singled out two elements of our way of being Christian. First, he pointed to what he called *filoxenia*—the love for the one who is different and for the stranger.

Second, he spoke of our particular way of interpreting our being a Roman reality: "You, even when you are far from Rome, in another country, you are Roman." This is certainly not meant to be an imperialist, centralist, or Romanocentric vision of life and of religious experience. On the contrary, I would say that it is rather a sense of debt and an explicit bond with the one who is not Roman. It is the opposite of provincialism, without becoming a cosmopolitanism without roots. For us, it means to be Christian, to be Catholic, to be open to the universal and not to be a prisoner of one's own particular situation. It is also a way to (seek to) live without enemies, without having to raise walls at a time when this is a strong temptation for everyone in the Western and advanced societies and at a time when every church reality too is tempted to live by identifying the enemies.

The community seeks to live without enemies and without scapegoats at a time when the temptation of the fortress nation and the church refuge is strong. We have come to understand that in this logic the enemies can be the foreigners, the gypsies. Indeed, they can be any-body or everybody. They can be invented enemies, because the presence of the enemy fills the vacuum of one's own identify and seems to free one from the burden of taking responsibility for living.

This *filoxenia*—this love for the stranger, for other peoples and for the one who is far away—represents something that is profoundly intimate, deep within the life of the Church itself.

The life of the Church points one continually to these dimensions of bonds, above all with the peoples and the countries in the South of the world. The culture of solidarity is being considered more and more as an accessory, and yet we see it as ever more precious. The Christian Churches constitute an impressive body of concern, thought and solidarity with the South of the world, and that is very important.

Moreover, the community believes that *filoxenia*, which involves welcoming the stranger who is close to us, is one of the primary demands of our times. Living together with other people becomes a normal condition of social life; *filoxenia* can give all of us the taste for living together with the one who is close and the one who is far away.

From its own experience, the San Egidio Community has come to see *filoxenia* as profoundly and intimately linked with the work for peace, and also with ecumenism and interreligious dialogue.

The community is convinced that even in what seem to be our turbulent societies—but which in the final analysis are still rather peaceful and protected, lay Christians cannot but feel the challenge of the distant countries that are suffering from wars or conflicts. Faced with the dramatic images from these conflicts, we ask ourselves what can we do. Sometimes we come up with drastic solutions that put our consciences at rest, but too often these solutions are unreal and only add more war to the existing war.

We in the community have come to believe that if on the international level many people—even small populations—can make war, so too it should be possible for many people also to make peace. All of us can work for peace.

Our own experience with Mozambique has taught us that it is possible to work for peace and succeed. It is possible to work through channels of friendship and of disinterested help to create the spaces where it becomes possible to think of the so-called "impossible peace." The small ones of this earth are like San Egidio, armed only with credibility and without having any particular interests to defend except, of course, peace. It is possible for such to build up the synergy for negotiations among the interested parties and the countries that are friendly to them.

Such work for peace, in our experience, is not something that often hits the front pages of the papers. Indeed, as I recall the Mozambique peace process, I remember that it hardly ever reached the front page of the papers until right at the end.

In my view, this work for peace is a particular challenge today, especially after the fall of the Berlin Wall in 1989, which also opened the road to so many conflicts around the globe. (N.B.: There are thirty-six major conflicts in the world today, each with more than a thousand deaths per year as a result of the conflict; over 80 percent of the victims of these wars are unarmed civilians, and 80 percent of these are women and children).

Right now the San Egidio Community is making an effort to prevent genocide taking place in Burundi, as happened not so long ago in Rwanda. And after a strong and discreet effort of peace, the process of peace brokering in Guatemala was unlocked in Rome, at San Egidio headquarters, and there is now a concrete possibility that 1996 can mean peace in Guatemala after thirty-four years of civil war.

The community has been working too in small ways over recent years to give peace a chance in the Sudan. And it has worked hard recently for peace in Algeria and has succeeded bringing together—in November 1994 and January 1995—the leaders of the main opposition parties to try to start up the peace process in a situation that seemed impossible. It is seeking to promote a political, not a military solution; it is working to prevent the annihilation of a people and the adversaries in a civil war which is above all else a war against civilians. The entire population seems to be held hostage in the cross fire of violence, and the elimination of members of religious orders and journalists seems something that pays dividends. We have pushed for the opening of negotiations between all parties, including the Islamic movement. The opposition leaders have now agreed on a common platform for peace on a democratic basis respecting the different elements in Algerian society.

In the atmosphere of Vatican II, Paul VI's *Ecclesiam suam* became like the Magna Carta of dialogue. This encyclical and John XXIII's pastoral and diplomatic "method" of searching for what unites and leaving aside what divides people are in some way at the source of these peace efforts. This pastoral and diplomatic method, evangelically inspired, brought us to the discovery of the possibility of transforming guerilla men into political men.

Yes, it is our conviction that each one of us can and should work more for peace. Indeed all of us have this one talent to spend, since we are not living in a situation of war or of insecurity for our lives. At the very least, we can support those who are working for peace.

San Egidio is something which does not belong only to San Egidio. "Your existence is a source of joy for us," said the Dominican Master

Father Timothy Radcliffe at the Mass for the twenty-seventh anniversary of the community last May. Speaking for the superiors of the Jesuits, Franciscans, White Fathers, and women religious of the Sacred Heart of Jesus, he assured them that San Egidio is "one of the contemporary forms of that evangelical dream that guided Dominic, Francis, Ignatius, and many other disciples to found new communities in this service of the Gospel."

In the same Thanksgiving Mass, Carlo Maria Martini, the cardinal-archbishop of Milan, said:

> I can remember, for instance, in the early '70s, walking one afternoon through the streets of Trastevere and thinking to myself about the division immediately after the Council between those who favored commitment to the poor and to the transformation of society, and those who put all the emphasis on spirituality and prayer; I said to myself there must be a way of reconciling these two approaches, a way of bringing together in one's life a sense of the primacy of God, of the word, of prayer and an effective charity shown in love for the poor, in presence to the poor and the most abandoned. . . .
>
> Some months later, it happened to be one of the first anniversaries of the community of San Egidio, through another chance encounter I met some of the community, and they told me about the community, indeed, better still, they invited me to come and see. Thus I began to understand and appreciate this living synthesis of the primacy of God, of prayer, of hearing the word, and, together with others, dedicating oneself in a real and effective way to the poor, and to studying the problems of society attentively and with discernment. . . .
>
> It is important that the original inspiration remain always clear, always alive, luminous before our eyes. Certainly the community of San Egidio has grown from its first beginning, has lived through many events, many occurrences, has expanded in its charity, in its attentiveness to the poor, to the needs of society. However, it has expanded not only in its original work—which was extensive even from the beginning—but in its other achievements. I think of all the ecumenical dialogue which has been carried on in big conventions of people of different religious beliefs. I think, too, of all the work which has been done for peace, bringing peace and the promise of peace to different continents.

To live without walls is important in today's world. But we realize that for a community, a church association or a particular Church to live without walls also means that it must live without walls with respect to other associations and communities. That is certainly the case. It also means to live without walls between the other Churches. Here the whole discussion about ecumenism enters in. So too does the whole subject of interreligious dialogue: Here again we are faced today with the great question of acceptance. I am thinking, for example, of our relations as Christians to Islam, to Judaism, to the other great religions of the world and the questions they pose for us.

Here I could speak at length about this whole commitment to dialogue that Pope John Paul II has called for. He singled it out as an important part of the Christian life and not just as an accessory element. The San Egidio Community took up seriously his invitation after the historic World Day of Prayer for Peace in Assisi, October 1986.

Since then the community has sought to carry forward the Assisi experience. Thus, the strong force of energy released then and rooted only in prayer—as the representatives of different religions prayed alongside each other in Assisi—this strong force has passed from Assisi to Rome, then to Warsaw for the fiftieth anniversary of the outbreak of World War II. It then went back to the Mediterranean coasts and from there to Brussels, hosted by Cardinal Danneels, and then to Milan, where Cardinal Martini was the host. From there last August it moved to Jerusalem for the historic first meeting of Jews, Muslims, and Christians in the Old City of Jerusalem to discuss the destiny of the Holy City, which now seems to be under dark clouds again. Finally, in October the meeting was held in Florence.

In our view, the interreligious dialogue is not only a challenge for the present generation of Christians, it will remain so also for some future generations. This is so because of the changing nature of the conflicts in our world and because today, after the collapse of the East-West wall, some are even considering seriously the building up of other walls such as between North and South.

The South of the world means Islam, mainly, while the North includes Western Europe, lay and Christian. We cannot share such thinking. Indeed, we believe that at this level the dialogue should be carried forward by concrete communities, by concrete worlds, through friendship, faithfulness, and culture. Because there is no friendship if there is no culture. If there is not much culture, one cannot understand the other; moreover, there is no culture without feeling and friendship.

We must avoid being at peace with a vision by which we look on the East as Slav and a little fanatical, and look upon the South as a wholly fundamentalist and integralist Islam. We need first of all to be able to distinguish so that we can unite and above all understand. We need also to begin to understand the different expressions and nuances so that we can talk and dialogue.

It is in this way that the Church can become what Pope John XXIII called "the village fountain." We are speaking of the global village, but also of the city or the country in which we are living. But the Church is not the whole village, it is not everything; but it can become a place where the people of the village can stop by for clean water, for water that comes from afar and brings with it tastes, echoes, tensions and passions of distant worlds.

The village fountain is perhaps, as in some Byzantine places, the holy fountain where one can buy images of the mother of God and where all come, all the citizens, the sick, the rich and poor alike, pilgrims and traders, to be cured of their diseases, of their closures and their egoisms. Today the Church, every community, can serve as a city without walls. It can do so in the measure in which it accepts knocking down and not justifying its own walls but, on the contrary, in the measure in which it accepts spending itself to open bridges. We, in the Community of San Egidio, like to try to be in harmony with this village fountain, and we are content to be able to spend ourselves for this end.

9 The Cost of Charism

■ *James W. Douglass*

(The facts in this essay are accurate as of June, 1996)

Although I was in Rome during Vatican II, I never met Cardinal Suenens, but I have met him in the Spirit moving through all of the other authors in this volume.

In *A New Pentecost?* Cardinal Suenens wrote:

> Faith teaches us that suffering is the seed of life. It is perfectly normal, then, that the sufferings of the Church at this moment should give rise to great hope: no day was ever so pregnant with hope for the future as was Good Friday. Pascal was not afraid to write: "It is a happy time for the Church when she is sustained by nothing other than God." This same thought is taken up by Father Caffarel when he says: "The hour of suffering is the hour of God. The situation is hopeless; this, then is the hour for hoping. . . . When we have reasons for hoping then we rely on those reasons." He tell us we should rely "not on reasons, but on a promise—a promise given by God. . . . We must admit that we are lost, surrender ourselves as lost, and praise the Lord who saves us."[1]

Cardinal Suenens knew the Spirit of Jesus can transform us beyond belief . . . at the cross. That Spirit-given hope in inconceivable miracles at the darkest moments of our lives, at the cross, is the background for this essay.

The subject is the cost of charism, especially the charism of prophesying in action the nonviolent kingdom of God.

[1] Leon Joseph Cardinal Suenens, *A New Pentecost?* trans. Francis Martin (New York: Seabury Press, 1975) xi.

The great Jewish scholar Yeshayahu Leibowitz wrote:

> A prophet foretells but what ought to take place. The prophet presents a
> future which must be striven for, and which one must attempt to bring to
> fruition, without any guarantee that this will actually be realized . . .
> Every prophecy deserves to happen—and it depends on [humankind]
> whether those things which deserve to happen will or will not happen.[2]

These words apply to Jesus' prophecy of the nonviolent reign of God.
The keys to understanding Jesus' prophecy are to recognize, first, that
it is contingent, not predetermined, and to recognize, secondly, that it is
our responsibility to pray and strive for its fulfillment on earth. "Thy
kingdom come, thy will be done *on earth* as it is in heaven."

Have you ever lived in a country where the people's loyalty to the
spirit of that country was measured by love, especially love of enemies? How might we live as if we were already in such a country of the
Spirit, such a world of the Spirit, as if it were no farther away than our
hands?

Jesus tells us, "I say to you that listen, Love your enemies, do good to
those who hate you, bless those who curse you, pray for those who
abuse you" (Luke 6:27-28).

What is the cost of prophesying by our actions a nonviolent world of
the Spirit, a world where the guiding Spirit of conflict becomes love of
enemies?

Again he tells us, and in fact leads the way for us: "If any want to become my followers, let them deny themselves and take up their cross
daily and follow me. For those who want to save their life will lose it,
and those who lose their life for my sake will save it" (Luke 9:23-24).

Jesus' prophesy of love means the nonviolent transformation of the
world. It is a prophecy that each of us makes in words each time we say
the Lord's Prayer. But it is a prophecy whose future will be done on
earth only if we begin to allow God's fire of enemy love to blow
through us as a community. This is what Cardinal Suenens understood
so profoundly—the miracle of the Holy Spirit through the cross. The
charism of prophesying with our actions what we say in the Lord's
Prayer bears with it a cost. The Spirit of Jesus gives simultaneously
prophecy, rejection, and death. When Martin Luther King prophesied
nonviolence or nonexistence, and lived out that contingent prophecy
by resisting the Vietnam War and mounting the Poor People's Campaign, he was rejected and killed. If prophets are consistent in pro-

---

[2] Yeshayahu Leibowitz, *Notes and Remarks on the Weekly Parashah,* trans. Shmuel
Himelstein (Brooklyn, New York: Chemed Books, 1990) 186–87.

claiming and living nonviolence as the will of God, their listeners give them death, which is then God's gift as well.

But when God gave Jesus death, the disciples wanted nothing to do with the cost of his living prophecy. His execution by the state shocked and terrorized his followers, just as it was meant to. His resurrection also shocked them. But it did not revive them. They were still so cross-shocked, so numbed by death that they could barely believe the life before their eyes.

Pentecost is *the disciples'* resurrection, a resurrection through fire.

This Suenens Symposium is about that fire, so I've been thinking about fire. A sudden, roaring fire blowing through one's house or one's very being is as terrifying as a public execution. Such a fire threatens to end life and burn everyone up. But the fire of Pentecost began life and brought everyone together. In fact the fire of Pentecost brought the different peoples of Jerusalem together—a miracle in any age. It was the fire of God's all-inclusive Love that burned through the conflicting languages that day, and can do the same in our day. The fire of God's love was the life that exploded right out of death itself—Jesus' death—and gave the apostles life. The death we have been numbed by has in it a living fire of Total Love that is our resurrection.

Do we believe that? Or, more to the point, do *I* believe that?

In a sense the only sin for a Christian is *not* to believe in that Resurrection by Fire.

I am guilty of that sin.

When I returned from Iraq during Easter week 1996, just before our plane touched down at JFK Airport I became ill. For the next three weeks, I had stomach cramps, diarrhea, and a profound lack of energy that kept me in bed at my home in Birmingham, Alabama. I mention this because when I finally saw a doctor my symptoms suddenly disappeared without treatment. I think I was spiritually ill from the suffering and dying children I saw everywhere in Iraq. I had seen an executioner's cross. I saw an empire today executing an entire generation. I was overcome by death. I think I was spiritually ill from not believing deeply enough in those children's resurrection, from not really believing in the resurrection of Jesus and of all of us.

The Food and Agriculture Organization has estimated that over six hundred thousand children have died so far from the United Nations sanctions against Iraq. Those sanctions are five and a half years old. They began before the Persian Gulf War. In 1996, the sanctions were modified by a United Nations agreement that will finally permit Iraq to sell a portion of its oil on the world market, part of which will go toward war reparations to Kuwait and Saudi Arabia and part of it toward food and medicine to suffering Iraqis. But the overall sanctions will remain in effect. That United Nations agreement will save thousands of Iraqi lives. But the limited help it will give Iraq within the continuing sanctions will fall far short of twenty million people's needs. United States policy makers hope that the United Nations agreement will institutionalize the sanctions by reducing the number of dying Iraqi children to a less visible, more tolerable level. The sanctions are killing, and will continue to kill, not their target, Sadaam Hussein, but the innocent people, mainly children, who are caught between the United States of America and their own government.

On my Holy Week trip to Iraq, I struggled with despair from seeing again, as I have on previous trips to Iraq, countless malnourished, ill children dying in hospitals without medicines or medical technology because of the sanctions. I don't like to think I despaired. But after I returned from Iraq somewhere deep inside me, in a place deeper than my thoughts, for a while, faith shut down. My body put me to bed, telling me what I wasn't telling myself, that faith was on hold.

But death itself has within it a living fire of Love that is our resurrection.

Our only sin is not to believe in that Resurrection by Fire.

I'm alive again now. The strange part about my resurrection is that I'm alive again also because of what I saw in Iraq. I died because of the death I saw in Iraq, and I was raised finally because of the life I saw in Iraq, a fire of Love which burned up the death in me.

I went to Iraq as a member of a little group called Voices in the Wilderness. In January a few more than one hundred Americans signed a statement saying that we considered sanctions that kill hundreds of thousands of children to be immoral. We said we would openly violate those sanctions by collecting medicines and taking them to Iraq. The Treasury Department then sent us a letter saying we were liable to twelve years in prison and a million dollar fine if we did what we said we were going to do. That is what a few of us did do during Holy Week.

Sr. Anne Montgomery, Sr. Eileen Storey, and I went first to Amman, Jordan. From there, loaded with suitcases and boxes stuffed with thousands of dollars worth of medicines, we took an overnight bus across the desert to Baghdad. When we reached the border of Iraq, the government inspector did not just seize our medicines for his government's own distribution. He said we could deliver our medicines as we wished. In Baghdad we were joined a day later by three more members of our group, Kathy Kelly, Fr. Bob Bossie, and John Landgraf. They had piles of mail bags filled with more medicines. We took much of the medicine directly to the poorest children's hospital in Baghdad, Qadissiya Hospital, in the area known as Sadaam City. Two million Iraqis live in Sadaam City. One million of them are children—all served by Qadissiya Hospital.

I am afraid that most of the children we saw in Qadissiya Hospital are now dead. These were children who were, first, malnourished because of the sanctions. They had picked up illnesses derived partly from a contaminated water system that was destroyed in the Gulf War and has never been adequately repaired because of the economic embargo. Like thousands before them they had then come to a hospital with virtually no medicines or medical technology because of the sanctions. They have died or are dying. An entire generation of Iraq is perishing.

But let me tell you the other side of my experience of Iraq, life that came from the midst of death.

It is represented by Dr. Mahir Jallo, the inspiring director of Al Hamdahya General Hospital at Qarah Qosh. Dr. Mahir told us:

> We have a severe shortage of vaccines and critical drugs. Only a few emergency operations can be performed—two or three a week. There can be no elective surgery until better days. The water supply comes and goes daily. The purification machines fail, and there are no spare parts. Communicable diseases spread. Typhoid, para-typhoid, and cholera are increasing, and other diseases that were very limited before, such as tuberculosis.

Yet Dr. Mahir was smiling as he told of beginning a large program at his hospital to encourage breast-feeding. He hoped U.S. friends would provide educational materials to help with the program: "We must always be hopeful," he said, "and give all we can from our lives to pass through these hard times. Always the light will be on the way."

I asked Dr. Mahir when was the last time an American doctor had visited his hospital. He said quietly, "I have never had an American doctor visit my hospital."

Besides visiting hospitals, Anne Montgomery, Eileen Storey, and I experienced the grace of worshiping in Iraq during Holy Week. In the all-Christian village of Qarah Qosh near Mosul, we joined thousands of desperately poor Iraqis trying to squeeze into the Syrian-rite Church of the Virgin Mary. Others crowded the windows or peered over one another at the doors. On the steps of the altar children sat watching and listening, as the priest glided among them. Then on both Holy Thursday and Good Friday, for three to four hours the people chanted and sang the words of the Gospel back and forth across the packed church, in both Syrian and their native Aramaic. Jesus was there as I had never seen him, from his very language to the pure faces of his people—a people that flowed out from that church beyond counting.

The people of Iraq may be dying, but there is a flame of life that burns within them. It is the flames of faith, the faith of Muslims and Christians in the living God, a faith that lives on and deepens no matter what happens to them at the hands of political leaders.

I think of my Christian friend Jamil, a retired geophysicist living with his wife Adeeba, and two sons in Baghdad. Before the sanctions, Jamil's and Adeeba's government pensions were worth $1,250 a month tax-free. Today they are worth $10 a month. As a result, Jamil and Adeeba sell their furniture and family possessions to sustain themselves.

Jamil told me a Muslim story to illustrate how he maintained hope as a Christian. It seems that Moses was the only person who talked with God. Moses asked God if he could be God's agent, giving everyone his or her needs, for just one day. God agreed. At the end of the day Moses asked, "How did I do?" God said, "You forgot that little urchin at the bottom of the sea."

"The point," Jamil said, "is that God remembers everyone, even the smallest urchin in the sea."

"We leave it to God," Adeeba added, "God will never forget us. God will never forget his servants."

"If I am a true Christian," Jamil said, "I must love my enemy. I must forgive my enemy. And I must do everything I can for my enemy. This is my attitude in life. What I pray each day is, give us this day our daily bread. And I pray, forgive me my sins as I forgive others' sins against me. This is all I can do."

I want to say that this Iraqi faith does not fit our preconceptions about faith, any more than the killing of children fits the righteousness of our politics toward Iraq. While I was in Qarah Qosh, I asked one of the local Iraqi Dominican sisters if Sadaam Hussein had ever visited there. She said, yes, but only once. She added: "He doesn't have to come here. He knows that he has our support."

I was told repeatedly by Iraqi Christians that they have more freedom to worship there than they would have in any other Middle Eastern country. The situation in Iraq is not simple. There is religious freedom, at the same time as there is political repression. Sadaam Hussein's government is building churches and monasteries for Christians and mosques for Muslims. Iraqi Christians compare the religious freedom they enjoy to the repression of Christians by our Gulf War allies, Saudi Arabia and Kuwait.

The faith of Jamil and Adeeba, the faith I witnessed in Qarah Qosh, is a faith that has overcome my sense of death from the children I saw dying in the hospitals. I believe the hundreds of thousands of innocents who are already gone are alive in God, and I believe their lives can raise us to life so that we can stop an evil policy. A policy that kills masses of innocent people in order to get at one man is evil. It is also counterproductive. It has in fact strengthened the power of that man. Maybe the Iraqi children who have died to us but who live in God can teach us how to really believe in God. God is present or absent in the means we choose. Maybe the children's experience of the sanctions can teach us that the means is the end in the process of becoming. Our chosen means, killing them, is *not* the way to change the government over them in a benevolent direction. Believe me, their parents do not agree with such a means. We might not believe in it either if it were our children being sacrificed to an economic embargo around the United States that was designed to change the leaders and the policies of our government. What we sow in Iraq today is what we shall reap in Iraq and the world tomorrow, someone and something far worse than Sadaam Hussein.

A United States diplomat commented on the recent United Nations agreement with Iraq by saying, "The United States intends to hold Iraq's feet to the fire to assure that this agreement is not violated."

The people of Iraq have had their feet held to the fire for five and a half years, but beneath that fire of death, there is a living fire of Love that is our resurrection, too.

I believe that living fire of Love burns just as deeply here in the United States, when we are willing to take on suffering in resistance to the killing of the innocent.

Our only sin is not to believe in that Resurrection by Fire.

I believe there is a scene in the Gospels prior to the crucifixion which can help us to interpret further the meaning of our Resurrection by Fire. It is Jesus' transfiguration.

A transfiguration is a change in form, a transformation. A transfiguration can be a positive change in form, as when a caterpillar becomes a butterfly, or it can be a negative change in form, as when a city is destroyed by an atomic bomb and becomes a nuclear wasteland. A transfiguration can also be an astounding change in form, as when the cross of an executed Jew becomes a way of life for his followers.

Consider the transfiguration scene in Luke's Gospel. We are told that the two great leaders on the mountain talking with Jesus, Moses and Elijah, "spoke of his *exodus*, which he was about to fulfill in Jerusalem." Luke has make the unusual choice of the Greek word *exodus* for Jesus' death because that death would accomplish a new exodus, recalling that of Moses and his people. Jesus' new exodus would lead all of God's people out of a still greater bondage than that of Egypt, a human bondage to violence. At Jesus' cross God absorbs an empire's means of execution without retaliation, thus revealing through Jesus the nature of a nonviolent cross—suffering love and forgiveness of enemies: "Father, forgive them for they know not what they do."

The transfiguration of Jesus on the mountain is a symbolic anticipation of his transfiguration on the cross, and the transfiguration of violence itself by a divinely given nonviolence. Jesus' prayer on the mountain is his acceptance of the cross that he knows is coming. His transfiguration is God's blessing on the one who has accepted the way of the cross, his new exodus.

Just as the cross of an executed Jew was transfigured, so were the atomic bombs at Hiroshima and Nagasaki transfigured.

We sometimes fail to realize the miracles God has accomplished for us through history. I believe it is a miracle that the atomic bombings of Hiroshima and Nagasaki did not result in a hatred of Americans, and a resentment similar in consequences to the resentment Germans felt after World War I which led to the rise of Hitler. Why did the atomic bombings of Hiroshima and Nagasaki *not* lead to a world-destructive hatred and resentment? How were the people of Hiroshima and Nagasaki transfigured in their death as Jesus was in his?

I believe the transfiguration of our nuclear history happened especially through the charism of forgiveness as it was lived out by a Catholic doctor at Nagasaki, Takashi Nagai, and his wife Midori Nagai.

Dr. Takashi Nagai was dean of the radiology department at the University of Nagasaki on August 9, 1945. Although severely wounded from the A-bomb, Dr. Nagai extricated himself from the ruins of his medical school, organized a band of surviving doctors, students, and nurses, and led them in serving the sick and dying for three days until Nagai himself collapsed.

Dr. Nagai then recovered sufficiently to make his way to his own home. He found it burned to the ground. He also found the corpse of his beloved wife Midori, with a rosary clutched in her hand. Just as Jesus on the mountain had anticipated his execution on the cross, so had Midori in her home at Nagasaki anticipated her death from the atomic bomb. After the A-bomb attack on Hiroshima, Midori felt rightly that Nagasaki would be next. She had only just managed to evacuate their two children to the country before returning to the Nagai home and her own death. Like many of the residents of the Urakami district of Nagasaki, the Nagais were devout Catholics.

The A-bomb at Nagasaki had in fact fallen almost directly on the Urakami Cathedral, dedicated to the Virgin Mary. The cathedral was both the center of Japanese Catholicism and the symbol of a centuries-old history of martyrdom. That the worst impact of the A-bomb had been absorbed by the cathedral and by a Catholic community surrounding it that was sustained by its own tradition of martyrdom, Takashi Nagai took as providential.

On November 23, 1945, an open-air Mass was held for the dead of Nagasaki beside the shattered Urakami Cathedral. The bishop asked Dr. Nagai to speak. What Nagai said that day to "bandaged, limping, burn-disfigured, and demoralized Catholics" is shocking:

> Our church of Nagasaki kept the faith during four hundred years of persecution when religion was proscribed and the blood of martyrs flowed freely. During the war this same church never ceased to pray day and night for a lasting peace. Was it not, then, the one unblemished lamb that had to be offered on the altar of God . . .?
>
> How noble, how splendid was that holocaust of August 9, when flames soared up from the cathedral, dispelling the darkness of war and bringing the light of peace! In the very depth of our grief we reverently saw here something beautiful, something pure, something sublime. Eight thousand people, together with their priests, burning with pure smoke, entered into eternal life. All without exception were good people whom we deeply mourn.
>
> How happy are those people who left this world without knowing the defeat of their country! How happy are the pure lambs who rest in the bosom of God. Compared with them how miserable is the fate of us who have survived! Japan is conquered. Urakami is totally destroyed. A waste of ash and rubble lies before our eyes. We have no houses, no food, no clothes. Our fields are devastated. Only a remnant has survived. In the midst of the ruins we stand in groups of two or three looking blankly at the sky.

Nagai concluded his talk:

> "Blessed are those that mourn for they shall be comforted." We must walk this way of expiation faithfully and sincerely. And as we walk in hunger and thirst, ridiculed, penalized, scourged, pouring with sweat and covered with blood, let us remember how Jesus Christ carried his cross to the hill of Calvary. He will give us courage. "The Lord has given; the Lord has taken away. Blessed be the name of the Lord."
>
> Let us give thanks that Nagasaki was chosen for the sacrifice. Let us give thanks that through this sacrifice peace was given to the world and freedom of religion to Japan.
>
> May the souls of the faithful departed, through the mercy of God, rest in peace. Amen.[3]

---

[3] Takashi Nagai, *The Bells of Nagasaki,* trans. William Johnston (New York: Kodansha International, 1984) 108–9.

I agree with Takashi Nagai's critics that the evil for which we as humans are responsible cannot be attributed to the will and grace of God. Yet as uncritical as Nagai's thinking is in this respect, his focus on the redemptive nature of suffering is as profoundly Gandhian as it is Christian. Nagai's emphasis on redemptive suffering offers a corrective shock to our pragmatically oriented Western nonviolence.

Until his death in 1951, Takashi Nagai lived in a little hut in Nagasaki, which he called *Nyokodo,* "love your neighbor as yourself." There he prayed, received visitors, and wrote twenty books, beginning with his best-selling *The Bells of Nagasaki.* One of his best-loved books contained his letters to his children, whom he knew would soon become A-bomb orphans. In each of his books the overpowering theme is God's love for us, and our love for one another, as the basis of peace. Like Gandhi, to whom he was often compared, Nagai identified the Sermon on the Mount as the practical charter for world peace.

Besides being a scientist, poet, and father, Nagai was a master of calligraphy and painting. An ink painting he did of Midori suggests the transfiguration of Nagasaki, which his and her charism of forgiveness have accomplished in history for you and me. In the painting, Midori, like Mary, is on a cloud being assumed into heaven. She is dressed in a wartime blouse she was wearing when the A-bomb exploded over Nagasaki. And the cloud on which Midori is standing is itself a mushroom cloud.

Takashi Nagai wrote that he discovered the depths of God's friendship by walking with God through Nagasaki's nuclear wasteland. It was Takashi Nagai's walk of forgiveness that transfigured the atomic bomb, just as it was Jesus' prayer on the cross, "Father, forgive them for they know not what they do," that transfigured a Roman means of execution into a way of life for us all, a resurrection from violence.

Our only sin is not to believe in that Resurrection by Fire.

10 | Some Reflections on Leon-Joseph Cardinal Suenens

■ *Bishop Kenneth B. Untener*

Along with being a great thinker and a great theologian, Cardinal Suenens was someone who took delight in the fortuitous confluence of little things. For example, it meant a lot to him that he was born on the feast of the maternity of Mary. And when, as his mother was being buried and her body lowered in the grave, the Angelus bell of the nearby church rang at that moment; it rang late. And Cardinal Suenens always felt that it was the hand of God, arranging things so that the bells would ring as his mother was being lowered into the grave. What he'd make of having this conference in the shadow of the Rock N' Roll Hall of Fame, I don't know, but those are the kinds of things in which he took delight. And so, for him, it would not be a mere coincidence that this particular gospel lands on this event, with its strong verbs of a God going outward: love, gave, send, save. That was the kind of God that Cardinal Suenens so believed in, and he, the extroverted, outgoing person, relished that.

Nor would it be a mere coincidence for him that Trinity Sunday lands in the middle of this event. Cardinal Suenens was a man of the Trinity. Now, you might think perhaps better put, a man of the Spirit, but it is our belief that since the birth, death, resurrection, and ascension of Jesus, you cannot have one without the other. And it is the Spirit that most of all tunes us in to the fullness of this great mystery that is God, who is Trinity. In our thoughts we can isolate the Father, more likely isolate the son, but when we think of the Spirit we tend to let the whole reality of God flood upon us. Because he was a man who loved the Spirit, Cardinal Suenens was a man of the Trinity; because he was someone who so loved the Spirit, Cardinal Suenens was one who had a sense of the height and the breadth and the depth of the great mystery that is God.

In John's Gospel, when Jesus speaks of the depth of the mysteries of God, people are always missing it. Nicodemus in this passage misses it. The Samaritan woman at the well misses it. Pilate misses it. The disciples miss it over and over. Cardinal Suenens did not miss it. It was most of all his sense of the expansiveness of the mystery of a God beyond comprehension that gave him his wonder and awe as he faced the Church and faced the world. Listen to these four quotations that characterize some of what I am talking about:

I. He said: "We must look at the world of the twenty-first century, which is already dawning, with new eyes, with the eyes of Christ." Because of his awareness of the wideness of God, Cardinal Suenens was never afraid of the future. Cardinal Suenens never looked at the future with trepidation; for him, it was simply the unfolding of a wider horizon which was always necessary.

II. He said: "In these times we must all behave as non-infallible seekers." It was that attitude that helped him be so comfortable with ecumenism, because we were always, always inadequate in our understanding, and there is a wideness to God which includes more than we understood.

III. He said: "We must give the Holy Spirit a chance to be both the faithful one, par excellence, and the revolutionary one, whose breath is new life." He believed in that old saying—The Church gives birth to the Church every day, always being born to a fuller appreciation of its mystery. He was never afraid of reform.

IV. And finally, he said after the Council: "It is a new springtime for the Church, but it is a late February, early March springtime. We are still having heavy showers and early morning frosts, but we are moving along." He had a realistic optimism, and it characterized his approach to the Church and his approach to the world, for both were God's.

Did you ever think of how the words to songs don't have the same depth of meaning when they are spoken without music? For example, if someone just spoke "Silent night, holy night, all is calm, all is bright," it doesn't do it. The music brings out the richness of *silent, holy*. Or to recite, *"Edelweiss, Edelweiss,* every morning you greet me, small and white, clean and bright, you look happy to meet me," doesn't do it either. The Spirit could be compared to the music that makes the things of our faith come alive with the depth and the meaning that comes from the great mystery that is God.

It is the music of the Spirit that makes the doctrine of the Trinity more than a doctrine. It is the music of the Spirit that speaks of the Risen Jesus, not a retired Jesus who is simply watching his fixed and finished Church play out its history. It is the Spirit, it is the music of the Spirit, that makes our traditions more than dead memories. It is the music of the Spirit that makes our teachings come alive. Sometimes we've got the right words but we forget the music. And sometimes, sometimes, the Spirit gives us the music when we don't have the words. Sometimes we have a sense that this is in tune with what God wants of us, but the words are not in our tradition, and we must tune in, carefully, together, to the music of the Spirit.

Cardinal Suenens was who he was because of the music of the Spirit in him, and because of that he was music to our ears. He would not find it a coincidence that we shall sing at the end of this celebration (singing), "Let us bring the gifts that differ, and in splendid varied ways, sing a new Church into being one in faith and love and praise." I never knew when I decided to use the analogy of music that it would all fit together in that fortuitous confluence in which Cardinal Suenens takes such delight. Let us "sing a new church into being, one in faith and love and praise."

11 The Charism of Cardinal Suenens

■ *Archbishop William J. Levada*

On May 7, 1996, *The New York Times* carried the following obituary: "Leo Joseph Suenens, whose public and behind-the-scenes leadership at the Second Vatican Council made him a major architect of 20th-century Catholicism, died yesterday in Brussels. He was 91. Active to his last day, the retired archbishop of Malines-Brussels and primate of Belgium was planning to attend a symposium in his honor at John Carroll University in Cleveland at the end of this month."

We are here in Cleveland. He is not. May our sadness at his absence, coupled with our joy at having known him—or of him, make this symposium in his honor a worthy tribute to this distinguished son of Belgium and of the Church. Cardinal Leo Joseph Suenens, at this evening prayer of the Church tonight we commend you to the mercy and love of the God whom you served so faithfully and so well. May this entire symposium, whose title "Retrieving Charisms for the Twenty-First Century" is surely the most "Suenens" of themes, be our abiding tribute to you *in memoriam.*

For me to stand before you this evening to give this keynote reflection on "The Charism of Cardinal Suenens" is truly a daunting task. In the first place, many of you will wonder why I am presuming to replace the advertised keynote speaker, Cardinal Godfried Danneels, Cardinal Suenens' successor as archbishop of Malines-Brussels. The blame must be placed squarely on Cardinal Suenens. Notice that I hasten to exonerate Cardinal Danneels from blame for his triple-bypass surgery. In his May 28 letter to me he wrote, "My health is improving steadily, but I don't yet fully resume my activities." Thanks be to God for his successful convalescence.

When Cardinal Danneels was advised that it would be unwise for him to attend this symposium so soon after his surgery, Cardinal Suenens suggested that I be asked to substitute for him. If I were in your place, I would surely be disappointed too, and I can assure you I am the first to say that I am no adequate replacement.

The program as originally conceived called for Cardinal Suenens himself to give a response to Cardinal Danneels' talk. That dialogue itself would be worth a trip to Cleveland. After accepting Dr. Donnelly's invitation to substitute for Cardinal Danneels, I wondered what I should say that might provide something for Suenens to respond to, but was tranquil in the thought of that kind man who would never embarrass his friend and indeed who had such wit as to find the makings of a silk purse even when presented with a sow's ear!

My friendship with Cardinal Suenens began as a working relationship, since he had been invited by Pope Paul VI to "accompany" the new Catholic charismatic renewal. As an official of the Congregation for the Doctrine of the Faith, I was one of those at the Holy See who had responsibility for liaison with the movement. As he "accompanied" the renewal, he invited me to accompany him—to Dublin, to Paray-le-Monial and Taizé in France, to Nice and Paris and Brussels, and especially at Rome: In his company I grew from admiration of him to know and like him.

Since becoming a bishop I have only been able to stop in to see him in Brussels too rarely and was planning just such a visit when the symposium provided a welcome opportunity to see him here in Cleveland, a visit we both indicated in our correspondence earlier this month we were looking forward to. "It will be a great pleasure to refresh our so good memories of the past," he wrote. Indeed, Eminence, it would have been!

Cardinal Suenens has written much in a style which is never harsh about people, but always frank. In his single line about me, in *The Hidden Hand of God*, he says of me, "He was very much on our wavelength and became our friend."[1]

To be on Cardinal Suenens' wavelength is no mean boast, as I am sure will be witnessed at this symposium. And while I know there are many, even at this conference, who were better friends and could serve his memory more eloquently, my only regret is that this invitation came late and in the midst of my first five busy months as archbishop of San Francisco, thus compounding my limited ability to do justice to the theme and to the man. But he above all was realistic in his expectations: After offering to provide me a copy of his "three books of 'memories,'

---

[1] Leo Jozef Suenens, *The Hidden Hand of God—The Life of Veronica O'Brien and Our Common Apostolate*, (Dublin: Veritas, 1994) 256.

including the last one about our King Baudouin," he remarked in his letter, "but of course you don't have to read all those pages! . . . And you don't have to give a eulogy with only [good] qualities!" No, it is true, that speech has already been given by Cardinal Danneels himself in his moving homily at Suenens' funeral in the Cathedral of St. Michael in Brussels on May 11.

In Spiritu Sancto

Where to begin in summing up this man, who was born in 1904 and died in 1996—a life which almost coincides with the twentieth century? After many false starts and prompted by our annual celebration of the feast of Pentecost this past Sunday, I have decided to take his episcopal motto *In Spiritu Sancto* as a kind of golden thread with which to weave together the varied and complex facets of the life and times of Cardinal Suenens.

The commentator on Suenens has a distinct advantage: In his autobiographical *Memories and Hopes*,[2] published in 1991, he has provided his reader with recollections about the principal events of his life. The other two books of "memories" are *The Hidden Hand of God—The Life of Veronica O'Brien and Our Common Apostolate*, published in 1993, and *Baudouin, King of the Belgians*,[3] published earlier this year. Not only do these three books of "memories" give evidence of a truly prodigious memory, with a special fondness for humanizing personal anecdotes; they also astonish me at the organization and completeness of his files, from which he was able to produce a lifetime of key documents! Both the style and the substance of his reflections in these books, as in others, highlight what is for me another "charism" worth commenting on: He displays a sense of confidence, both in himself and in the work of the Holy Spirit, which seems to me to offer a charism worth "retrieving" for the twenty-first century.

This quality is evident in his many books, for example, on the laity (*Theology of the Apostolate of the Legion of Mary*, 1953) and on religious women (*The Nun in the World*, a rather inept English title for *La Promotion Apostolique de la Religieuse*, 1962). Another book written to counteract the movement to substitute social action for evangelization, *The Gospel to Every Creature*, was described by then-Archbishop Montini of Milan, in his introduction to the Italian translation, as "courageous and optimistic."

---

[2] *Ibid.*, *Memories and Hopes* (Dublin: Veritas, 1992).

[3] *Ibid.*, *Baudouin, King of the Belgians—the Hidden Life* (Ertvedle, Belgium: FIAT Publications, 1996).

In Spiritu Sancto: The Holy Spirit was the ground of his confidence and optimism, and provided the common theme for his singular achievements not only as a diocesan bishop and primate of his country's episcopate but also in living service of the ecumenism and the collegiality which became such important themes of Vatican II. As a successor to Cardinal Mercier, whose Malines conversations were an early benchmark in Catholic-Anglican ecumenical relations, he was a dedicated and optimistic ecumenist. So on the fortieth anniversary of the Malines conversations, it was characteristic that he would introduce a favorite ecumenical saying into his homily during a visit to the archbishop of Canterbury, Michael Ramsey: "What is difficult, we can do right away; what is impossible will take a little longer."[4]

He was one of the major architects of Vatican II, for which Pope John invited the Catholic world to pray, "Renew your wonders in our time as for a new Pentecost." For Suenens, "the council was above all an event—a breath of the Holy Spirit, a breath of renewal."[5] And he was the indispensable guide and shepherd of the charismatic renewal is its early years and set it on a firm course as a movement in and for the renewal of the Church in the Holy Spirit.

In Spiritu Sancto: By temperament and conviction, Suenens lived his episcopal motto in a remarkably consistent way. For him the Holy Spirit was the soul of the Church, never a force for destruction, always a force for renewal and building up. It illustrates as well his abiding devotion to Our Lady, as this passage taken from his reflections on becoming the new archbishop of Malines-Brussels in 1962 shows:

> My motto "In the Holy Spirit and in Mary" acquired new meaning day by day. At the heart of the Creed is a profession of our belief that Jesus was born of the Holy Spirit and of Mary. This is not a matter of past history. We must extend this mystery into the church, through all time, and never dissociate the institutional church from the charismatic church—these are but two aspects of a single reality.[6]

Vatican II

One of the delightful aspects of preparing this symposium address was the opportunity it afforded me to review again the extraordinary time that Vatican II was in and for the Church. In his biography of Pope Paul VI, Peter Hebblethwaite writes that "toward the end of the second

---

[4] *Memories,* 208.
[5] *Ibid.,* 148.
[6] *Ibid.,* 59.

session [of the council] it was possible to believe (as certainly Ottaviani believed) that [Pope] Paul had fallen under the spell of Suenens. He was the star of the Council. His speeches on charisms, on the restoration of the diaconate and [on] the age of retirement [of bishops] had all proved extremely effective."[7]

How does one get to be a "star" of the Council? A look at the record reminds us how great events in history are not the outcome of determinate forces, but quite contingent upon persons and circumstances.

For one thing, Suenens' background and position favored his ability to make a significant contribution. He was fifty-eight when the Council began, was familiar with Rome and with Latin (the language of the Council) from his student days, spoke French, Dutch, and English fluently, and had been named both archbishop and cardinal within a year of the opening of the Council. Early in his priesthood he had been assigned to teach philosophy at the diocesan seminary in Malines and was vice rector of the University of Louvain during World War II, taking over as interim rector for over a year when the rector was imprisoned by the Germans.

In the university setting he came to know Msgr. Gérard Philips and several other theologians who would provide the theological expertise to undergird the *aggiornamento* recommended by Pope John XXIII. He had lengthy experience in administration of a major diocese as auxiliary bishop and vicar general since 1945 and as apostolic administrator after the death of his predecessor, Cardinal Van Roey. He was furthermore an internationally recognized author, whose stature as bishop was well known.

For another, he was clearly seen by Pope John as a person who could bring a necessary fresh perspective to the work of the Council, in order to ensure that it did not simply become a rubber stamp of the status quo which the Roman curia would likely seek to guarantee in the interest of institutional preservation. The elderly Pope John, chosen as an "interim" pope in 1958 to succeed Pius XII, announced—less than three months after his inauguration—the convocation of an ecumenical council. The reaction was general surprise, and in not a few quarters, genuine shock.

Suenens loved to recall the story Pope John told him of his own secretary Msgr. Capovilla's less-than-enthusiastic reaction to the proposal. The Pope said to him, "You are saying to yourself: The pope is too old for this sort of adventure. But Don Loris, you are far too cautious! When we believe that an inspiration comes to us from the Holy Spirit,

[7] Peter Hebblethwaite, *Paul VI—The First Modern Pope* (New York: Paulist, 1993) 365.

we must follow it: What happens after that is not our responsibility."[8] How it must have reminded him of a favorite memory of his own bishop when he was a seminarian. Cardinal Mercier told the young Suenens one of his favorite quotes from Bishop Pie of Poitiers: "When caution is everywhere, courage is nowhere to be found. Our ancestors were not so quiescent; we shall die of prudence yet, you'll see."[9]

Just weeks after appointing him archbishop, Pope John named him a cardinal, as Suenens recalls, "in order to make it possible for me to be involved in the preparatory work for the council as a member of the central preparatory commission."[10] Another anecdote serves to illustrate why Pope John needed to rely on non-curial cardinals like Suenens. When he asked the Pope during a meeting of the commission why he appointed the prefects of the Roman congregations to chair the Council's commissions, remarking that this "could only inhibit the council members in their work and in their discussions," the Pope laughed and said, "You are quite right, but I didn't have the courage [to do otherwise]."[11]

Suenens recalls how the interventions by Cardinals Lienart of France and Frings of Germany at the opening session of the Council set a new tone. Both objected to the lists of commission members prepared in advance by the curial cardinals and asked that the Council members themselves determine this membership. The standing ovation they received from the bishops made their proposal prevail. Suenens observed, "To a large extent, the future of the council was decided at that moment. John XXIII was very pleased."[12]

Not all were so pleased with Suenens, however. While secrecy prevailed at the Council (*pace* Xavier Rynne) and no doubt disagreements in philosophy and perspective remained gentlemanly (no beard-pulling at Vatican II, unlike Trent), Suenens was thought by some to be too progressive and too blunt. Although he could never verify it, Suenens tells the story himself about a superior general who reported to Pope John on the providential spread of the wonderful apostolic works of her community. Genuinely impressed, the Pope is supposed to have asked if there was anything he could do for her. No fan of Suenens' book *The Nun in the World*, she is reputed to have said, "Holy Father, you could give me the head of Cardinal Suenens on a silver platter!"[13]

---

[8] *Memories*, 65.

[9] *Ibid.*, 21.

[10] *Ibid.*, 59.

[11] *Ibid.*, 71.

[12] *Ibid.*, 68.

[13] Elizabeth Hamilton, *Suenens—A Portrait* (Garden City, N.Y.: Doubleday, 1975) 79.

He had the trust of John XXIII. And working with Cardinal Montini on the preparatory commission and steering committee earned him the trust of the future pope as well. His contribution was fundamental to the direction of the council.

At the first session, there were fully seventy documents prepared in draft form to be submitted, to the Council Fathers, covering the most serious issues to minor changes in canon law. Suenens proposed a reduction in the number of documents, clustering them around themes —he found a natural grouping of seventeen subjects. He further proposed that the Council should be organized thematically around a central vision which could be explained to the Church at large and to the world, in order to satisfy the hopes and expectations aroused in so many quarters by the unique event. It will not surprise us to learn that Suenens himself received the task to flesh out this proposal.

Suenens prepared a detailed series of recommendations, suggesting that the Council should respond to the hopes of the waiting world by dealing with a double range of issues: "One series of issues would concern the Church *ad extra*," he wrote, "that is to say, the Church in relation to the world of today. A second series of issues would deal with the Church *ad intra*, that is to say, the Church as she is in herself, again with a view to assisting her in fulfilling her mission in the world."[14] He added a number of practical indications for streamlining procedures of the Council and ensuring the application of its teachings after the Council.

The coordinating group, Montini in particular, approved and encouraged the plan. The Pope adopted its basic insight in his radio message *Ecclesia Christi, lumen gentium* a month before the opening of the first session.

Still, rejecting the preparatory work of the curial commissions at the first session was not enough to give the Council a sense of direction. The indications of the Pope's failing health, together with the vast number of speeches and disparate subject matter, all contributed to a sense of drift. Cardinal Montini wrote to the Pope asking for greater coherence and structure for the Council and reminded him of Suenens' plan; Pope John sent Suenens a copy of the letter, as if to say "full speed ahead."

Toward the end of the first session of two months' duration, Suenens presented the outline of his plan in a speech to the Council Fathers. The plan recommended that the Council focus on the theme of the Church *ad intra* to clarify her evangelical nature, her work of prayer, sanctification, and teaching; and on the Church *ad extra*, looking at the expectations of the modern world, the family, the needs of the poor and the demands of justice, and social and international issues, with special

---

[14] *Memories*, 141.

attention to religious freedom and war and peace. This speech had an important effect on the Council, giving the assembled bishops a much-needed sense of direction and hope.

After the close of the first session of the Council in December 1962, Pope John displayed once again his great confidence in Suenens by having him personally go to the United Nations to present the encyclical letter *Pacem in terris*. He was extremely well received by the world body, not to mention by public opinion, especially in the United States.

Pope John also assigned tasks to the coordinating council to get ready for the second session. To Suenens he entrusted the schema on the Church *ad intra* (which would become *Lumen gentium*), and the schema on the Church *ad extra* as well. Suenens invited Msgr. Gérard Philips of Louvain to work on the draft of *Lumen gentium* with a group of Belgian theologians; he personally followed the work and participated in the decisions which led to its organization in its present well-known form: the mystery of the Church, followed immediately by a second chapter on the People of God; only then did the draft begin the lengthy discussion of the episcopacy and papacy, collegiality and of the place of priests, religious and laity as part of the People of God.

During the second session of the Council, Suenens gave what Hebblethwaite calls "one of the most effective speeches made at the council."[15] He urged that the draft of *Lumen gentium* bring out the charismatic as well as the ministerial nature of the Church, stress the role of "prophets" as those who inspire people to live the Gospel, explain the interlocking roles of pastors and charismatics in the Church better and proclaim St. Paul's doctrine of the freedom of the children of God. This speech was fundamental for the shaping of paragraph 12 of *Lumen gentium*. Nor was the ecumenical significance of this speech overlooked; the bishop representing the patriarch of Moscow told him that the focus on charisms "could be a starting point for the work toward unification of the Churches."[16]

His success with *Lumen gentium* was not to be replicated with the early process of drafting *Gaudium et spes*. The schema on the Church and the world turned out to be unsatisfactory; eventually it was to be assigned to another commission not under Suenens' responsibility.

Pope John XXIII died the day after Pentecost in 1963, having seen only the first disappointing session of the Council. But his great contribution was recalled in the extraordinary homily in his memory Suenens was asked to give by the newly elected Pope Paul VI at the opening of the second session in October. A few significant passages

---

[15] Hebblethwaite, 355.
[16] *Memories*, 141.

will have to suffice: "When he was elected, John XXIII might have seemed to be a 'transitional pope.' He was indeed transitional, but not in the way expected nor in the ordinary sense of the word. History will surely judge that he opened a new era for the Church and that he laid the foundations for the transition from the 20th to the 21st century."[17] "For him," Suenens went on, " the council was not first of all a meeting of the bishops with the pope, a horizontal coming together. It was first, and above all, a collective gathering of the whole episcopal college with the Holy Spirit, a vertical coming together, an entire openness to an immense outpouring of the Holy Spirit, a kind of new Pentecost."[18]

Not only did Pope Paul give Suenens the singular honor of preaching this homily before the bishops in council and thus before the whole world, but he had him at his side on the balcony the evening of the announcement *Habemus papam.* Moreover, when the time came for the new Pope's first Angelus, he invited the visitor in his study, Suenens, to stand beside him at the window of the papal apartment.

He further chose Suenens to be on the steering committee as well as one of the four council moderators. He clearly knew his value as a leader among the bishops and as one who could provide the practical strategy needed for the council to succeed. Having worked together on the central preparatory group and the steering committee in the first session, Pope Paul and Suenens knew each other's vision and goals.

Suenens remarks that Montini was more interested in the Church *ad extra*; Pope Paul also maintained throughout his pontificate a keen interest in liturgical reform and renewal, which was not a theme that attracted Suenens' interest and energy. What Paul VI did not share with Suenens was the latter's passion for a new vision of the Church as the people of God, for the role of the laity and for episcopal collegiality to be applied in practice in addressing the challenging issues of the day. It was Suenens who orchestrated the dramatic consultation which showed the overwhelming support of the council fathers for a text *de ecclesia* which would highlight episcopal collegiality. As Kilian McDonnell, O.S.B., observed, it is not hyperbole to call Suenens the "apostle of collegiality."[19]

Postconciliar Years

In 1968 Suenens published what was perhaps his most popular book, *Co-responsibility in the Church*, which was not a manifesto for power

---

[17] Suenens, *A Man Sent from God—A Homily Delivered at the Opening of the Second Session of Vatican Council II, in Memory of Pope John XXIII,* (Dublin: Veritas, 1992) 3.

[18] *Ibid.,* 10.

[19] Kilian McDonnell, O.S.B., Book Review, "Memories and Hopes" *Worship* (1992–93) 543.

sharing in the Church so much as a plea for structures and practices which guaranteed dialogue and open communication. It was this question of consultation which caused the growing tension with the Pope. On two of the most sensitive issues of the early postconciliar period, priestly celibacy and birth control, Suenens urged the Pope more than once to make use of the collegial structures of the Synod of Bishops for discussion of the questions with representation from the episcopal college.

After the encyclicals *Sacerdotalis coelibatus* (1967) and *Humanae vitae* (1968), when Suenens continued to press for collegial discussion of the issues, there was no doubt a strain in his relationship with the Pope. Hebblethwaite calls him "a thorn in Pope Paul's side."[20] Suenens insisted that he did not see his public voice as dissenting from decisions of the Pope nor as a matter of ideological conflict, but rather as a frank plea for the practical implications of a lived collegiality in the Church. He probably failed to see that for many in those days, ideological conflict was strong and intentional, and as Avery Dulles has recently concluded, their public dissent was very damaging to the Church. But his own charism for public relations and his remarkable ease with the media led him to value open communications as part of the "way" for the Church in the new era of Vatican II.

One cardinal wrote to him suggesting he resign; he declined the invitation. For Suenens, this cooled relationship with the Pope was a mutual cross, but never tinged with personal animosity. It resulted from his conviction about the importance of the Council's vision of pope and bishops, of the pope as head and member of the college of bishops.

Sometimes he was even called a "rebel" cardinal. But he preferred the treasured memory of Fr. Walter Burghardt's introduction at a conference in New York:

> Today's speaker does need an introduction: He is not all you have heard. He is not an enemy of Pope Paul; but he has written with bold accuracy: "The greatest day in the life of a pope is not his coronation but his baptism, his mission to live the Christian life in obedience to the Gospel." He is not turning the Church into a democracy; but he does insist that ministry is the task of all Christians, that what today's Christians need is co-responsibility.[21]

The Synod of Bishops was a new organism in the Church, recommended by Suenens and other bishops at the Council in order to provide a structure in which the Church's bishops could continue to experience

[20] Hebblethwaite, 5.
[21] *Memories*, 255.

and live *Lumen gentium's* doctrine on collegiality in a concrete, practical way. Some had proposed that the Synod of Bishops have a deliberative vote, much in the manner of an ecumenical council. The theological problems relating to the world's bishops deliberating through representatives—a kind of on-going ecumenical council *in absentia*—proved an obstacle too great to overcome to implement this view.

Suenens knew the value of the new Synod of Bishops as an instrument of affective collegiality at least and was a participant in every Synod of Bishops from the time of the Council until his retirement as archbishop in 1979, as well as in the special synod of 1985 to mark the twentieth anniversary of the Council. At the first synod Suenens recommended the establishment of the International Theological Commission, again envisioning a new structure which would provide an instrument of dialogue and consultation for the postconciliar Church.

While the issue of birth control would await discussion until the 1980 synod on the family, after Suenens' retirement, the issue of clerical celibacy was discussed at the synod in 1971. Here Suenens sought to open up the possibility of a "double clergy," as he calls it, "the one celibate and the other married." I think his own reflection on this synod is important, especially in view of the suggestion made by Hebblethwaite of a seemingly inexplicable change of heart in which Suenens "abandoned the 'liberal' or 'progressive' camp."[22] About the 1971 discussion of priestly celibacy, Suenens wrote: "The synod proved that such a possibility is not yet accepted within the Church of the Latin rite. A majority of the bishops (107) voted against this idea; however, a substantial minority (87) were favorable to it, under certain conditions. All agreed that the final decision, concerning both the appropriateness of such an option and its practical applications, should rest with the pope. Pope Paul did not want to go in this direction; nor does the current pope, John Paul II."[23]

Suenens himself points to a renewed relationship of trust and confidence which began with his papal audience in the spring of 1972, when Pope Paul and he discussed a theme dear to the hearts of both: ecumenism. He wrote a letter to the Pope reflecting on this audience, which marked "a turning point in our relationship, since the problems of the council were from here onward increasingly replaced by new concerns. These were to include, in particular, preparations to receive the charismatic renewal movement, which was then at its earliest stages in Catholic groups in the United States."[24]

---

[22] Hebblethwaite, 5.

[23] *Memories*, 251.

[24] *Ibid.*, 253.

Reflecting on the death of Pope Paul in 1978, whom he knew so well and with whom he worked closely over two decades, Suenens observed: "From time to time, Pope Paul and I had differences of opinion, but these never in any way affected my loyalty to him. Pope Paul was profoundly aware of his responsibility, and this awareness often seemed to overwhelm him. . . . He loved the Lord passionately and served him to the extreme limits of this strength—often in particularly difficult circumstances, in a troubled and torn world."[25]

The Charismatic Renewal

Modern Pentecostalism began in 1906 in a small black Protestant Church on Azusa Street in Los Angeles. It has had an astonishing growth—first among Protestants in the United States, and in the latter decades of this century, across all denominations in Latin America, Africa and indeed throughout the world. Fr. Kilian McDonnell, O.S.B., the Collegeville Benedictine who is both theologian and chronicler of the movement, has recently opined that by the year 2000 the number of Pentecostals of all denominations will far exceed the number of Protestants and Orthodox combined.

The first group of Pentecostal Catholics experienced the gifts of the Holy Spirit in the manner unique to Pentecostalism at Duquesne in Pittsburgh in 1967 and at Notre Dame in 1968. By 1972 Cardinal Suenens personally encountered the charismatic renewal, the preferred terminology for Catholics and mainline Protestants, for the first time during a visit to the United States. He was immediately taken by this encounter, appealing as it did to his keen desire to see the Church flourish as in a new Pentecost through the work of the Holy Spirit. For him this amounted to a life-long goal.

In many ways Suenens was an unlikely person to carry the banner for the Catholic charismatic renewal. Personally reserved, even shy, at times almost overly intellectual, he was profoundly touched in his own personal experience and in assessing the fruits of the Holy Spirit in so many Catholics (and Protestants, too, I should add) whose spiritual journey had been deepened and advanced through the renewal. Cardinal Danneels captures it perfectly in his funeral homily:

> How could a cardinal with a face that did not show many emotions, with a straight and immobile stature, with a grave and steady voice, find himself at ease in the midst of a crowd that sang, danced, clapped hands and spoke in tongues? Was it a late life conversion to fantasy and imagination

---

[25] *Ibid.,* 321–22.

in a man who had been until then too rational and responsible? No. Rather, he perceived in this revival a return to the Church of the Acts of the Apostles about which he had always dreamed—with a taste for the Scriptures, spontaneous prayer, joy, a sense of community, the stirrings of the Spirit, the proliferation of charisms. The renewal gave the legitimate role of the heart and the body back to the spiritual life of Christians.

Suenens dialogued with the Catholic leadership of the new movement—Ralph Martin, Steve Clark, Kevin Ranaghan, Fr. Jim Ferry in the United States, and in Europe as well. He made a singular contribution by explaining the renewal to the pope and the curia, and by alerting its leadership to what I would call their "amnesia" about the gifts of the Holy Spirit to the Church: the Eucharist, the Blessed Virgin Mary, the pope as visible center of unity, the scope of Catholic teaching and practice.

From 1974 to 1986 Suenens composed a series of six "Malines Documents," which still serve as a guide to the renewal, with precious insight into its possibilities and its needs. *Charismatic Renewal,* with Kilian McDonnell as lead consultant, was followed by *Ecumenism and Charismatic Renewal* (1978). In 1979 *Charismatic Renewal and Social Action* was written in collaboration with his longtime friend Dom Helder Camara of Brazil. In 1982 he wrote *Renewal and the Powers of Darkness*, with a foreword by Cardinal Joseph Ratzinger. The final two documents treat two specific issues the renewal had to deal with: an overreliance on introspection, in *Le Culte du Moi et Foi Chrétienne* (1985); and the controversial phenomenon *Resting in the Spirit* (1986), sometimes also referred to as "slaying in the Spirit."

1975 marks the year of the renewal's "coming of age" in the Catholic Church. Thanks to Veronica O'Brien's urging of the cardinal and the cardinal's convincing recommendation to Pope Paul, the renewal was invited to have its world congress at Rome on Pentecost during the Holy Year. As Fr. Walter Abbott notes, during the 1975 Holy Year "the charismatic renewal was decisively accepted into the Catholic Church when Pope Paul endorsed it in St. Peter's Basilica on Pentecost Sunday."[26] Hebblethwaite concludes, "Suenens won another battle."[27] It is also fair to say that Suenens was the man of the hour for the renewal. His patient, intelligent, ongoing dialogue showed many in the charismatic renewal how to integrate their new enthusiasm for religious experience blessed by the gifts of the Spirit into the faith and practice of the one, holy, catholic, and apostolic Church.

[26] Walter Abbott, S.J., "For a Cardinal's Birthday: A Note on Women in the Church," *America* (Aug. 13, 1994) 5.

[27] Hebblethwaite, 612–13.

Charisms for the Third Millennium

On July 14, 1979, less than a year into the pontificate of Pope John Paul II, Suenens submitted his resignation as archbishop of Malines-Brussels. It was a duty which he, above all, would not neglect or refuse, since he had been the first to publicly call for the retirement of bishops. While the council heard his plea without enthusiasm, Pope Paul VI introduced the rule, *motu proprio.*[28]

On January 4, 1980, he was succeeded as archbishop by Godfried Danneels, then bishop of Antwerp. His has been an active retirement, as his many books and lectures throughout this period will attest. His successor has publicly stated what Pope John Paul II said to him as he began his ministry, "Cardinal Suenens played a crucial role during Vatican II, and the universal Church owes much to him."[29]

At this symposium we look to the twenty-first century and the third millennium of Christianity. I was asked to speak to you about the charism of Cardinal Suenens. I have tried to be reasonably thorough, and I hope reasonably objective, in the time given to me. I know that he was genuinely looking forward to this very symposium on retrieving charisms for the twenty-first century to find the new insights and new directions of the Spirit, who blows where he wills.

By way of conclusion, I would recall again Suenens' singular achievement in providing direction for the Council in its earliest days, when he outlined a simple framework for its deliberation and the council decided to concentrate its work around the central theme of the Church as such—*ad intra and ad extra.*[30]

It seems to me that he models a very significant charism to be retrieved for the new millennium: an ability to frame the question properly. Of course our society and its media already have a political framework for characterizing religious statements: They are usually cast on the grid from liberal to conservative. The frame of reference is most often the current political campaign, with comments as thoughtful as a sound byte. The Gospel message handed on in the living tradition of the Church is either unknown or so far in the background that it is unrecognizable as a frame of reference.

In my view, even in the Church people tend to mimic the secular frame of reference, with its penchant for labels. I suggest a moratorium on labels in the Church and a retrieval of the unified vision of the coun-

---

[28] *Memories,* 141.

[29] Walter Abbott, S.J., "For a Cardinal's Birthday: A Note on Women in the Church," *America* (Aug. 13, 1994) 5.

[30] *Ibid.,* 354.

cil, which did not issue a "conservative" *Lumen gentium* and a "liberal" *Gaudium et spes*.

To frame the question properly for these last days of our advent before the Jubilee of the Year 2000 and for the third millennium, we would be well served to focus more clearly, and with greater unity as Catholic Americans, about our task as *sacramentum mundi*—the sacrament of Christ in the world.

In his apostolic letter *Tertio millennio adveniente*, on preparation for the Jubilee of the Year 2000, Pope John Paul calls the Vatican II, in which he participated as auxiliary bishop of Krakow, "a providential event, whereby the Church began [to prepare] for the jubilee of the third millennium."[31] In commenting on the series of Synods of Bishops begun after the Council, he says:

> The theme underlying them all is evangelization, or rather the new evangelization, the foundations of which were laid down in the apostolic exhortation *Evangelii Nuntiandi* of Pope Paul VI, issued in 1975 following the third general assembly of the Synod of Bishops. These synods themselves are part of the new evangelization. They were born of the Second Vatican Council's vision of the Church. They open up broad areas for the participation of the laity, whose specific responsibilities in the Church they define. They are an expression of the strength which Christ has given to the entire people of God, making it a sharer in his own messianic mission as prophet, priest and king.[32]

John Paul relates the themes of Catholic social doctrine to the new evangelization, continuing the vision of *Evangelii nuntiandi*, which proposed "evangelization" precisely as a Gospel vision which embraces the Church *ad intra* and *ad extra*. It thus transcends the categories of dialectical perspective of action and reaction which characterize so much of modern political thought and strategy, of liberal vs. conservative as a dominant framework.

To enable and to serve this new evangelization, Vatican II provided its providential clarification of the true nature of the Church, so that knowing who she is, the Church might be better able to be the *sacramentum mundi*. The pluralism of contemporary society challenges us more than ever today to know and say why we believe in Christ and who we are as Church.

For this reason the question of Catholic identity is necessary and central both for the Church as a whole and for each individual disciple

[31] Pope Paul II, apostolic letter *Tertio Millennio Adveniente* (On Preparation for the Jubilee of the Year 2000), 18.

[32] *Tertio Millennio*, 21.

within the community. In the face of the well-documented religious ignorance among Catholics in America, I think we must look more urgently at the task of how well we form ourselves as Church for our mission in and to the world. What Cardinal Newman called for more than a century ago in England—a well-formed, well-educated and convinced Catholic laity—will be more than ever a necessity in an increasingly democratic and pluralistic world of the third millennium.

Fr. Benedict Ashley has suggested that we pay more attention to the "documents" of this Catholic identity: the teachings of the Vatican II as developed through the Synods of Bishops and their resulting apostolic exhortations, and particularly as presented in an integrated manner, updated with the teachings of Vatican II, in the *Catechism of the Catholic Church*. In his 1994 McGinley lecture at Fordham, Fr. Avery Dulles, a symposium speaker, called the catechism "the boldest challenge yet offered to the cultural relativism that currently threatens to erode the contents of the Catholic faith."[33]

Put another way, the broad task of the new evangelization, the Church's mission, requires the concomitant task of ongoing catechesis, I might even say a "new" catechesis, to provide the indispensable foundation for effective engagement in the Church's mission in the world, which is the baptismal vocation of the laity.

Framing the question for the next century and the new millennium in this way, as our readiness for the challenge of the new evangelization, will ideally bring us to an ongoing participation in the new Pentecost envisioned by Pope John XXIII and Cardinal Suenens for Vatican II.

In his final chapter of *The Hidden Hand of God*, Suenens gives us quite consciously his last testament: "As I look to the future, I cannot avoid stressing the role of the Holy Spirit in the Church of tomorrow. He is always 'the life-giving Spirit,' in the fullest meaning of the words. This is the idea I would like to emphasize by way of farewell."[34]

Cardinal Suenens, tonight we thank you for the charism—the gift—your life has been for us as Church. In our farewell to you, may we pay to you the tribute you so kindly gave to your friend John XXIII in your homily at Vatican II: "At his departure, he left us closer to God and the world a better place for us to live."[35] *Requiescat in Spiritu Sancto.*

---

[33] Avery Dulles, S.J. "The Challenge of the Catechism," Laurence J. McGinley Lecture (New York: Fordham University Press, October 1994).

[34] *The Hidden Hand of God*, 329.

[35] *A Man Sent from God*, 13.

12

Remarks of
Joseph Cardinal Bernardin

■ *Cardinal Suenens Awardee 1996*

I first met Cardinal Suenens in 1967 in Atlanta, where I was an auxiliary bishop. He had come to Atlanta at the invitation of my bishop and episcopal mentor, Archbishop Paul Hallinan, who many of you know was a native of Cleveland. As always the cardinal was very gracious, but what struck me most was his insightful vision of the contemporary Church. I was reminded of his vision a couple of months ago when I read the first volume of what has been described, correctly, I believe, as a definitive history of Vatican II, edited by Professor Giuseppe Alberigo, in collaboration with an international editorial board of well known scholars. While I knew the very significant role that Cardinal Suenens had played during the Council, I had not been so familiar with his many contributions to the preparatory work described in the first volume, announcing and preparing Vatican II for a new era in Catholicism.

Today, we need an authentic vision of the Council's teaching because of the tensions and division within the Church. I am further convinced that Catholics need to focus more intently on the conciliar teaching, probing more deeply its meaning and it implications for the life of the Church, as well as that of the world in which we live. Now at first that may seem like a statement of the obvious; after all, what have we been doing for the last thirty years? But consider what is happening. There are some who feel that the conciliar teaching is depleted, that is, both the Church and society have moved far beyond it. What is needed, they say, is Vatican III, and already their eyes are turned to what a new council can do. Indeed, some of them already act on what they assume a new council would do. There are others, however, who are committed to restoring things to the way they were before the Council. For them the

Council was a well-intentioned effort that has not turned out too well. They tend to ignore or even repudiate its teaching. There are still others for whom Vatican II is only a name. They do not fully understand the Council's teaching and often fail to see its relevance to their daily lives.

Perhaps I have over-simplified matters, but I think all would agree that the two more extreme tendencies exist, and they create tensions within the Church. It is my conviction that we do not fully understand all the implications of the Council's teaching, and for that reason we have not adequately implemented it. While much has changed in the past quarter century, it takes more than a single generation to assimilate fully the teaching of an ecumenical council, especially one whose purpose was primarily pastoral, one that addressed so many important topics and concerns. One of the difficulties in this instance is that in the conciliar documents, our traditional teaching is often presented alongside the newer theological and pastoral insights of recent decades. The great need now is to show how the two relate to each other, how the newer insights were a logical, legitimate and, indeed, needed development of our tradition. To fulfill this task we must be faithful to the values of both the old and the new. One cannot be emphasized at the expense of the other. Such a comprehensive approach to conciliar teaching, I believe, will prevent us from becoming preoccupied with single points in isolation from all the rest. It will enable us to see the full beauty and relevance of our heritage as it has developed under the influence of the Holy Spirit from the apostolic age to the present.

This process will require the best efforts of our theologians working together with representatives of other disciplines, and they must of course pursue their efforts in partnership with the ecclesiastical magisterium, which has the ultimate responsibility for affirming the faith of the ecclesial community. This international symposium on charisms is, I believe, a splendid example of how bishops, theologians, and people generally can work together to contribute to the development of this deeper understanding of conciliar teaching, in the context of reading today's signs of the times. As you know, for such efforts to be successful, much is required on the part of all who are involved: an appreciation of our heritage of faith, an openness to authentic doctrinal development, a correct understanding of the respective roles of the various disciplines in the magisterium, mutual respect and trust, and a willingness to work together in a collaborative fashion.

In accepting the honor that you have bestowed on me, I pledge to do what I can to help establish the ecclesial climate in which such collaboration can continue to take place. I trust that you will join me in accomplishing this goal, a goal that is so essential to the well-being of the Church, a goal toward which Cardinal Suenens devoted his life.

Contributors

Doris Donnelly is the director of *The Cardinal Suenens Program in Theology and Church Life* at John Carroll University. The author of several books including *Learning to Forgive* and *Spiritual Fitness,* and editor of *Mary: Woman of Nazareth,* she has also authored many articles. At John Carroll University, Dr. Donnelly is also professor of theology in the department of religious studies.

John C. Haughey, S.J., professor of religious ethics at Loyola University, has had a long association with Cardinal Suenens because of their mutual interest in the charismatic renewal. He is the author of eight books and many articles. For the last ten years he has been a member of the Vatican sponsored dialogue with Pentecostals.

Margaret M. Mitchell, associate professor of New Testament at The University of Chicago, is the author of *Paul and the Rhetoric of Reconciliation* and has published articles in *Novum Testamentum, The Journal of Biblical Literature, Harvard Theological Review,* and *The Journal of Religion.*

Avery Dulles, S.J., professor of religion and society at Fordham University is an internationally known theologian and lecturer and the author of seventeen books and over six hundred articles on theological topics. He serves on the International Theological Commission and is consultor to the Committee on Doctrine of the NCCB.

Mary Catherine Hilkert, O.P., associate professor of theology at the University of Notre Dame, holds special interest in theological anthropology, fundamental theology, and feminist theology. She is coeditor of

The Praxis of Christian Experience: An Introduction to the Thought of Edward Schillebeeckx and author of *Naming Grace: Preaching and the Sacramental Imagination.*

Barbara E. Reid, O.P., associate professor of New Testament studies at the Catholic Theological Union, centers her research on Luke-Acts, feminist biblical interpretation, and the use of the Bible in preaching. She is co-editor of *The Collegeville Pastoral Dictionary of Biblical Theology,* and author of two books: *Women in the Gospel of Luke* and *The Transfiguration.*

Wendy M. Wright holds a Ph.D. and teaches theology at Creighton University with expertise in the history and theology of spirituality and family spirituality. Among her books are *Francis de Sales* and *Jane de Chantal: Letters of Spiritual Direction,* and *Sacred Dwelling: A Spirituality of Family Life.*

Mercy Amba Oduyoye, a native of Ghana, was educated at Cambridge, United Kingdom, and holds a doctorate, *honoris causa,* from the State University of Amsterdam. She has served as visiting faculty at Harvard and Princeton. Her published works include: *Daughters of Anowa: African Women and Patriarchy,* and *Hearing and Knowing: Theological Reflections on African Christianity.*

Mario Marazziti is president of the Community of St. Egidio in Rome, which has been nominated for the Nobel Peace Prize for its peace efforts in Mozambique. He is the author of *An Extraordinary Life: The Story of AIDS, Solidarity and Hope.* He is a journalist responsible for cultural programming at RAI, the Italian Public Television Network.

James W. Douglass served as a theological advisor on questions of nuclear war and conscientious objection to Catholic bishops at Vatican II. He has taken part in peace missions to Israel, the West Bank, Jordan, Iraq, Zagreb, and Sarajevo. Among his books are *Dear Gandhi: Now What?,* and *The Nonviolent Coming of God.*

Bishop Kenneth Untener is a native of Detroit who serves as bishop of Saginaw, Michigan. He holds a doctorate from the Georgian University in Rome and is a frequent lecturer on theological and pastoral issues in many dioceses across the country. In addition, he publishes often in a variety of journals.

Archbishop William J. Levada, is a long-time friend and colleague of Cardinal Suenens. He serves the people of San Francisco as their spiritual leader.

Joseph Cardinal Bernardin, first recipient of The Cardinal Suenens Award and much beloved archbishop of Chicago, was honored for his faithfulness to the spirit of Vatican II.